Time stood suspended for an endless heartbeat. I cannot recall my thoughts, if, indeed, I had any. But other details are still clear: Joan, her face white, her eyes round and staring, pressing herself backward against the counter top, the coffee pot clutched in one hand; Matta, sitting up, looking at Wa intently; the throb in my arm and the feel of blood running wet and warm toward my wrist. And Wa, no longer himself, was transformed into a fighting wolf, standing ready to leap, and staring intently into my eyes with those uncomfortable yellow lenses of his, while his rumbling growl continued nonstop. His teeth were so fully exposed that his upper lip was wrinkled back to reveal the top of his red gums. He was a superstition come alive, Fenris, the giant wolf of Norse mythology, son of Loki, who had slipped the chain…

secret go the wolves

R. D. LAWRENCE

BALLANTINE BOOKS • NEW YORK

Library of Congress Catalog Card Number: 79-22709

ISBN 0-345-33200-8

This edition published by arrangement with Holt, Rinehart and Winston.

Printed in Canada

First Ballantine Books Edition: October 1983
Sixth Printing: April 1989

For the wolves of the world;
for their protection and understanding.
And for those people who seek to preserve
a magnificent animal from the predatory effects
of human greed and superstitious bias.

PROLOGUE

The letter was dated January 30, 1978. It reached me two weeks after being written, arriving at Watson Lake, Yukon Territory, the day after I had spent some time tracking a large wolf pack through the 45-below-zero forests of lodgepole pine that stretch into infinity in that part of Canada's northland. My Florida correspondent and the U.S. and Canadian mail services had picked an appropriate time to put the letter into my hands, for the missive contained a cry of help on behalf of a wolf:

Dear Mr. Lawrence:

Your letter arrived today, and it suddenly occurred to me that you may be the person to turn to for advice— advice on what to do with a wolf! The enclosed newspaper clippings tell the story. The letter to the editor was written by me.

Dog Control (the dog catcher) is still holding the wolf. It can't be destroyed because it is an endangered species, and I doubt that there is anyone in the area with the facilities or the know-how to provide the animal with a decent life. Could a wolf raised in captivity ever survive in the wild? Do you know of any sanctuary that could handle it?

Some of the men involved are incredibly callous and

the citizens are hysterical because the wolf is supposed to have eaten some pet dogs.

If you have any thoughts on the matter, you can write to the St. Petersburg Times, *or write me and I'll pass the information on.*

I'll write more about it later,   Joan

The accompanying newspaper clipping, dated January 19 and by-lined by *Times* staff writers Peggy Vlerebome and Steve Hasel, told the story:

LARGO— Dense underbrush, an armed posse, and a trained German shepherd dog brought an end Wednesday morning to the free roaming of a wolf that police say killed at least four dogs and terrified two small boys.

The wolf was captured near Walsingham Reservoir shortly after 11 A.M. by Wayne Robie, of Pinellas County Dog Control.

Robie said the animal was indeed a wolf and not a dog.

Only a few hours before it was caught, the wolf frightened two small boys outside Anona Elementary School in Largo and reportedly killed one dog and injured another near Seminole.

Police are "99 percent sure" that the captured animal was responsible for three other dog deaths in the last week.

The story then went on to describe how the wolf was captured and how it was later exhibited to groups of people whose dogs had been killed or injured.

This story, and subsequent clippings sent to me by my Saint Petersburg correspondent, reminded me once again of the ignorance and superstition that still persist in the minds of most city dwellers where the wolf is concerned.

It reminded me, also, that I had been equally ignorant and superstitious almost a quarter of a century ago...

My first close encounter with wolves in Canada took place on January 12, 1955, in a spruce forest in northwestern Ontario.

My activities that morning began routinely enough: up at

5:30 A.M., breakfast, the performance of a few chores, and then, dressed and hooded against a northern winter, out into the dawn to note the mauves and pinks that streaked the east and promised a bright, fine day.

Half an hour later, walking under a cobalt sky and facing a sun that was still suspended halfway over the tree line, I fancied that the glow with which the understory was bathed could easily be mistaken for the flaming of a distant forest fire. Except, of course, for the singular absence of heat. It was strange, I thought, that so much golden energy could not raise the mercury past the 30-below-zero mark. It was almost as odd that I should feel warm enough to undo the parka, slip off the hood, and remove my moose-hide mitts, for the cold was dry and there was a total absence of wind.

I felt good, full of energy. As usual, I was consumed with curiosity, greedily absorbing the sights and sounds and aromas of this rugged, beautiful land, forever seeking to learn more of its secrets.

The narrow trail threaded through a region of densely packed spruces that were, I knew, several centuries old, but that were still only medium-sized. Never would these evergreens attain maximum growth, for they were rooted in muskeg bottom, a spongy, waterlogged land filled with a sort of organic gruel manufactured over the ages from the carcasses of dead trees, plants, and animals; such bottomland offered scanty support to the spruces during the months when it was not frozen solid. As a result, the trees grew great, octopuslike masses of roots that, of necessity, took sustenance away from the trunks and branches and leaves. This, combined with the long, cold winters, kept the trees relatively small, each averaging some forty-five feet in height with a trunk diameter of eight or nine inches.

For me, this was both good and bad. At that time I earned my winter-living as a logger, cutting pulpwood to sell to a local mill; it was good because the logs were easier to cut and lighter to handle, bad because it was necessary to cut down a larger number of trees to make up one cord of wood.

On that particular January day I had almost finished cutting my quota of logs to fill the contract with the mill, and for this reason I was in no great hurry to reach the work site. I virtually dawdled, allowing myself plenty of time to study the wilderness, stopping occasionally to admire some of the more intricate

3

patterns sculpted on the snow or to examine the animal tracks that, since the previous day's sundown, had been superimposed on top of the homeward-bound, crisscross prints left by my snowshoes.

The trail had been busy over the night and early that morning. Varying hares, mice, squirrels, deer, a bobcat, and at least one pack of wolves had traveled the route in both directions or crossed it at different points, the marks of their journeyings leaving numerous messages stamped on the snow.

Within some of the trees ventriloquial gray jays chattered softly or whistled sharply as the mood seized them; boreal chickadees sang their dulcet little melodies. Not to be outdone, the ravens cawed and gurgled and cooed, alternating their lusty, cacophonous medleys with sounds that were amazingly like slurred human speech, as though the great ebon birds were actually greeting me with husky *howdoos*. When this happened nearby, I would stop and return the greeting, whereupon the avian owner of the so-human voice would stare down at me from its perch atop a scraggy spruce, raising a ragged crest and turning its head to follow me with one black, unwinking eye as I resumed my walk, the powerful beak looking like something carelessly carved out of a lump of anthracite.

Presently, when the sun had completely cleared the trees, I lengthened my stride and stopped less often. Ten minutes later I arrived at the place where my nearest neighbor was also cutting pulpwood. Harold Hanson was a Norwegian, his farm located about one mile from my own homestead. He was prosperous by my newcomer's standards, having settled in the regions when he was eighteen years old, fresh from his native land, many years before I took passage from England. In addition to a comfortable home and a nice herd of cattle, he also owned horses, on one of which he had ridden to work this morning, to arrive well ahead of me. His fire was already going nicely, and the coffeepot that was suspended over the flames by means of a tripod of green willow poles was bubbling vigorously and filling the air with the appetizing aroma of its strong brew.

He was sharpening an ax when I emerged from out of the trees. Giving the blade a final swipe with the whetstone, he looked up and waved toward the fire.

4

"Coffee. Sit." As short of words as he was sparing of gestures, he nodded slightly toward two log seats beside the blaze.

Sipping from tin mugs, we sat and chatted in a desultory sort of way for about ten minutes before I stood, emptied the dregs from the mug, and scooped snow into it to clean it. As I did so, I noticed that Harold had brought his .30-30 rifle. Noting my glance, he answered my unspoken question.

"Yesterday, I didn't bring it and, by yes-suss, didn't a big bull moose come steppin' out of the bush!"

I nodded understanding before thanking him for the coffee and turning with regret from the warm fire to resume my journey. It was long past the hunting season, but meat was always scarce in the backwoods, and none of us refused an opportunity to bag a bull moose or a buck deer if chance put one across our paths. Tomorrow I would bring my own rifle, provided that Harold didn't get the bull today, for we always shared our off-season kills.

It was two miles from Harold's site to mine, and what with dawdling along the way and stopping for the coffee, I arrived at my workplace later than usual. Belatedly anxious to get to work, I slipped out of my packsack, set it down on the pile of logs already cut, and made ready to start.

Moments later I finished notching a tree and was about to kneel, bow saw in hand, to cut it down when two wolf howls were voiced from nearby. The eerie, haunting cries had the power to immobilize my entire body. Both knees bedded in snow, left shoulder pressed against the scaly bark of the tree trunk, and bow saw suspended in midair, it seemed that only my heart was endowed with movement, as though it would make up with speed and noise what the rest of me was unable to achieve. In that attitude, trying to listen to the wilderness but hearing only the thumping noises issuing from inside myself, I felt the acrid taste of fear in the back of my mouth.

It took an enormous effort of will to make myself rise. Even as I was turning my head toward the place from where the frightening calls had come, more wolves howled from several other directions. With dreadful certainty I knew that I was inside a ring of timber wolves.

I *think* I exhibited a calm that I was far from feeling as I moved cautiously and stooped to exchange the saw for the ax so as to have something to defend myself with when the attack came—and I was quite sure that come it would! Now I put my back against the tree, there to stand apprehensively while the ululating calls of the wolves became occasionally punctuated by gruff and rapid barks.

Seconds later I saw one of the animals. It materialized suddenly between two trees no more than twenty or thirty feet away, a big, gaunt beast of a slaty gray color that stared unblinkingly at me with dark yellow eyes.

The creature stood stock still for only a few seconds, but that was enough time to note with clarity every detail of its appearance. It carried its head held high, mouth agape far enough to show the long, slightly curved tusks gleaming with reflected light; the pink, wet tongue lolled out of the corner of its mouth, a bead of spittle hanging momentarily on its very tip. The animal's ears were stiffly erect, aimed at me, the coarse guard hairs on its neck and shoulders, forming a thick ruff, were also erect, as was the hair along its spine. It left as it arrived, swiftly, silently, bounding fluidly into the forest to be hidden immediately by the trees and the underbrush. The howls and barks became louder, closer, and more frequent. The wolves were tightening the circle.

Since arriving in these backwoods fresh from the immigrant ship three months before this moment, I had seen and examined many wolf tracks, found the remains of their kills on several occasions, and listened to them howl often, but, until now, I had never seen a wolf outside of a zoo. Before today I had felt no fear of the wild dogs as I traveled through the wilderness; indeed, their haunting voices, heard as a rule in late evening or after dark, and some distance away, had always thrilled me, and I had longed to catch a glimpse of a wolf or two. But not like this! These wolves were too close; there were too many of them. They immediately awakened the memory of all the myths and exaggerated tales heard in Europe during my childhood, which, of course, I believed, and even embroidered with additional horrors produced by an active imagination. Many a deliciously fearful night did I spend in my darkened bedroom inventing gigantic, ravening wolves every one of which was intent upon feasting on my flesh. Of course, in my imaginings, I always got away and left in my wake a number of dead or injured killers; and if at times the phantoms I created threatened to get out of hand, my parents in the living room could always be relied upon to dispel the too-real fears. Long before I passed my teens, these childish fancies were forgotten, or so I thought. Now they all came rushing back, evoking images of the wolf as a ravening, man-hunting creature endowed with great strength and almost magical powers, a veritable symbol of evil. Pure nonsense, of course, but how does one rid oneself of years of superstition when brought suddenly face to face with the physical manifestation of such mythological beings? It isn't easy. For me, it wasn't possible at that particular time.

Soon after the howling began, and following the glimpse of the first wolf, four others showed themselves, copying almost exactly the actions of their companion. But, to my relief, the pack didn't appear disposed to attack. Not yet, anyway. Instead, the wolves continued to howl and to bark with increasing frequency, a furious, hysterical sound, quite unlike the latration of domestic dogs, that was voiced in staccato bursts. I found this more intimidating than the querulous and plaintive howling.

The minutes passed, the expected attack did not materialize; I moved away from the tree, walking slowly and swinging my head from left to right in a vain attempt to keep all the animals under constant observation. Ax held ready, I worked toward the piled logs, which were stacked almost five feet high. I climbed on top. From here, I reasoned, I would have a better chance of defending myself.

For a seemingly endless time—it could have been five minutes or half an hour—the status quo endured. The pack continued to howl and bark; individual wolves showed themselves periodically between the trees. There were eight or nine wolves, I estimated, my nerves becoming more tightly strung every time one of the great beasts emerged to view.

Finally I could stand the tension no longer. Ax in one hand, a stout club picked up off the ground in the other, I walked away from the log pile, not bothering to fasten on the snowshoes. I actually felt less fearful as I moved toward the trail mouth, preferring the grim prospects of an immediate showdown to the nerve-racking vigil on top of the logs.

Great was my relief when the circle of wolves opened to let me through—though I suppose it didn't exactly open; those animals nearest to me simply refrained from running across my path. In any event, they didn't attack.

7

On the trail, walking as quickly as circumstances allowed and trying to look in all directions at once, my fear lessened. When I had placed some two hundred yards between myself and the logging site and realized that the wolves were becoming quiet and were not following, my confidence began to return. I was still apprehensive, but now I didn't look around so often, contenting myself instead with periodic halts during which I searched the surrounding forest, listening intently for sounds of pursuit.

By the time I had covered about half a mile, all the wolves stopped calling. At the cessation of the last primordial howl the wilderness became a place of intense silence interrupted only by the noise of my breathing and by the crunch of my boots in the snow. In this way I reached Harold Hanson's logging site.

My neighbor had, of course, heard the howling, but after almost thirty years in the backwoods, he hadn't paid much attention to the sounds. Indeed, he seemed quite indifferent to them and looked at me as if he thought that my imagination had run away with my common sense. Detecting this unspoken reproach and feeling somewhat foolish now that the wild dogs weren't circling me, I didn't stress the incident. Instead, I asked him for the loan of his rifle, promising to share with him the twenty-five-dollar bounty, paid by the Ontario government for each wolf killed, if I was able to shoot one or more of the animals. Motioning for me to help myself to the gun, he dug into his parka pocket and scooped out a handful of shells. Armed now and feeling very brave, I retraced my route.

I don't suppose that much more than two hours elapsed between the time I quitted the logging site and my return to it with the rifle, but during this interval the wolves had gone. Emboldened as much by their absence as by the gun in my hand, I scouted the surrounding forest.

The trampled snow, covered with tracks, proved that I had not imagined either the incident or the number of wolves in the pack. The numerous tracks in the snow tended to confirm my estimate of eight or nine. After I measured the distance between the log pile and the tracks, I found that at one point during their circling, a few of the wolves had come to within fifteen feet of me. Moments later the tracks led me to the source of all the commotion.

At a place seventy paces from the log pile lay the remains of a deer. The wolves had made a kill not long before I arrived to interrupt their feeding; hungry, tantalized into a frenzy by the taste of blood and meat, the pack had combined to drive me away.

There wasn't much left of the whitetail, just bones, bits of hide and sinew, clumps of bloody fur, and the top part of the skull gnawed clean of skin and meat, a grotesque mask of death in which yet reposed one glaring eye. I shuddered, unable to refrain from imagining my own head lying there, its gray white skull tinged red in places, awaiting the ravens that would come to administer the last rites by picking it clean. Even now a number of the big birds were perched in the trees around the remains, clearly disturbed and annoyed by the human intrusion. They sat in solitary ire or in clusters of twos and threes cawing and rasping their impatience.

Like all the other kills the remains of which I had found during my wanderings, these leftovers were scattered over a relatively wide area, their distribution resulting from individual wolves seizing a part of the prey and carrying it some distance from their pack mates so as to eat undisturbed. The snow was a patchwork of red blood and rufous hair within an irregular circumference of some 250 square feet; inside this feeding area lay the meager remains of the prey. The deer's hair was scattered all over, looking, except for the blood that stained the bigger clumps, rather like a liberal fall of extra-long, dead spruce needles. Patches of saffron-hued snow marked those places where some of the wolves had left their scent; the outline of a big body dented the snow wherever a wolf had lain. Looking up at the ravens before turning away from the leftovers, it occurred to me that the birds would find little here to clean up.

That day's experience created a deep impression on me, but it was not until several years later that I was to understand just how fully I was influenced by those wolves. At the time (and perhaps this was the most significant lesson to be learned from the encounter) came the realization that wolves, even under severe provocation, will not attack a man. With a lot of luck and some fast ax work I might have been able to defend myself against one or two wolves, but against an entire pack I would have stood no chance at all if they had elected to charge.

9

With the exception perhaps of a threat to their cubs, no greater provocation could be offered a pack of wolves than to interrupt them at a meal. Not only had I done this, but I had lingered a considerable time, damned near *inviting* them to attack, however unwittingly. Instead of rushing in for the kill, as I had fully expected them to do, the wolves resorted to a bluff that was remarkably effective. When their strategem worked, I was allowed to go in peace, and they returned to the meal that had been so rudely interrupted.

Before that winter was over, I was treated to one more close-quarters encounter, though this was of quite a different nature, involving only one wolf—or, at least, only one that I was *aware* of.

It happened in late February when I was returning home at dusk from another part of the wilderness that surrounded the homestead. I had been checking traps, none of which had produced a yield, and I was about three miles from home, snowshoeing along my outbound trail within the deep shelter of a large belt of lowland cedars. That was my first year as a trapper of furs, an occuptaion I had already found distasteful and that I was to abandon before too long. I remember that I was silently debating the morality of the thing while trudging home empty-handed, secretly rather glad that the traps had failed.

At one point I slowed down to look at a stand of particularly large cedars that would yield a number of good electrical poles could I but haul them out to roadside so as to sell them. Turning my head, I thought I heard the sound of soft footsteps behind me. I stopped, did an about-face, and scanned the darkening forest. The trail was empty, no movement disturbed the quiet of the tightly packed trees. I shrugged, put it down to imagination, and resumed the journey. But when the slight noise was repeated only a few moments later, this time punctuated by the sharp sound made by a cracking twig, I realized that I was being followed by something fairly large, for by now I knew enough about the wilderness to be aware that the lesser animals of the forest would be too timid to track a human. In any event, their progress through the soft snow would not have been audible unless such an organism was very close indeed.

Once again apprehension fanned the imagination, its cause this time not a pack of wolves but an *unknown* thing. Tenderfoot that I was, the concept of a mysterious beast tracking me through the solitude of a penumbral forest was able to evoke more fear than the wolf pack had done. Unarmed except for a hunting knife, I felt very vulnerable and helpless, too inexperienced and confused to realize that, with the exception of wolves, which I now no longer feared, or bears, which I knew were sleeping in their dens, there were no other carnivorous animals in those forests powerful enough to pose a threat.

I kept on traveling at my normal pace, but I tried to set down each snowshoe as quietly as possible, at the same time listening for, and hearing occasionally, the stealthy tread that continued to keep pace with mine.

I stopped suddenly and turned around at the same time. Caught in the act of gliding behind the shelter of a clump of trees, the big, black timber wolf was close enough to allow me to determine that he was a male.

My apprehension vanished. I was instantly intrigued and much interested in the wolf. I spoke to him, keeping my voice low and gentle, as though I was talking to a strange, but not unfriendly, dog during a chance encounter. The wolf didn't respond like a dog might have done, but he didn't go away either; thrusting himself deeper into the cover of the full-skirted cedars, he remained still, facing me, his only visible parts one gleaming eye and the edge of a snow white patch he carried on his chest. We remained thus for perhaps thirty seconds, then I turned and resumed my homeward course, walking more slowly. Presently I heard him move; he was following me again.

The wolf was still dogging me when I reached the homestead's clearing three-quarters of an hour later, but he advanced no farther than the edge of the trees. It was almost dark by now. On turning around when I was about fifteen yards into the clearing, I managed to catch one more glimpse of him, a shadow darker than all the others, seen against the snow, a *moving* shadow that melted back into the forest.

The wolf captured in Largo, Florida, a female, was given to a small, private zoo, my correspondent said in a letter I received in March 1978. She concluded, "I doubt that any of us can change the fate of the animal now, but I'll keep you posted if

11

there are new developments. In the meantime I'm pretty upset about it."

I knew how she felt, remembering how determined I had been to see to it that Matta and Wa should return to the wilderness as soon as they were able to take care of themselves.

CHAPTER ONE

The disreputable canoe swooped around the bend of the Mattawa River, its small outboard motor coughing and wheezing asthmatically. The occupant of the craft sat hunched in the stern, facing backward and evidently trying to administer first aid to the ailing engine. He was so preoccupied with the task that he was blind to the turbulence that lay ahead, an area of fast, choppy water created by the narrows into which the canoe had been disgorged.

I yelled. In another few moments the old boat was going to swing broadside to the current and be precipitated into a wide, turbulent reach of the river, where it would almost certainly swamp. Either the man didn't hear me or he was too busy to pay attention. The outraged motor emitted one last, agonizing shriek and died.

My own sixteen-foot Chestnut sat nearby on the bank; in its bow was a hundred-foot coil of Manila rope. Putting down the fishing rod without attempting to retrieve the line from the water, I hurried to get the rope, so as to have it ready to throw to the canoeist when he was trundled past by the current.

When I turned away from the Chestnut, I saw the man abandon the motor, reach into the craft, and take out a broken paddle. With this ineffectual tool he began to try to control the runaway, which was already exposing its port side to the thrust

13

of the current; he didn't stand a chance. If he didn't swamp soon, his only hope of coming out of the predicament with a relatively dry skin and without losing the contents of the canoe lay in my ability to throw the rope far enough out to allow him to catch it.

I called again. This time he looked up. I held the rope up high so he could see; now he waved, aware of my intention as he redoubled his efforts in a vain attempt to turn the canoe toward shore.

The water was roiling, some of it already slopping over the exposed side; twice the canoe almost tipped, only to be saved on each occasion by some caprice of the current, but by the time it was almost abreast of me and close enough for the throw, it had reversed direction and was being swept downriver stern first. I flung the rope, watching it uncoil as it sped across thirty or forty feet of water. The throw was good; the descending line passed over the canoe, caught on the starboard gunnel, and slid toward the man, who grabbed it and held on as I pulled him in. But a good many gallons of cold river water spilled over the side before the craft was safely aground.

In the interval between the appearance of the canoe around the river bend and the moment that its stern touched the shore, I found myself reflecting on the man's carelessness, thinking that only a greenhorn would trust himself on a fairly fast river in such a canoe and add to his foolishness by relying on a decrepit motor, his only other means of propulsion being a broken paddle.

I tipped the leg of the motor to get it out of the sand, then looked up, seeing the man for the first time. He was an Indian. I am always irked by irresponsible people who risk their own lives and the safety of others during travels through the wilderness; now I was close to anger, because such riverine carelessness exhibited by an Indian was doubly offensive. I had always admired and respected the aboriginal North Americans for their knowledge of the wilds and for giving the world the canoe, a craft that, for me at least, is *the* most marvelous, adaptable, and safe means of water transport of them all. But this fool whom I had rescued was utterly incompetent, when, by tradition and heritage, he should have been an expert.

I was about to tell him so when I smelled his breath. He was quite drunk. As though to prove it, he fell full length in the sand when he tried to step out of the beached craft, there to lie giggling as the broken paddle, which he was clutching when he stood up, fell into the water and was swept downriver.

I hauled the canoe higher up the bank, noticing as I did so that it contained a variety of junky impedimenta and a half-filled sack that was soaked in blood and river water. Something inside the bag was moving. The Indian was now on his feet and initiating a step toward me. At that moment I heard a low, pathetic mewling sound coming from the gory bag.

"What have you got in there?"

"Makekun-shish. Nesho."

I knew enough Cree to understand the short answer. *Makekun*: "wolf"; *shish*: "young"; *nesho*: "two." He had two wolf cubs in the sack.

"Where's the blood coming from?"

"Keisays skwao makekun," which, literally translated, means "old woman wolf"; the mother, I inferred. "I get that one wolf good. Then skin 'er. Bring back *shish* to sell," he explained further.

Taking an unsteady step toward me and thus exposing my nostrils to the reek of alcohol and other odors that emanated from his person, he patted my shoulder.

"By damn, you bloody good booger with a rope. Gotta have a drink!"

His words were slurred, his speech clipped, but he had more English than had first been apparent. Staggering to the stern of his canoe, he reached in and produced a bottle of rye whiskey that was almost half full. As he did so, I bent down and took hold of the sack, lifting it out of the boat to cut the string that bound its neck. The Cree was saying something, but I paid no attention, too concerned with opening the bag so as to look inside.

It was at first hard to distinguish between the living pups and the bloody bundle of wet hide that had been the bitch wolf, but when I forced myself to reach into the mess, my fingers at once encountered the tiny, quivering cubs. I took them out and held them against my chest, trying to give them some warmth and comfort, and feeling through my shirt the spastic shivering that seized them, a rapid, pulsing series of shakes that issued from deep within their bodies, undoubtedly brought about by fear, shock, and cold. They were pathetic little beings, soaked to the skin in river water, their fur matted by the blood of their mother, each about eight or ten inches long, sooty gray in color, and quite blind.

The Cree, swaying on his feet, had the bottle tipped to his mouth, his head well back as he guzzled whiskey. Looking at him and feeling the shaking of the cubs that were even then working their mouths as they sought frantically for their dead mother's teats, I became so angry that I would have struck him had I not been holding the wolf pups. I turned away, walking to my canoe, beside which my gear was stacked. From the packsack I took out a towel and wrapped the cubs in it, then placed them gently inside the Chestnut, in the sun. I spoke to the Cree.

"You'll never get those pups alive to Mattawa, let alone sell them."

"Have a drink. I owe you. Hey, mebbe you want to buy dem *shish*?"

I had already determined that the cubs would stay with me, but this wasn't the time to show my interest in them. Pretending an indifference I was far from feeling and because tipplers like to drink in company and I wanted this one in a good mood for the bargaining that would soon start, I swallowed my anger and accepted the proffered bottle, wiping its neck thoroughly before taking a sparing sip, slowly, so that it would appear as though I was drinking a good measure.

Half an hour later our deal was made. I paid the Cree twenty-five dollars and the oldest of my three paddles (I never travel with less) in exchange for the cubs. By now the whiskey bottle was almost empty, but it was the Indian who had drunk the lion's share.

Money in pocket and paddle in hand, the Cree wove a course to his canoe and dropped the paddle into it. He now removed the dead motor from its place in the square stern and entered knee-deep into the water to stow the engine in the bow. That done, he returned to shore, paused long enough to drain the rye bottle and to toss it into the Mattawa, then pushed the canoe into the water. He climbed into the stern, settling himself on the seat, whereupon his weight immediately ground the keel into the sand. I stepped forward and gave him a good shove, sending the craft into the current, The river took hold of the

16

canoe and started it on its way, my former companion paddling unsteadily. That was the last I saw of him.

I stood pensive for some moments, trying to recall something, some nearly hidden memory that nipped at my conscious mind as it tried to surface. Then it came to me. I had bargained with an Indian in similar fashion on another occasion. The circumstances were different, and almost twelve years had passed in between, but on an afternoon in the autumn of 1956 I paid to Alfred, an Ojibway Indian, twenty dollars for my wolf-dog Yukon*; we had also sealed our compact with a drink, though on that day it was wine instead of whiskey that we shared.

The mewling cries of the cubs returned me to the affairs of the moment, and as I walked back to the Chestnut determined to do what I could for the two cubs, I wondered about my "bargain." The odds were stacked against the survival of the little wolves. It appeared that, once again, my heart had ruled my head and I had been parted from twenty-five dollars of hard-earned money and a paddle worth another ten dollars for the sad privilege of nursing two moribund wildlings, the responsibility for which was immediately to deprive me of eight more days of holiday, because now I was going to have to cut short my stay here so as to get the pups home quickly. There I could care for them properly, if they lived that long.

During my conversation with the Cree, who was a trapper and ran a line somewhere to the northwest of where we met, he told me how he had killed the mother wolf and taken her pups. He had neglected to pull his traps at the proper season, which is usually done just before breakup, and had returned to his line in early May to take care of the omission. It was while he was doing this that he noticed a newly dug wolf den halfway up a sandy knoll.

When all his traps were collected, he returned periodically to the den area in the hope of shooting one or more of the wolves; but the wary animals eluded him. Shortly after the bitch gave birth (and was thus reluctant to escape with the other members of her pack when the man showed up), the Cree made his last trip, camping near the knoll for two days. He knew

---

*See: R. D. Lawrence, *The North Runner* (New York: Holt, Rinehart, and Winston, 1979).

the bitch was in the den, but he delayed killing her because he hoped that by waiting he might be able to shoot one or more of the other wolves. So he found a place from which he could watch the den unseen, deep within a thick clump of evergreens.

The wolves weren't fooled. They stayed clear of the den area during the day, coming only in the dead of night to bring food for the nursing bitch. Tired of his vigil and afraid that if he waited any longer, the mother wolf would probably carry her blind cubs away from the den and hide them elsewhere, he stood vigil only until the female made one of her periodic appearances at the cave mouth, undoubtedly aware of the man's presence and uneasily watchful because of it. When she showed herself, he shot her through the head and afterward crawled into the lair, to find that it contained three pups. One was the runt of the litter and, in his own words, "kinda sickly." He gathered up the two healthy pups, cracked the ailing one on the head with a stone, skinned the mother and the dead cub, and left. An hour or so later he got into difficulties with the river.

Wolf fur is far from prime at that time of year, especially when it belongs to a nursing female. The Indian knew this, of course, but he wasn't interested in the hide. He killed the mother and pup for the twenty-five-dollar-a-head bounty money that the government of Ontario paid for dead wolves; the two pups he kept alive to sell to a pet store, expecting to get fifty dollars each for them, a considerably inflated figure that was no doubt introduced for bargaining purposes.

I confess to having felt satisfaction from the knowledge that this coarse and brutish man would not realize his expected profit. Yet I regretted the need to reward him at all for his butchery. But reflecting about it later, I found that I could not really blame him. The fault lay with our society and with a government that, because of political expediency, persisted in paying blood money in this supposedly enlightened age.

By the time that the Cree and his canoe had disappeared around a bend of the river, I had unwrapped the cubs and was already wiping them off, anxious to get them dry as soon as possible, afraid that they would get pneumonia otherwise. When most of the moisture was removed from their bodies, I bundled them up again, this time using a down-insulated vest I had brought with me against the chill of the backwoods nights.

Snuggled inside this garment, the little wolves didn't cry as often or as shrilly, but they continued to make soft, almost catlike mewling sounds.

There was no means of knowing when they had last fed from their mother, but regardless of this, some warm milk would help them build up body heat. There was a bag of powdered milk in the food pack, and my fire was still going fitfully. Adding fuel, I put some river water in a pot to boil; making ready the milk took only a few moments, but as I waited for the water to become hot, I suddenly realized that getting the fluid into the cubs was going to present problems. At home, on the 350-acre farm that my wife, Joan, and I owned, there was an assortment of gear and utensils designed for the caring of wild strays, including feeding bottles and a variety of nipples that I had myself made from clay molds and liquid latex. With these, animals as small as newborn mice and as large as moose calves and bear cubs could be nursed. On this trip, my equipment did not contain any of these items.

Joan had gone to visit her mother in Manitoba for two weeks, and I, feeling the need of a time of solitude, had elected to spend fourteen days canoeing and camping up and down the Mattawa River, a short tributary of the Ottawa River that lies some two hundred miles north of Toronto. This was a rare indulgence for me in those days, for, what with holding down a full-time job that required me to commute eighty miles each way by car to get to and from the office, writing at home, doing the many chores associated with the preservation of the 350 acres of almost-wild land, and pruning and caring for a large maple bush that was tapped each spring for the syrup, there were not many opportunities to get away for more than a day's solo fishing. And as if all that were not enough, a continuing procession of orphaned or injured animals and birds that were delivered to our care by various police departments as well as by individuals kept both of us additionally busy.

It began locally at first, when residents in our area learned of our commitment to nature and brought occasional foundlings that were in need of attention. Then the word spread, and because the various animal shelters would not take in wild strays and the zoos were usually overstocked with the common denizens of the Ontario forests, our farm became the refuge for a wide variety of fascinating creatures. More recently there had been a lull in the flow of foundlings, and it was for this reason that Joan had gone to visit her mother and I had gone after the bass on the Mattawa.

Learning by trial and error what to feed each orphan, how much, and how often was something that preoccupied me considerably at first, but at this point I prided myself on the ability to make up a formula, or diet, for almost any kind of animal.

As I busied myself measuring out some powdered milk in readiness for mixing it with hot water, I knew that if the cubs survived, Joan and I would have to care for them at least one year, perhaps longer, by the end of which time we would be extremely fond of them. Much sadness could be forecast for North Star Farm when the young wolves left to take up life in the wilderness—perhaps something I should have thought about *before* buying them from the Cree. But then, we had experienced this kind of emotion many times during the past five years.

After the water boiled for ten minutes, I took it off the heat and set the pan to cool in the shallows of the river. As it was doing so, I completed the dismantling of the camp, begun before breakfast, following a decision to move downriver to select a new fishing spot.

Taking down and folding the tent, I kept trying to think of some way to get the milk inside the little wolves, but it was not until all the gear was stowed in the canoe that I was forced to accept the solution that suggested itself almost at once but that I was reluctant to implement at first: I was going to have to use my mouth as a container and to let each pup suck the tip of my tongue as I dribbled milk down it. Not a pleasant prospect. But by now I was fairly philosophical about such things, having been taught by a succession of orphaned animals to adopt a purely clinical attitude when engaged in tasks that would otherwise have been repugnant.

It is always helpful to know the approximate age of a young wild animal when preparing to feed it for the first time if one is to determine with some accuracy such factors as the strength of the formula, the amount that is to be fed, and the frequency of the feeding. From my brief observation of the pups, aided by the knowledge of wolves acquired over the years, I was able to make a fairly accurate guess at their age, their subsequent development showing that I was no more than a couple of days out either way.

In Ontario, most wolves mate between the first and third weeks of March, though some mate earlier, perhaps in late February, and others, usually females breeding for the first time, do so as late as mid-April. Gestation takes between sixty-two and sixty-three days on the average, but, here again, some pups come into the world as early as fifty-nine days after mating and others don't emerge until sixty-six or sixty-seven days after they were engendered, the variations being as capricious as they are in the case of human infant births.

Wolf cubs, like dog puppies, are born blind, deaf, and, if not altogether devoid of a sense of smell, with limited olfactory powers. Yet they have well-developed taste buds and are highly sensitive to physical changes in their environment, being quick to detect differences in temperature and texture as well as to feel pain, cold, heat, comfort, and unusual vibrations occurring in their immediate surroundings. At this early stage in their lives the cubs are helpless and vulnerable. They cannot yet regulate their own body temperature, and they are therefore particularly vulnerable to cold, succumbing to exposure or to pneumonia if they become severely chilled. To complicate their lives further, the pups can only drag themselves around with their front legs, their hindquarters being relatively incapable of controlled movement. On the positive side, they do seem to have a well-developed sense of balance, and they grow with remarkable rapidity when properly nourished.

Weight at birth varies from half a pound to one pound, yet, by the time their eyes open eleven to fifteen days after birth, the cubs already weigh three pounds or more—but rarely more than four pounds—and when they begin to hear for the first time, twenty days after coming into the world, they may scale as much as eight pounds. By then, too, their back legs are strong enough to hold them upright, and they begin to go outside for short trips, watched over by their mother and by the other adult pack members. Even their coats have changed at this stage of development. At birth all cubs are dressed in fine, sooty or blue-gray fur, but by the time they take their first wobbly steps outside, this has become thicker, woolly in texture, and is beginning to show the hues that each pup will acquire when fully adult.

21

Aware of these things, I guessed that the cubs were more than five days old and less than fifteen: If they had been younger, their back legs would have been less developed and they would not have weighed as much; if they had been fifteen days old, or older, their eyes would have been open. In my pocket diary I estimated their age at seven days, which meant that their mother must have mated some time between the third and fourth weeks of March, or rather later than most of her kind in that part of Ontario. Perhaps this was her first litter? If so, it might account for the small number of cubs born to her, though this was by no means certain, because wolves will produce as few as two pups or as many as fourteen, there being many factors that influence the size of a litter.

I was mixing the milk and water as I was thinking about these things, careful to make a weak solution, because cow's milk, even when skimmed, is usually too strong for young animals unless it is well diluted. Lastly, I took a big swig of the stuff and, as I felt the temperature of the liquid in my mouth, decided that this method of feeding the little wolves had at least one advantage, despite its many drawbacks: The formula would be continuously preserved at body temperature.

With cheeks puffed out like an overloaded chipmunk, I thrust a hand into the bundled vest and closed my fingers gently on the first pup encountered. Sitting in the sun and cradling the cub against my chest, leaning against the canoe, I made sure the pot of formula was handy before lifting the wriggling little animal, cupped in both hands, and bringing its questing mouth up to my own. I eased my tongue through compressed lips.

With amazing alacrity and more vigor than I would have believed the cub capable of, my tongue was seized greedily and immediately subjected to some quite painful sucking, becoming pulled out of my mouth a good deal farther than nature ever intended it to go. Before I could bring matters under control, the little wolf had filled its mouth with tongue as well as milk, immediately choking and spluttering. This allowed me to extricate my lingual appendage and to be more cautious the next time I offered it to the frantic little mouth. Learning by trial and error, I at last discovered the correct techniques. Matters now proceeded more or less calmly, and the first cub slowly filled its stomach with one full mouthful of milk, only *some* of which was spilled down its chest and onto my clothing.

Eventually the little beast was done; and I had gotten my first taste of wolf-on-the-hoof, as it were, a savor that I can only liken to the odor that emanates from a very wet, and not too clean, dog.

Both pups were fed in this manner, the second one behaving more decorously than the first, though distinguishing itself by ingesting two mouthfuls before it permitted me to return it to its nest without screaming. All that now remained to be done was to clean from each matted little body the milk spills that were mixed with the remains of their mother's blood. For this I used a cloth dipped in warm water, swabbing each unwilling waif before rubbing it as dry as possible with a towel. As a separate ritual at the end, I massaged gently around the genitals of both pups to stimulate the moving of bladder and bowels, a task that would have been routinely performed by their mother's tongue but that I elected to do with a cloth dipped in hot water.

During this chore I was able to determine that one cub, the smaller, was a female, the other a male; it was he who fed last and who proved the less excitable but the hungrier of the two.

Now I held them on my lap, covered by my hands, waiting for them to answer "the call of nature," hoping at the same time that I would be quick enough to feel its onset before the cubs messed in my lap. It was during this waiting period that their names occurred to me. The female would be called Matta, the male Wa, after the river on the banks of which they came into my care.

As things turned out, the cubs did their duty admirably on the grass, and after they were comfortably wrapped up, first in the towel, then in a square of plastic and, lastly, in the down vest, which was thus protected from accidents, I launched the canoe and began to paddle downriver to the town of Mattawa, where my car was parked.

The drive home from Mattawa took five hours. It should have taken three, but the extra time was used up during four stops, each called for by the cubs in peremptory voices. No longer was I worried about their chances of survival. Indeed, since their first feed, the two appeared to be getting increasingly

23

lusty, hungry, and damnably impatient, characteristics that, had I but known, were to govern the state of things to come.

It was fortunate that I had prepared a good supply of formula to take with us on the journey; it was equally fortuitous that my kit contained several towels with which to mop up and swab two pups who appeared able to urinate out of all proportion to their intake of liquid. Prior to the fourth stop, when we were only half an hour from home, I resisted the importunings of my wards until I could stand their wailings no longer, thinking as I pulled off the road in defeat that of all the animals I had raised to date, these two were by far the noisiest and the most demanding.

But when I discovered that in addition to their liquid output the cubs had also produced a liberal amount of pastelike feces that was plastered all over them, I felt their demands were not unreasonable. But I wished they had contained themselves for just a little longer! The towel supply had now run out. I used a shirt, a pair of boxer shorts, two small packages of Kleenex, and a pair of socks. Even then, and as I lifted each pup in order to give it mouth-to-mouth sustenance, it smelled, and *tasted*, like an unclean goat pen in the Algerian Casbah.

Within five minutes of the farm gates I had a sudden and rather disturbing thought. In my anxiety over the cubs, which began the moment that I learned they were bundled in the gory sack with the hides of their mother and sibling, I had completely forgotten about Tundra; which goes to show just how anxious I was, because Tundra, a one-hundred-pound purebred Alaskan malamute, was not easily forgotten. Indeed, he was a much-loved monster who had the run of the house as well as a forty-by-seventy-five-foot enclosure added to the back of the building, complete with a basement-window entrance indoors. On the very few occasions when Joan and I went away without him a neighbor would feed him once a day and make sure that his giant water container remained clean and full.

On those occasions when he remained at home alone, his usual practice was to begin howling like his wolf ancestors the moment that he heard the sound of the returning car's engine, which he could recognize while the vehicle was some considerable distance away. As the car neared the farm, he would dive indoors through the basement window, clatter upstairs, scattering rugs as he went, and then wait, gathered by the front door like a tiger about to pounce on its prey.

As soon as the door was opened wide enough to allow him through, Tundra would leap, and if whoever faced the entrance wasn't careful, he or she would end up on the floor, to be kept there by one hundred pounds of muscled dog, who stood on top, the better to lick every inch of exposed skin. Afterward, when he was dislodged with difficulty and his victim was again upright, care was still required, for malamutes, as well as wolves, love to nip, *ever* so delicately, with their front, cutting teeth, delivering tiny pinches that demonstrate abiding allegiance within canine social circles, but which can be extremely painful when administered to the fleshier parts of the human anatomy.

But it wasn't Tundra's welcoming habits that disturbed me as I neared home. The cause of concern was the dog's tendency to eat things. All northern sled dogs are inveterate hunters; Tundra was no exception. He grudgingly respected those wildlings under our protection, provided they were not too readily available to him; but every time a new boarder arrived, he had to be chained until the stranger was settled in the barn or in one of our other buildings for convalescents. When the dog was released again, he was allowed to smell my hands and clothing so as to get the new scent, then he was taken, on his lead, to inspect the latest acquisition. From then on, all would be well, provided his domain was not violated by any of our wards.

If, on the other hand, and as occurred on two occasions, I arrived carrying a new waif and Tundra wasn't secured, he would begin to greet me, then would stop fussing when he got the alien scent. Immediately after that he would become a hunting predator. The first such occurrence ended without too much fuss, because it happened that I was bringing home a baby weasel that had been slightly injured. The very small *Mustela rixosa* reposed in my coat pocket, leaving my hands free to deal with our dog's exuberance. But weasels own senses at least as keen as those of the canines, and the one I was carrying quickly detected its danger and deposited in my pocket a quantity of highly odoriferous musk. This pestilential habit is common to all members of the clan and is resorted to during moments of stress or excitement. Still, no great harm was done.

I was slow to learn by experience that time. It took the second confrontation to warn me that Tundra could not be allowed his freedom during those first moments when a new animal was introduced to the farm. That particular incident produced a broken chair, one well-bruised leg (Joan's), and an extra hole in the hide of a cat who had already been run over by a car and who was definitely not in need of further blood-letting. That the affair had a happy ending was only due to the cat's ability to leap on top of the refrigerator and to the fact that it had inherited more than the usual quota of feline lives. It went on to recover and to become the pampered pet of an English lady living in Toronto, although it always walked with a limp.

Because the cubs were so small and so helpless, they were going to require constant attention for the next few weeks. The only effective way of ensuring that they got it was to keep them in the house, a place that was very much a part of Tundra's personal domain. How would he react to the small wolves? This question contained the cause of my concern.

The dog's deep and long-drawn howls reached me as I drove through the farm gates. By the time I pulled up outside the house, my ears detected the last clattering noise, telling me to expect Tundra, in the crouch position, on the other side of the door. On the seat beside me the cubs were quiet; I left them there as I made sure that all the windows were closed, opened the door, and got out of the vehicle. On the porch, I stepped to the front door and put the key in the lock. With the practice of experience, I turned the key, pushed the door open hard, and slipped sideways to place myself flat against the wall of the house, all in one movement.

Practically at the same instant that my back encountered the wall, Tundra came through the doorway, twisted in midleap, and stood before me on his hind legs, one massive paw on each of my shoulders. He was about to try to lick me when he evidently picked up the odor of the wolves that clung to my clothing. Now he nosed into my chest, moved down to my stomach, allowing his front legs to drop back to the floor. Intrigued as he was with the telltale scents, he didn't realize until it was too late that my right hand had slid around his wide leather collar. But then, knowing the routine well by this time, the dog tried to wriggle free, not wanting to be chained up while the source of those tantalizing sniffs was secreted away.

Following me unwillingly to the machine shed, to the wall of which his thirty-foot-long chain was fastened, he suffered himself to be secured; but though deprived of his freedom, he still had a voice. He used it, loudly and continuously and mournfully, filling the yard and quite a number of square miles of adjacent wilderness with the age-old, primordial cry of the wolf.

When I opened the front door of the car to transfer the cubs to the house, they appeared to be reacting to the calls, perhaps able to feel the sound vibrations, or perhaps because their hearing was beginning to emerge. However it was, and whether or not they *could* detect Tundra's calls, the pups were moving agitatedly inside their wrappings, crying their thin wails.

CHAPTER TWO

On arriving home early that evening and after carrying the cubs into the house, I had cleaned them up and settled them into one of the many nesting boxes made for just such purposes. The cubs weren't fed on this occasion, having consumed a goodly amount of milk-and-water less than an hour earlier. When the little wolves were settled, curled up one against the other and seemingly about to go to sleep, I busied myself preparing a quantity of formula ahead of time, now using Olac, a human-infant product that contained all the necessary vitamins and supplements; I had found it to be an excellent diet for young wild animals when given in the right proportions to body weight. This done, I put together on a tray the utensils that were to be reserved for the cubs from now on: one sixteen-ounce glass measuring jug, two eight-ounce feeding bottles equipped with puppy-sized nipples, an old electric coffeepot, long since relegated to duty as a formula warmer, a one-gallon insulated jug that would later be filled with hot water for mopping-up purposes, a roll of paper towels, and a jar of Vaseline for lubricating and soothing overworked orifices as occasion arose. Lastly a box of rice Pablum was added to the total, a little of which would be mixed with the Olac formula for the time being. Later mixed-grain Pablum would be substituted— the rice cereal helps prevent loose bowels in addition to supplying a little extra nourishment, but the mixed-grain variety becomes the staple part of the diet until a young animal begins to eat the foods that nature designed for it.

Earlier, before placing the pups in the nesting box, I weighed and measured them. Matta weighed one pound twelve ounces, and was twelve inches long from tip of nose to end of tail, this appendage measuring three and a half inches in length. Wa weighed an even two pounds and was fourteen inches long, his tail accounting for three and three-quarter inches of the total. These details were part of the first entry in the "wolf log," as I referred to it, a chart that was to record the vital statistics of the cubs as well as details of personality and physical development. On a separate sheet food intake was to be logged, at least until the cubs passed through the critical stage of infancy, a time between birth and the twenty-first or twenty-second day of life, the wolf neonatal period. By then, they would be able to see, hear, scent, and walk; they would also have developed their milk teeth and would be able to start eating solids.

While I was engaged with the formula mixing and tray preparation, Tundra had been howling, a continuous ululation that after the first five minutes began to get on my nerves. When the cubs started to make their own peculiar little noises and thus told me that they were not about to go to sleep just yet, it seemed that this would be as good a time as any in which to introduce Tundra to the wolves and to impress on him sternly that Matta and Wa were now a part of our household and were not, on any account, to be eaten.

Because I knew Tundra well, I prepared the scene before bringing him into the house. Taking an old blanket and folding it in half twice, I put it on the floor in one corner of the kitchen, transferring the pups to it. If he were allowed to sniff them while they were confined in the box, he would push down hard with his nose the better to ingest their aroma; he had a hard nose, he often used it powerfully, and I was afraid he might injure the pups. By putting them out in full view and by restricting him with the lead, I hoped to be able to control his nasal eagerness. I was nevertheless somewhat worried when I went to fetch him. I would have preferred Joan to be present, so she could have hovered protectingly over the cubs. But I knew that unless I allowed him to meet Matta and Wa tonight, he would continue howling.

Malamutes, it is to be noted, are generally able to pull twice their own weight when hitched to a sled. One of their breed, on a short haul from a standing start, set a record in Alaska when he moved a sled loaded with 1,100 pounds during the annual sled-dog trials. I had no illusions about what was going to happen as I fastened Tundra's lead to his collar *before* taking his chain off: He would immediately lunge forward, and unless I was able to dig in my heels and lean backward at the moment of his first charge, I would be propelled toward the house at a fast run, provided I didn't fall on the way.

I succeeded in stopping his charge. Sliding my left hand down the lead until it was some four inches above his collar, I pulled upward, taking most of his weight off his front legs; in this way I was able to control him, and we moved toward the house at no more than a fast trot, though accompanied by the dog's stertorous breathing sounds, which, to the uninitiated, would have suggested that Tundra was being strangled to death. Inside the house I was more in control. The floors were composed of tongue-and-groove hardwood sanded to a smooth finish and polished; on top of this, Joan had placed a variety of rugs. The combination of slippery floor and movable rug furnished an admirable curb for the dog's exuberance, even if he always attempted to make up lost ground by increasing the speed of his pumping legs. This wasn't very good for the floor *or* the rugs, but it protected the furniture from collisions with human and canine bodies.

Tundra was led into the hall, through the living room, and into the kitchen, which is my euphemistic way of saying that he dragged me along while he followed the effluvium of wolf that guided him unerringly to where the cubs lay huddled on the blanket. Now, a dog's tail was designed by nature to serve many purposes as well as to decently cover those parts over which it normally hangs, man's experiments with interbreeding to the contrary notwithstanding. In the case of malamutes and other sled dogs, who emerged, in all probability, after camp dogs became inadvertently crossed with wolves during the misty days of prehistory, the tail has become unnaturally curled, though that is not to say that this appendage cannot revert to its ancient and original position. It can, and does, frequently.

But during moments of intense excitement, or when in harness, or when exhibiting dominance, sled dogs curl their tails into exceedingly tight spirals, managing, nevertheless, to wag them when occasion demands, the rate and duration of the wag depending largely on the importance of the reason for it and upon the personality of individual dogs. In Tundra's case, extreme, pleasurable excitement resulted in a prolonged series of swift, short wags of his spiraled tail, but whether the pleasure resulted from, say, the anticipation of being let off his lead to play with Joan or myself or whether it stemmed from the imminent eating of some living tidbit unfortunate enough to come to his notice could only be determined by the physical circumstances.

As the dog scrambled frantically toward the cubs, his tail was going in the prescribed, extreme-pleasurable wag. But I couldn't tell whether he was happy to meet the cubs or whether he wanted to eat them. For this reason I hung on grimly, lifting him even higher off the floor so that his front feet were actually two inches or so above the boards. In this position, wagging furiously, wheezing and gasping, he tried to lower his head, nostrils siphoning audibly, ears pricked forward, his back haunches actually quivering under the strain. Slowly and apprehensively I began to lower him, trying to be ready to pull him away or to force him to drop a victim should he snap one up from the rug. Already I was regretting the experiment.

When his panting jaws were inches away from the cubs, to my utter amazement, his tongue emerged, and he tried to lick them. I let him down until he stood on all fours again, and I eased the tension on the lead. He lowered his head, nosed each pup very gently, and then began to lick them painstakingly and thoroughly, over and over, turning them with his nose when he felt he had completed one side to his satisfaction, doing the other, wagging his spiral in quivering little jerks and at great speed. And the pups lay there clearly enjoying the experience!

I removed the lead, pulled up a chair, and sat down to watch. Tundra immediately lay down, put one paw on either side of the pups, and contemplated them fixedly. If one so much as wriggled, it was immediately licked, and I noticed that though their fine guard hairs were damp, the under fur remained amazingly dry. They certainly looked better after the dog finished grooming them, much better than they had when I had com-

31

pleted my clumsy attempts to rid their fur of feces and caked-on blood.

Matta lay on her back with her fat, pinkish belly aimed at the ceiling, small mouth agape as she snored quietly. Wa was crawling sluggishly, pulling himself along with his stumpy forelegs, his inching progress taking him toward Tundra, who was curled up at one end of the blanket that was spread on the kitchen floor. The dog's neck and head were erect, his ears pricked forward; his intelligent eyes moved constantly as he glanced first at one cub, then at the other, in between sparing a second or two to direct his gaze at me.

The little she-wolf was couched between her self-appointed protector's big paws, not because she had positioned herself there but because the dog had arranged himself in that position. Wa, unlike his sister, made no attempt to go to sleep. He was near Tundra's right foreleg when the dog lay down and when an accidental movement of his head brought the cub's nose into contact with the dog's hair, Wa scrabbled toward the leg. It took him precisely three minutes by my watch to negotiate the two-inch-high obstacle and tumble down onto the blanket on the other side of it, there to lie on his stomach for another minute, his back legs splayed out behind, his front legs entangled one with the other, while his blunt-nosed little head nodded jerkily up and down in the rubbery manner of very young puppies.

Tundra watched him attentively. Once he reached down and licked Wa, the merest flick of the tongue, before he turned away to deliver an equally token lick to Matta, as though anxious to ensure an even division of his attentions.

Wa started to crawl again, but now he was aimed away from the dog, moving so painfully slow that I found myself straining for him, wanting to help him, the kind of urge that grips an adult who is watching a small child as it tries to perform some intricate function for the first time. Controlling myself, I continued to watch, fascinated not only by Wa's actions, but also by Tundra's behavior during the last half hour.

As closely as I could judge after watching him carefully, Wa's rate of progress approximated an inch a minute and since he was some four feet from the edge of the blanket, I didn't attempt to turn him back. But Tundra did. After Wa had traveled three inches, the dog leaned sideways, twisted his head so the top of his nose would connect with Wa's back, and nudged the cub closer to his extended foreleg. This rather unceremonious boost landed Wa upside down, and for a moment the cub lay there, front legs waving in the air, his back legs hanging flaccidly on the rug; then the little wolf heaved himself over, landed back on his stomach and resumed his lethargic crawl. This time, however, his nose pointed toward Tundra's stomach, and his rate of speed seemed to increase fractionally, as though he could sense the dog's body warmth.

At that moment Matta whimpered in her sleep, and Tundra dropped his head swiftly and licked her, stroking his ham-pink tongue over her from groin to chin several times, until she became quiet. Wa kept crawling.

It was now 10 P.M.; I was ready for bed. But I wanted to watch Wa a little longer, curious to discover his intentions. At the same time, I was most interested in Tundra's behavior, and delighted by it, too! Clearly the dog had appointed himself the guardian of the cubs, no doubt obeying some ancient, hidden pack instinct, some leftover, paternal trait inherited from his wolf ancestors. Be that as it may, I thought, and whatever the reason, I was considerably relieved.

Reflecting about Tundra's behavior, I supposed I should have anticipated something of the kind: Hadn't Yukon proved to be a most solicitous father? Of course, *he* was half wolf, which species, I knew, took its family responsibilities most seriously, so much so, in fact, that cubs are looked after and watched over by all adult pack members rather than by their parents alone.

Dragging himself forward with his tiny front paws, Wa spent five laborious minutes in getting to the long, outer hairs that adorned Tundra's under parts, but once there, he seemed to accelerate his progress, thrusting his way into the hirsute jungle at a point somewhat to the south of the dog's navel.

Tundra turned his head and looked at the cub briefly, then swung around to fix his gaze on mine as though to say, "It's okay, I'll take care of him."

I felt as if I was being patronized! His manner was like that of a person who has been offended by another, but who is too well brought up to argue with the offending party, electing to show through exaggerated decorum that good breeding forbids altercation with those of a lower social standing.

"You sanctimonious humbug! How was I to know you wouldn't eat them?" I grinned as I pretended to scold, and he had the grace to wag at me.

It was at this moment that Wa, finding his mouth in close proximity to one of the more tender parts of Tundra's anatomy, decided that he would essay a tentative suck or two. The effect on the dog was electrifying. He leaped up so quickly that he sent Wa rolling onto the kitchen floor and dislodged the sleeping Matta, who wound up under my chair. But when both pups began to wail pitifully, and even before I could rise to take a hand in the matter, Tundra became once more paternal. In two swift, sure movements, he reached under the chair, picked Matta up in his mouth and replaced her on the blanket; as swiftly, he rescued Wa and put him beside his sister. This done, he lay down again, taking up his old stance, and immediately began to lick the cubs. Moments later they were both quiet. Tundra now put his head down just beside his left front paw and closed his eyes. But his ears remained on the alert.

Still wanting to turn in for the night, but loath to disturb the peaceful trio, I sat and watched them, thinking my thoughts while waiting for the pups to become hungry again. They would, I knew, announce their appetite with those querulous little wails that could carry a surprising distance.

One of the matters that preoccupied me as I sat in vigil was the need to ensure that the cubs got just the right amount of properly balanced nourishment. If they were fed too much, or if the formula was too strong, they could become seriously ill, perhaps die; if they were fed too little, or the formula was too weak, they faced the same dangers. Yet I could only guess at the proportions of the formula and the frequency of feeding. Fortunately, I had done quite a good deal of such guessing over the years and to date I had not lost an animal because of improper diet.

It's all so simple in nature! Most mammals born and raised in a den by their mothers are allowed to suckle pretty much on demand and feed on a little-and-often basis. The nourishment they ingest from a healthy mother is always in balance. When a human takes on the task of fostering such animals, alternatives must be found, but what these are to be depends largely on the species and not a little on the temperament of the individual, for animals, just like human beings, develop their own idiosyncrasies—if they are not actually born with them, that is.

Wolf cubs grow rapidly; they are great eaters as a result, increasing their demands daily. I knew this, but what I didn't know was how to distinguish between the demands of need and the demands of greed. In the end, I decided not to waste energy attempting to ponder the imponderable. I would do as I had been doing all along: I would use the boiled-egg method to determine the quantity, as well as the strength, of the formula each cub would be allowed to ingest at any one time. It was, after all, a simple method that had so far worked every time. It came to me in a moment of intuitive acumen one day as I was wrestling with this same dietary problem while feeding twin raccoons. Joan, taking one of them from me to clean it up after it had gorged, remarked that its belly was "like a hard-boiled egg." When the greedy one was seized by copious diarrhea the next day I knew that the hard-boiled-egg belly equaled too much formula, a soft-boiled-egg belly meant too little, and a medium-boiled-egg belly was just right. The same method applied to bowel movements, medium being the desirable state of plasticity.

By the time these things coursed through my mind, the cubs were beginning to stir, causing Tundra to sit upright again. I yawned, scooped up both pups, and whisked them into the nesting box preparatory to taking them upstairs to the bedroom, where they were going to have to sleep for the next week or so in order to facilitate night feeding.

Seeing that his wards were being taken away, nothing would do but that the dog had to sleep upstairs as well. As I climbed the stairs, followed by Tundra, I feared that slumber was going to be fitful for a while.

In the bedroom, I placed the nesting box on top of the bedside table, at first intending to leave the cubs there, where I could reach them easily. The tray I had planned to leave on the floor, also within reach, but now that Tundra had joined the party I realized that the tray would have to be hoisted out of harm's way. The dog wouldn't willfully interfere with the formula, but he would almost certainly trample all over everything. A moment's thought solved the problem. I opened the drawer in the table, transferred the cub's bedding into it, and settled Matta and Wa in their temporary, nighttime quarters. The tray was placed on the tabletop. That done, I fed the cubs a light meal, a procedure that evoked Tundra's interest when they refused the bottle and, too weary to argue, I once more used my mouth.

It was gratifying to have Tundra available and willing to do the mopping up and b-b (bladder and bowel) stimulation, not only because I had found this a somewhat tedious chore but also because he could do it more quickly and far more effectively. It pnly took him a few minutes to complete the task that night, but when the cubs were placed in the drawer, the lights were extinguished, and I climbed into bed, Matta and Wa began to wail.

As soon as the first reedy sounds emerged from the partly closed drawer, Tundra lifted himself from his place beside the table and tried to stick his nose through the gap, rising on his hind legs the better to do it and managing to knock over the contents of the tray with one of his front paws. In vain did I tell him to "go sit" as I rescued the tray; he was beyond the reach of human orders, his innate concern for the pups dominating all else. In the end I had to take Matta and Wa out of their impromptu *chambre à coucher* and put them in bed with me, curled up on my diaphragm, where they were able to feel the pumping of my heart and to draw comfort from it. Peace was restored in this manner.

Dawn was breaking when I opened my eyes believing that a particularly vivid dream had awakened me. I lay for some little time in that bemused state between sleep and awareness, trying to recall in more detail the incubus that still caused me to feel as though I had stood in a downpour while something attacked my right armpit. When I remembered the cubs, I knew I had not been dreaming.

They had wet me several times, and Matta, I discovered on extending my exploratory left hand, was even at that moment attempting to suck milk from my armpit, working her mouth so vigorously that she had actually caused a reddening of the skin.

Too sleep-drugged to want to fuss with the coffeepot and the nursing bottles, I gulped cold formula, warmed it in my mouth for a while and lifted Matta to my lips, selecting her first in case she should seek to continue sucking on me. Wa, meanwhile, was lying on his back, beside my thigh, opening and closing his mouth wetly, as though tasting his breakfast already. At that moment the U.S. cavalry galloped up the stairs: Tundra, probably feeling too hot lying on the rug, had evidently gone to his favorite place, the basement, a remarkably cool area where, especially in the heat of the summer, he normally spent considerable time. He had heard me stir and now came up with his customary energy.

Sliding into the bedroom on "two wheels," he leaped onto the bed, narrowly missing Wa with one of his great paws, stepped on my abdomen, and stuck his nose in my face the better to observe and to lick Matta. When I freed one hand from the cub's body and punched him—I could not talk at the moment—he turned his attentions to Wa, licking *him* instead. This pleased me; Wa was soaking wet. So was Matta, but nothing could be done about that just then.

"Here, clean this one up now," I said to Tundra when Matta allowed herself to be parted from my tongue.

While the dog was washing the she-wolf, Wa began to ingest formula, doing it with his usual, deliberate slowness. Halfway through the feed he disgraced himself by depositing in my hands a revolting mess, delivered amid small, explosive noises and a great deal of sotto-voce grunting, all of which he managed without missing a suck. As I hastily put him in the drawer in preparation for ridding myself of the odoriferous porridge, at the same time warding off Tundra, who was immediately drawn to the scene of the action, Matta, unattended and probably feeling neglected, copied her brother's actions, making *her* mess on the sheets. At that, I roared my disapproval. Tundra, knowing the signs, leaped off the bed and clattered downstairs, all the way to the basement, through the window, and out into his pen.

It took an hour and a half to set everything to rights. During this interval the cubs were sponged more or less clean, then handed over to Tundra in the kitchen, where he licked them spick-and-span. In the meantime I changed the bed and myself, thrust the soiled laundry into the washing machine, and had a shower. Feeling less irritable and more awake, *and clean*, I brewed coffee, fried eggs and bacon, made toast, and took the lot outside, ordering Tundra to "stay with the cubs!" when he made to follow me.

The morning, which I had been too busy to observe thus far, was fine and warm, one of those balmy June days that are cool enough to subdue the ardor of the mosquitoes yet warm enough for human comfort. The birds, at the height of the nesting season, were exceptionally active and in good voice, except, perhaps, for the raucous blue jays, who immediately came to beg from my table, Our resident chipmunk, christened Scruffy—because he was—also made his presence known, emerging from his lair under the machine shed just as I was about to take the first mouthful. But I was ahead of him, having brought along a supply of peanuts and sunflower seeds, some of which I arrayed on the picnic table before sitting down. Scruffy was at least five years old, the chipmunk equivalent of Methuselah, and seemed able and ready to go on living for a long time to come. He was Tundra's pet hate. No matter how hard the dog tried to sink his teeth into the audacious and tempting body, Scruffy invariably escaped, diving with weasel-like speed and agility into any one of a dozen or more bolt-holes he used when seeking sustenance in the yard.

All chipmunks are indefatigable. I once tested Scruffy, or tried to, by taking a huge supply of sunflower seeds outside and allowing him to help himself. This was done in the interests of science; I wanted to discover the quantity of food that a chipmunk would normally take to its burrow. When Scruffy showed no signs of giving up after he had ferried away three quarts of sunflower seeds and one pound of peanuts, I ended the experiment. But I gleaned one bit of scientific data when I took the time to count out two hundred sunflower seeds and watched while Scruffy stuffed his cheeks, for when I counted the remainder, I discovered that he had crammed sixty-three seeds into his pouches.

I finished eating and began to make notations in the wolf log, but when I realized that I didn't know how much liquid could be contained in my mouth at one time, I returned to the house and sucked up water until my cheeks were distended, then spat it all out again into a measuring jug: two and a half ounces was the extreme capacity of my particular facial container. Thus I calculated that Matta, between now and the time I first fed her yesterday, had consumed almost ten ounces of food; Wa, during the same period, ingested closer to twelve. I noted these figures under *June 8*, with a reminder that they were by no means conclusive because I had no idea how much the cubs had obtained from their mother before she was killed. Under *June 9*, beginning with this morning's feed, I marked two and a half ounces for each cub; beside this, I set down the total amount that I had decided to allow them to ingest during the next twenty-four hours: eleven ounces for Matta, twelve ounces for Wa. After that, the amounts would be marginally increased every twenty-four-hour period, depending on the cubs' state of health and condition of their bowels. The last entry made that day showed both sets of bowels to be in good working order, the consistency of their output qualifying as "medium." In a notebook, I began to record details of the personality and temperament of each cub, together with the more outstanding features of their physical development, a task that kept me busy for the next five days, for the cubs made rapid progress.

Wa was the calmer of the two up to this time; he seemed to be more easygoing and placid. Matta was quite excitable, easily disturbed. It was impossible to determine with any degree of certainty, but it appeared that neither cub was actually aware of the radical change in their circumstances. Once they were taken out of the sack by the banks of the Mattawa and given food and comfort, they exhibited no signs of serious agitation. Lacking the ability and experience to sense and recognize danger, they showed no fear, reacting only to hunger and physical discomfort, their behavior patterns regulated by their nervous systems. Cold, sudden disturbances in their immediate physical surroundings, the need for food and drink, and the lack of immediate contact with another living body caused them distress, but, insofar as I was ever able to determine, they were either unaware of or unconcerned by the loss of their mother. These things did not surprise me, for by then I had observed similar reactions when caring for other infant animals, and I had already concluded that creature comfort is at first the only need capable of eliciting response from the very young of all species, human infants being no exception. Love, fear, anger, hate—all come later as the faculties become more developed.

On that particular day, Matta and Wa were still protected from the cares of life by the lack of two, and the poor development of one, of their five senses; that is to say, they could not hear and they could not see, while their sense of smell was at best rudimentary; but they could taste and they could feel.

I was interested to note that, though evidently unable to pick up noise, they were yet able to *feel* the vibrations of sound. First becoming aware of this when Tundra howled as we arrived home, I performed an elementary test: Sitting near them, I spoke directly into the nesting box in a voice slightly louder than normal; the cubs showed signs of agitation. Next I positioned a mirror so that I could see them while my head was turned completely away and I spoke in a louder tone; both pups remained unconcerned. I did this several times, always with the same results. The question I was aiming to answer, of course, was, Were they really unable to hear? Lacking audio-testing equipment, I could not answer the question with any degree of certainty, but if I was to accept the conclusions of experts in this field, I had to believe that wolf cubs do not begin to hear until they are some four weeks old. By the same token, since sound produces definite and measurable physical vibrations, it did not appear unreasonable to suppose that the cubs, like many other animals, could feel these.

It was, by contrast, easy to determine that Matta and Wa were unable to see; their eyelids were gummed shut. But they could detect light. From six feet away they reacted to the beam of a five-cell flashlight focused in their nesting chamber, and they always became momentarily startled when exposed suddenly to light at night or to intense sunlight.

Neither was there any doubt that they could smell, if poorly. The day after they came into my care, they were able to detect the odor of formula when this was two or three inches away from their noses. By June 13, they could detect the scent from a distance of five feet. The cubs' increasing ability to scent the formula and their obvious recognition of its meaning led me to conclude that the ability to reason develops quickly in wolf cubs: The formula differed in odor, taste, and texture from their mother's milk, but Matta and Wa soon associated these things with their comfort.

I felt great satisfaction on that particular morning as I finished reviewing the progress made by the cubs during the time elapsed since their arrival at the farm. On the fifth day, my notes concluded,

Formula consumption at June 13: Matta: twelve ounces Olac (one teaspoon to seven teaspoons of water) containing two tablespoons of mixed cereal Pablum for each eight ounces of liquid. Wa: fourteen ounces ditto. Cubs accepted bottle for first time last night: trumpets! Both sets of bowels are normal, stools firm but not hard, i.e., medium. Matta averaging two movements per twenty-four hours, Wa goes between two and three times, usually two good ones and one token. Bladders of both still producing copious, light yellow urine, but this appears normal, without noticeable odor unless sniffed closely, then usual smell for this waste. No irritations observed; fur in top condition. From tomorrow on will mix half a teaspoon cod liver oil per sixteen ounces of formula daily. Feeding frequency: six times daily: first feed 6 A.M., then every three hours; Matta receives two ounces each feed, Wa gets two and one-third ounces.

In future, cubs to be weighed only once a week. They don't take kindly to this, showing considerable agitation and crying constantly; Tundra put in basement during this activity—too much of a nuisance with his fussing and interference. Cubs now sleep *all* night in the nesting box on floor beside the bed. Tundra also in the room, but he leaves sometime during the night to go to basement.

Teeth of both cubs beginning to show, like the points of needles; gums slightly inflamed, purplish red around the teeth. Ears are still floppy.

The next day I had to go to the Toronto airport to pick up Joan, a round trip of slightly more than two hundred miles. The cubs would have to come along. Should I take Tundra as well? I debated this for a while, but when I remembered his solicitude for them and, since their arrival, his propensity to make a great fuss when he wasn't with them, I thought he might as well come too.

Before setting out, the pups were fed, washed by Tundra, and placed inside their nesting box, which would travel on the front seat beside me. When Matta and Wa were settled, I packed emergency supplies of paper towels, hot water in the insulated

41

jug, and a one-pint Thermos containing warm, ready-mixed formula. Letting Tundra into the back of the station wagon and giving him a big beef knucklebone to keep him quiet, at least for a time, I collected the cubs and left the yard.

As planned, we arrived early at the airport, allowing time to give the wolves an extra feed to keep them quiet while I waited for Joan. Again Tundra mopped them up, removing first the wet they had made on the journey and lastly, after each was fed, slurping off the spilled formula that tended to dribble from the sides of their mouths and course down their chests. Wa was the last one to receive the dog's attentions, and after he joined his sister in the box, I got out of the car, told Tundra to "watch them," and left for the arrivals building. On the way I smiled slightly, thinking that my admonition to the dog had not really been necessary. He had taken his role as guardian very seriously indeed.

Tundra was not by nature a savage dog, but he was extremely possessive. He would allow strangers to enter the yard, but he would not let them go onto the porch to knock on our door unless one of us said it was okay. Neither would he let a stranger depart if, once in the yard, the visitor found we were not at home. He didn't bark or fuss; he simply planted himself in front of an intruder and stared fixedly at him. His message was eminently clear. The cubs would be well guarded in my absence, and, because I had removed the lid from their box, would be tongue-fussed if they so much as whimpered.

An hour or so later, as Joan got near the car and began to make her usual noises for Tundra's benefit, she spotted the box.

"What have you got *this* time?" she asked in mock resignation, trying to open the passenger door before I had unlocked it.

Tundra must have scented or heard us before we came into view. He was standing on the front seat, straddling the nesting box and wagging his tail furiously, waiting for the door to open so he could properly great Joan. It was because of his position that my wife was unable to see inside the box and thus determine its contents for herself. I unlocked her door but left it shut, going around the front of the car to open my own door, intending to reach over and secure Tundra's lead before Joan got in. But she was impatient to see the latest additions to North bowl for

Christy

Star Farm and she didn't wait. An instant later dog and wife landed in a heap on the asphalt, there to remain until I got to them to untangle the melee. When order was restored and Tundra was secured by my hand around his collar, Joan, automatically wiping her face where the dog's wet tongue had made contact, opened the car door and bent over the box. Watching over her shoulder, I saw that Wa was lying on his back and yawning prodigiously and Matta was sucking gently on one of her brother's back feet. Joan dissolved into maternalism.

Her eyes, when she turned to look at me, shone with instant love, then filled with tears. She turned back to the waifs, murmuring endearments, and put her hands gently into the box to stroke both cubs at the same time. Matta and Wa accepted this as fitting tribute.

Knowing animals as I did, I insisted that from that moment on Matta and Wa were aware that they had an absolute sucker, metaphorically as well as factually. Joan denied it indignantly, maintaining that she *never* spoiled any of our foundlings. However this might be, my wife was then and there transformed into a doting she-wolf. Or as close to one as any human being can possibly become.

CHAPTER THREE

Matta and Wa were now almost seven weeks old, according to my calculations. But whereas when they first came into my care I was unsure of my estimate, now I could state with some degree of certainty that they had been born about the end of May, probably the thirtieth. This became evident the evening of Joan's return home when, at about six o'clock, I noticed signs of agitation in Tundra and in Wa.

As was by now usual, the dog lay in the corner of the kitchen where the blanket was spread, attending to his charges with a patience and love so palpably devotional that it often brought tears of joy to Joan's eyes.

Sitting in the living room making entries in the wolf log, I lifted my head to look into the kitchen when a low whine was voiced by Tundra. I was in time to see him stand up, head lowered toward Wa, who was moving jerkily across the rug shaking his head from side to side. The dog's attitude reflected so much concern that I got up immediately and went to see what the trouble was, followed, of course, by Joan.

Wa's eyes had opened! At least, they hadn't opened fully, but the lids were slitted, revealing the sparkle of a pair of rather worried, slaty blue orbs that caused their owner to move his head whenever the direct light from overhead impinged on the newly exposed pupils. I hastily flicked the switch and turned on a more subdued desk lamp. Then, not wishing to miss a moment of this enthralling event, I sat on the floor beside Wa, determined to remain there all night if need be in order to record the stages of sight development, Matta, meanwhile, was still quite blind; not one vestige of a crack could be detected between her gummed lids.

That was June 14. The pups were approximately two months old. We decided there and then to settle on a birthdate and, perhaps arbitrarily, picked May 30. When Joan brought me the wolf log—selfishly, I refused to go and get it myself in case I would miss something—I entered into it the date of birth, followed by a question mark in brackets that was never to be removed and was always ignored; then I recorded the opening of Wa's eyes. Afterward, the long vigil started.

By dawn, when I considered that Wa's eyes were opened wide enough to justify the term *fully*, I put both pups into their nesting box and trudged upstairs to snatch a few hours of sleep, noting, however, that Matta was still blind. The interval between the first slitting of Wa's lids and the final opening, some ten hours later, offered disappointingly little information.

The process was infinitely slow. Wa, startled and plainly uneasy during the first half hour of sight, soon became accustomed to the new and—surely!—wondrous sense, but apart from using his so-recent gift to glance myopically around himself, his behavior altered in only one regard. His back legs, though still weak, were now able to sustain his entire weight, and herein lay the greatest change in the cub now that he had some sight to guide himself by. Unlike Matta, who tottered on all fours for short distances but was liable to blunder into obstacles, the new Wa moved purposefully for the first time by 8 P.M. on the night of the fourteenth, much to Tundra's consternation.

If the cub's ability to see was a strange novelty to him, it seemed even more strange to the dog, who felt it his duty to pick up the straying wolf whenever he got close to the edge of the blanket; and since Wa immediately began to explore again when he was dumped beside his sister, Tundra was kept on the go almost constantly, never slackening his efforts but clearly concerned by this change in one of his wards. I was rather amused by the dog's behavior, especially when he would look at me, as near to frowning as a canine can get, as though expecting me to take a hand in the affair, to help him control the wanderer.

As far as I could determine from my observations of Wa that night, the most important change occurred when he realized that sight allowed him to direct his wobbly footsteps, thus awakening the latent urge to explore, the curiosity of life so essential to growth and development in all creatures. Only exhaustion stopped his wanderings, and then for not more than half an hour or so, time he spent sleeping between Tundra's paws, beside his sister.

The natural result of so much unaccustomed exercise was that Wa's appetite increased almost instantly, a fact that was communicated to Joan and me before seven o'clock the next morning, after I had slept no more than two hours. Making his keening hunger-wail while Matta still slept, awakening first Tundra, then me and Matta, and, lastly, Joan, Wa could hardly wait to clamp his jaws on the nipple of his bottle, becoming considerably agitated during a feed for the first time.

He consumed eight ounces with greed and gusto, a quantity that brought him close to the hard-boiled-egg belly. In the meantime, of course, Matta added her voice to the new day, and poor Tundra, recognizing at once the increased tempos of Wa's demands and the additional excitement exhibited by Matta, drove himself into a state bordering on frenzy. The dog couldn't stay still. At first he tried to interfere while Wa was having his breakfast, but when I became cross, he devoted himself to Matta, licking her into silence, but so profusely that she started to whimper before he was finished; this made the dog all the more excited and caused me to speak to him again, whereupon he dashed downstairs with a great clatter only to wheel around in the living room and come galloping back upstairs, to jump on top of Joan and to attempt to lick her face. Now it was my wife's turn to scold him, and he again dashed away, repeating his earlier maneuver. Fortunately, Wa had finished eating when Tundra galumphed up the second time, so the dog was able to direct his paternal urges to their proper course as he washed the cub thoroughly.

Matta opened her eyes the next night at precisely 9:03, in the middle of her last feed of the evening. She was lying spread-eagle on my towel-covered lap, head up, front paws pushing against my hand rhythmically as she sucked. It happened that

I was looking down at her when she ingested some formula down the wrong pipe and sneezed hard. And her lids opened, fully, just like that! For a second or two her rheumy blue eyes stared into mine uncomprehendingly, then she let go of the nipple and tried to bury her head in my lap.

Putting the bottle aside, I quickly covered her with my hands, and she became quiet, but when, some moments later, I began to lift my hands, she panicked once more. Now, having covered her head again, I slowly parted first one finger, then another, allowing a little light to seep into her shelter each time, but when she still reacted with panic, I asked Joan to put the lights out. At this point Matta seemed to recall that she had not yet finished swallowing her four ounces of formula, and she began searching for the teat. Joan picked up the bottle and put the nipple in Matta's mouth, holding the container and the cub while I eased out from under and went into the hallway to switch on a light, thus allowing a more gentle illumination to enter the kitchen.

Matta didn't stop feeding this time, but she did react, fidgeting more than usual, slopping formula out of the corners of her mouth, and at times choking when she ingested too hurriedly and the stuff went up her nose. In the end we decided not to worry her further by attempting to record her visual progress and instead put her and Wa into the nesting box, fixing a lid on its opening. The little bitch was going to require more time to become accustomed to her gift of sight.

This was not unusual. In the wild, cubs almost certainly opened their eyes in the darkened den, becoming accustomed to the filtered light coming from the entrance. Later, when better able to walk, they gradually approach the source of illumination. Our cubs had opened their eyes while the artificial lights were on, and though Wa had quickly adjusted, being the calmer and more phlegmatic of the two, Matta became alarmed and would have communicated her fears to her brother had we tried to force her to accept electric light.

Two days before, June 13, both cubs had been weighed and measured and the details noted in the log: Matta scaled three pounds four ounces, and measured 13¼ inches; Wa weighed five pounds one ounce, and was 15½ inches long. That night, after the cubs were put to bed, I filled in the additional details in the log, noting that Wa had opened his eyes twenty-seven hours before his sister, but that she, probably because of the sneeze, had opened them fully from the start. At this time, too, I was fairly sure that the cubs were starting to hear, if indifferently. There was no doubt about their ability to scent, for both were able to pick up the aroma of the formula when this was being mixed, even if they were in the living room and the food was prepared in the kitchen. And the teeth were now poking through the gums, not fully developed yet but already sharp as needle points in the front.

A week later, by June 21, both cubs demonstrated that they could hear well enough to respond to outside sounds, especially when our resident flock of blue jays came to the window feeder and shrieked at each other there as they observed the pecking order. The day before this, at the weigh-in, Wa scaled eight pounds three ounces, a gain of three pounds two ounces in one week! Matta did almost as well, weighing five pounds ten ounces, or two pounds six ounces more than the previous week. By now, too, both pups were able to walk quite well and were keeping Tundra busy as they rambled around the kitchen.

The dog no longer put them back on the rug, but he tried to keep track of both of his wards at once, and since they almost never went in the same direction, poor old Tundra dashed from one place to another, getting underfoot while Joan was trying to prepare meals and becoming almost as great a nuisance to her as were the cubs, who were often in danger of being stepped on.

Matta was now 14½ inches long, including a 4¼-inch tail, while Wa measured 16¾ inches and had a tail ¼ inch longer than his sister. Vision had considerably improved in both pups and their slaty blue eyes missed very little of what was going on around them. Sometimes the expression of those rather startlingly colored orbs seemed inordinately serious, especially when greeted by some new object; at other times, young as they were, pure mischief shone out of both sets of eyes, particularly when one pup, or both at the same time, attempted to chew on the fur of Joan's favorite slippers with teeth that were not yet fully formed.

On the morning of June 22, Wa's mouth proved to be full of his new teeth when I gave him the bottle, but Matta took another three days before all of hers completed their growth; once again the she-wolf's physical development was slower than her brother's, though this was by no means unusual. She would catch up in time, even if she would always be smaller than Wa (females are usually about 20 percent smaller than males).

With the development of scent, sight, hearing, and teeth, to say nothing of their back legs, our two waifs began to strengthen their individual personalities and to gain great confidence.

Wa was the daring one from the start. Nothing was too insignificant to escape his inspection, and no part of the ground floor of the house was proof against his visits. Matta, the nervous type, advanced in stages, exhibiting great caution when confronted by newness and not stirring a step until she had satisfied herself that it was safe to do so. Often, though she wanted desperately to follow her brother, she could not force herself to do so, yet she would stand spraddle-legged and whine pitifully, which sound was studiously ignored by Wa but drove Tundra to distraction—as well as Joan!

At this stage the cubs learned to play and run as well as to growl, and it was fascinating and often hilarious when they ganged up on Tundra, chewing at whatever part of his body they could most easily reach, while emitting their baby growls. The dog, at first, didn't know what to make of this, and he would rise and go lie down in some other part of the house. But not for long.

Locating him by scent, the Terrible Twins, as Joan now called them, homed in on the long-suffering dog as though they were tied to him by some invisible string, running in mock charge over the last few feet of floor and diving at him with baby ferocity. Again the dog would get up and seek sanctuary elsewhere, thereby starting all over again what I am sure was the wolf equivalent of hide-and-seek, for it was clear that Matta and Wa, much as they loved to chew on Tundra, loved even better the finding of him and the last, would-be fierce charge.

Once the area of the ground floor, that is, living room, hallway, and kitchen, had become familiar territory to Matta, she didn't hesitate to run and trot all over it, yet she showed little disposition to go toward the front door when this was opened. Wa, on the other hand, always tried to get through the doorway at every opportunity and soon learned to start for it when he heard the rattle of the latch. In this, I am sure, he was given confidence because he could detect Tundra's scent on and around it, and from my observations of him during those first weeks of his life at North Star Farm, I knew that the male wolf was going to prove exceptionally intelligent, resourceful, and perhaps too daring for his own safety. Matta was certainly endowed with a good intellect, but her bump of caution was equally well developed. As time was to show, these traits were inherent in each cub; they were not to change while they remained with us.

By the fourth or fifth day of their playing stage, the cubs bothered Tundra so incessantly that for the first time since he had taken on the responsibility for them he sought shelter in his basement redoubt, escaping there at intervals, remaining for periods that varied from an hour to two hours, and then returning to allow himself to be chewed, charged at, and generally molested, never once showing any anger toward the pups. In this regard he behaved rather like an adult wolf, for these animals are exceptionally patient with their young and also content themselves with moving away from the cubs when they become too bothersome.

The cubs were now able to eat meat and to chew bones, but they would not yet part from their beloved bottles. We tried several times to coax them to eat their Pablum and Olac formula, much thicker and stronger and in greater quantity, from a plate, but they steadfastly refused to do so. Matta simply backed away as though the plate and its contents was something quite dangerous; Wa was aggressive, growling his best growl at any human hand that tried to hold him near the food, then, when released, stepping boldly into the pap and squatting in it, plastering his behind and legs while at the same time focusing his blue eyes on me and whining his most pathetic and plaintive complaint. After the fourth such experiment, we gave up (for the time being), leaving Tundra to lick up Wa and the dishes, while the eight-ounce bottles, now two for each cub, were prepared.

The ingestion of raw meat was another matter altogether. All that Matta and Wa needed after they got the first taste was to sniff it from a distance and they galloped after it as though prepared to pull down their own prey. In this case, both cubs were equally bold, Matta refusing to take a backseat to her brother, a fact that Joan found out to her cost when she went to feed Wa a bit of raw beef without having an equal piece in her other hand for Matta. The bitch charged at her brother, and incidentally at Joan's fingers, snapped her needle teeth, and drew blood from my wife's index finger without, however, managing to take the meat away from Wa.

I was in the living room, so I didn't see the start of the affair, but Joan's loud "ouch" and a sudden outbreak of growling, the tempo of which I had not heard before, drew me to the scene. Joan just stood there, eyes wide, not knowing whether to suck her bleeding finger or separate the cubs, which had now locked themselves in combat; she was quite obviously more horrified by the first serious fight between the cubs than she was by the fact that she had been bitten. She looked as though she couldn't believe that her "darlings" were capable of so much fury, then turned some of the latter on me when I refused to separate the combatants.

In vain did I try to tell her that this was the first of many contests that would naturally ensue as the cubs grew and jockeyed for pack position. If I wasn't going to stop them, well, then, *she* would! Fortunately Tundra arrived to save our marriage, for I had no intention of allowing sentimentality to interfere with the course of nature.

Tundra, on the other hand, was a legitmate peacemaker, a role that he assumed with instant ease, as an adult wolf would have done in the wild. Wa became pinned by one of the dog's great paws; Matta was nosed to one side quite forcefully, so that she rolled a couple of yards along the polished kitchen floor. When both cubs cried their shrill protests at such ungentle treatment, Tundra at once relented. Wa was released and licked quickly, Matta was helped back to all fours by the facile nose and also licked. The two cubs joined forces immediately and started playing with Tundra, while I, the "brute who'd let my babies bite each other," got some meat for all three canines.

Two days before this incident Matta and Wa had been housed in a new nesting box, having outgrown both the old one and their place in our bedroom. That night, after the twins were settled in the kitchen and guarded as usual by Tundra, Joan and I went upstairs, still discussing the fight and my refusal to separate the cubs.

In the quiet of our room, I began to explain to my wife

some of the rather complex behavior patterns that govern wolf societies.

Matta and Wa were, of course, Ontario wolves, and thus Canadian by nationality—if animals have nationalities—but somewhere in their lupine past there must have been an American ancestor; why else would they have elected to show their independence on the Fourth of July? Joan insisted that this was coincidence; I wasn't so sure! But whether coincidence or because of some latent revolutionary tendencies, a definite change came over the cubs on that day, drawing itself to our attention during the weekly weigh-in.

Wa made himself hard to catch when the scales were brought into the kitchen but didn't resist my efforts when I placed him on the balance. He weighed exactly fifteen pounds, a gain of thirteen pounds in *four weeks*! Matta allowed herself to be caught easily enough, but she tried to bite me when I put her on the scales, though she submitted tamely enough when offered a bribe in the shape of a piece of raw steak (Wa got one also, at the same time); the little bitch weighed ten pounds two ounces and had gained eight pounds two ounces since June 8.

I let them play around the kitchen for a time, but when Wa grabbed one of Joan's furry slippers and made off with it, and Matta, not to be outdone, grabbed the other one while my wife was chasing Wa, we felt it was time to measure the cubs and put them back in the maple syrup evaporator house, a large shedlike building built on the edge of our maple bush where the vigorous and ebullient cubs were now spending their days, supervised by Tundra.

By concerted effort we cornered Wa, removing the slipper from his jaws. But when I tried to measure him, the cub wriggled and struggled, yelping loudly and causing Matta to drop her slipper voluntarily and to run and hide under the living room sofa. Clearly, Wa was not going to submit to the indignities of the tape.

"Well, I guess that ends the measuring sessions," I told Joan as I released the cub.

Almost as though my words were understood, Matta came out from her hiding place and aimed herself at the discarded slipper. But Joan was a little quicker this time, scooping it off the floor. As she was putting the coveted mules away, I picked up my hat and spoke the magic words:

"Walk time!"

Tundra had kept himself aloof from the earlier proceedings, but now he bounced to his feet and trotted to the hall, where his lead was looped over a hook, there to wait expectantly. Wa scurried to the door and positioned himself beside the dog, while Matta, ears pricked forward, gave up looking for the slippers and began to move toward the other two. I was about to open the door when Joan said she would come along also, and during the short wait that followed while my wife was getting a long-sleeved shirt as protection against the flies, both cubs began scratching at the door, which was something they had not done hitherto. Such bad manners evidently horrified Tundra; dropping his tail, he looked at me as though to disclaim any responsibility for the behavior of the cubs, knowing that I would not allow him to use his great paws in like manner. When I didn't do anything about the transgression of his wards, he reached out a hooked paw and pulled Matta away, bending his nose to do likewise with Wa. But the male wolf, having declared this Indpendence Day, snarled and snapped at the reaching nose.

Tundra's tail curled tightly, going from the extreme down position to the high, dominant one, as though powered by an invisible spring. He lifted his head only high enough to grab Wa by the scruff and to give him a complete and thorough shaking. Of course, our hero screamed his baby head off, and his racket brought Joan tumbling downstairs. When she saw what Tundra was doing, she turned on me.

"*Do* something!"

I shook my head. This she knew about. The scruff bite, the shake, these were the rituals of punishment in the canine world. Wa had asked for it, now he was getting it. And the harmless shaking was also a warning for Matta, who lost little time in seeking the shelter of her sofa hideout.

I myself had already had occasion to discipline the cubs in this manner, and although they cried as though they were being beaten with a club, I knew that the hurt was psychological and not physical. I knew also that this was necessary training for their future life in the wild, for without this discipline, which continues into adulthood as a strictly applied ritual, when a dominant wolf will deliver a token scruff bite and shake to an underling, Matta and Wa would quickly run into trouble on encountering wild wolves.

Tundra had punished Wa instinctively. After he dropped the cub following the shaking, which lasted only a few seconds, Wa flopped over on his side, tucked his short tail between his legs, and lifted the back leg that wasn't pressed against the floor. This was the surrender posture, equivalent to the "I'm sorry" of a human child. Tundra quickly licked the cub, and harmony was instantly restored. Sensing the peace with her already-effective radar, Matta popped out from the sofa. Now was the time to open the door and to lead the procession into the woods.

Joan was silent at first, clearly upset by Tundra's action, but as we discussed the pups, who now ranged ahead shepherded by Tundra, she saw the wisdom of my behavior. We had already thoroughly discussed the future of the two cubs, mutually agreeing that we would not keep them as pets and that we would seek to raise them as near to wild as was possible under the circumstances. If we were to do this, to equip them so that they could one day roam free and know how to live within their natural environment, it was necessary to teach them the facts of wolf life.

Matta and Wa had already given us much joy, amusement, and interest, but they had also posed many problems for us and had demanded much of our time and energy, to say nothing of our emotions. Of the two of us, Joan was the one who suffered most emotionally, because she had not had my experience in the wilderness and found it difficult to contain her pity and to smother her instinctive love when the pups got into trouble with Tundra or me or when, as during the meat incident, they fought each other.

We both knew by now that we had taken on an enormous responsibility that carried a stiff price tag of emotional anguish. But we both felt that whatever happened, Matta and Wa would one day go free and be as ready for their wild life as we could make them.

In this regard, because I felt it was necessary to fill a natural need, I had already begun to feed Matta and Wa by regurgitation, or, at least, by *pretended* regurgitation. At irregular intervals during each day I would cram hamburger wetted with milk into my mouth, go down on hands and knees, essay a "come here" *whoof* with a full mouth, and brace myself for the attack, because both cubs would dash up to me and begin to nip at my cheeks and neck, instinctively attempting to stimulate the regurgitation reflexes latent in adult wolves.

The first time I did this, Joan was out in the garden, the pups were wrestling in the kitchen. As soon as they smelled the meat coming out of the refrigerator, they stopped playing and stood still, eyeing me fixedly. I made a great show of stuffing my mouth amid many lip smackings and a few mock growls, then I dropped onto all fours and *whoofed* softly. Matta beat her brother to the post. Quickly, because her needle teeth drew blood, I opened my mouth, intending to spit out the mixture but she didn't give me a chance, thrusting her blunt little muzzle inside and grabbing whatever she could find. I didn't want my tongue to come between her fine teeth, so I drew back and let the rest fall to the ground, making sure I created two small mounds, so that Wa, who had meanwhile been nipping at my exposed neck, could also have his share. Joan came in at that moment, saw the cubs just finishing the last of the meat, then exclaimed loudly when she looked at me.

"What happened? You're bleeding all over your face and neck!"

I thought she was exaggerating. She wasn't. Looking in the mirror my face appeared as though I had tried to shave with a serrated, open razor; and my neck wasn't in much better condition.

I explained the wounds to Joan. She shook her head, suggested that I was carrying things too far, and immediately vetoed any further behavior of this kind on the grounds that people would begin to wonder about me if I went around looking like "a refugee from a slaughterhouse." But I felt that the cubs needed such stimulus as much as a human infant needs the fondling of its mother during the helpless stage.

"But we've got to figure out a way around the teeth," I told Joan.

That evening, after supper, I noticed that she was busy with some groundhog skins that I had tanned after their owners had foolishly walked in front of Tundra; she had been saving them to make herself some mitts. Now it transpired that she was

55

fashioning a sort of regurgitation helmet for me. I had been thinking along much the same lines myself but had hesitated to broach the subject just then.

About an hour later I was ordered to sit still for a fitting. The *thing* worked the first time. Unknown to me, Joan had used one of my old caps as the inner head side, stitching to it two wide flaps of hide, which were linked together by means of another, narrower band of groundhog fur, at a place corresponding with my chin. Thi was sewn to one side and secured on the other by a dome fastener, like a hairy chin strap. I looked ridiculous wearing it, but it was comfortingly furry for the cubs and offered excellent protection to me from those needle teeth.

Knowing our wolves by then, however, I allowed them to become acquainted with the headpiece, leaving it on the floor and letting them kill it dead several times after they had deduced that it wasn't likely to do the same to them. Indeed, so taken were they with the strange contraption, that Matta carried it in her mouth when I put the cubs to bed that night. And if the *thing*, as I continued to call it in preference to my wife's longer and rather revolting title, was a bit soggy and spiced with wolf aroma the next morning, the cubs rushed to it eagerly the moment I donned it to offer them their meal. But I did not allow either of them to stick their muzzles in my mouth again!

The following week, prodded by the fact that the cubs were clearly restless indoors, where we brought them every afternoon for their feed after they had spent the day in the evaporator house, I made two decisions: From now on they were to remain all day in the big sugaring-off shed, and I would construct a rendezvous for them in the maples, a place where they could accustom themselves to sleeping outdoors and where they could hunt small things while listening to the noises of the forest. At first we thought that Tundra should baby-sit with them, but in the end I decided to spend the first four or five nights with them, to make sure they became acclimatized to their new environment.

Thus, by mid-July, I led my wards to the readied enclosure, in which I had pitched the tent stocked with flashlight, sleeping bag, and pillow, and allowed them to make its acquaintance with Tundra. Later, just before dark, Joan came down, brought me a Thermos of soup and another of coffee, a bone each for the cubs and one for Tundra, and led the dog back, chewing as he trotted. A couple of hours later the mosquitoes began to find me, and I went into the tent, leaving the door open but igniting the pyrethrum powder.

The pups took to the rendezvous like a duckling takes to water, which was not surprising, for this has been the way of the wolves since the first howl lost itself in prehistoric space.

While the cubs are helpless during their neonatal stage, the mother takes care of them in the den, and the other pack members hunt for food and bring her rations back to her, either in their stomachs and regurgitating for her at the den entrance or carrying pieces of prey in their mouths. Later, when the pups are able to see, scent, and hear and are strong enough to walk short distances, they are led away from the den to a suitable rendezvous, where they will most likely spend the entire summer, or until they are strong enough to go with the pack on the hunt. Here, the young wolves are left alone when the adults are seeking meat and here they begin to acquire the skills and knowledge that will allow them to survive later on. If the den is kindergarten, the rendezvous is a combination of grades one, two, and three.

It was one of those hot, sultry nights in mid-July that Creation seems to have designed especially for the female mosquito. Not a breath of wind came to stir the leaves and the grasses, and a steamy warmth rose fitfully from the soil; the moon hung big and yellow, bedecked by a paraselene ring. But there was noise, a veritable farrago of sound: the whining drone of the bloodsuckers; the incessant croaking of the frogs; the maniacal shrieking of several loons disporting themselves on the lake across the larch swamp half a mile away.

From within the shelter of a spiky hawthorn, a catbird raised its mocking voice at intervals, now copying the sweet melody of the wood thrush, as suddenly reverting to its own kittenlike, mewling cry, then changing its mind in order to render some jumbled composition containing notes and trills stolen from a number of songsters; a male catbird it was, restless, probably hungry, definitely unemployed at night, and perhaps wanting to encourage his lady as she sat immobile and patient on her clutch of three or four blue green eggs in some neighboring tree or bush.

Louder than all the other voices of the night the cantos of

the whippoorwills continued monotonously, each of three woodsy-colored birds evidently eager to outlast the others as they repeated over and over the syllables from which their name derives.

Some ten minutes earlier Wa had walked into the tent and touched his cold nose to my cheek, awakening me in time to perceive the chunky outline of his sister as she, too, came into my shelter through the open doorway. The cubs appeared agitated, nervous, remaining within the confinement of the canvas despite the smoldering can of pyrethrum powder that I had lit before bedding down to protect me in some measure from the mosquitoes. The cubs sneezed repeatedly, their sensitive noses irritated by the slightly acrid smoke, but both pressed close to me.

I sat up and spoke to them soothingly and quietly, but I didn't give much thought to the cause of their concern. This was their first night in the forest; it was to be expected that the darkness and the many new sounds and scents they were encountering would combine to keep them in a state of alert tension. About to stroke them reassuringly, I heard the unmistakable crackling made by a heavy body moving through the undergrowth nearby. Then I heard a soft, husky snort, the kind of explosive noise that a person suffering from a heavy cold might unwittingly make when smothering a sneeze with a handkerchief. At that I arose, picked up a flashlight, and went outside, followed by Matta and Wa. I stopped, turned toward them before they emerged from the shelter of the tent, and growled at them, giving my deepest and best imitation of an angry dog, the wolf order to "stay" which by now the cubs obeyed instantly when it was voiced.

I knew what was out there, and why. Bears enjoy the taste of wolf cub, even to the point of raiding a den or summer nursery in the presence of the entire pack, a spectacle that I had once witnessed in the Yukon Territory; the dawn battle royal between five adult wolves and a big black bear lasted almost half an hour before the unscathed raider was forced to retreat and then run away at full gallop pursued by three of the wolves. None of the contestants was injured on that occasion, and the cubs remained safe in their den, but such encounters do not always end so well.

Adult bears, both black and grizzly, are endowed with such

thick, heavy coats that they are almost impervious to the powerful teeth of the wolves. The bear is swift and extremely dangerous, and one good swipe of its front paw will kill a timber wolf, or injure it so severely that it will die later. Only by force of numbers and by exercising all of their superb agility can a wolf pack defend its young from a bear attack, causing the raider to give up when he is repeatedly frustrated and perhaps bitten on paw or nose a few times. But once having given up and turned his back on his opponents, the bear invariably runs, and just as invariably is chased by several of the pack members until they feel that their enemy is far enough away from their territory.

It may well be that a few female bears go in for this sort of thing on occasion, but from my own experience I would say that it is the male of the species that is most likely to cause such trouble. Male, or boar, bears are loners—apart from the relatively short time that they spend with a female during the mating season—and are always on the lookout for the young of almost all species, their own included. They are extremely audacious and daring when hungry enough or when opportunity puts in their way some tender young animal.

As I stood outside the tent that night, listening for the intruder, I was determined that this bear was going to go away hungry.

The animal must have been standing still when I emerged, but within moments even *my* inefficient nose was able to pick up his scent, a smell I can only liken to the odor of pig. I switched on the five-cell light and began sweeping the surrounding forest, while speaking loudly.

Almost at once the bear turned around and began to run. My light just managed to pick up his fat rump as it was disappearing into the maples. Relieved, I began to walk around the wire enclosure, checking to see that our visitor had not breached the one-inch chicken mesh used to fashion an impromptu nursery, or rendezvous, for Matta and Wa. The wire was stapled to the trees, forming an irregular enclosure some sixty feet wide by eighty feet long, located just inside the maple forest and about two hundred yards from the house.

The wire fence was intact, and from close observation of the ground on the other side of it, I was able to determine that the bear had only just arrived when Wa came to wake me. This pleased me. It told me that the cubs, young as they were, had already become keenly vigilant and that, furthermore, they were exercising their reason, cautiously studying the normal sights, smells, and sounds of the bushland as these were encountered. When satisfied that the new sensory experience was harmless, they would ignore it if it offered no play challenge, or, after thorough investigation, would approach it and play with it one way or another, perhaps merely sniffing before turning away, or sniffing and pawing, or lastly, after the first two actions, biting at the object of their interest.

I had observed them carefully before going to lie down and had noted their reactions to each stimulus. Sound—alone or in conjunction with scent—was always cause for an alert when it was new to them. So was scent, and when they picked up what I called a silent odor, such as a dead insect, mouse droppings, or even the smell of urine deposited earlier by one or the other of them, they would react in the same way as they did for sound alone.

Such stimuli could be broadly classfied in two ways: sounds or scents that were known, but of little or no interest, such as the call of a bird in a tree (birds on the ground were later always investigated), or the smell of gasoline or some such "dull" odor; these were always picked up, logged, and then ignored; but noise and smells that were associated with food, or their "pack," in this case Tundra, Joan, and myself, were always treated with great interest. Likewise, I now realized, sound and odor interpreted as hostile elicited an escape reaction, much as these had done while Matta and Wa were confined to the house.

Sight was a relatively unimportant sense in the forest night, employed usually when the cubs were close to the object of their interest. They used their eyes, of course, but they obviously relied much more fully on their ears and noses.

Clearly, the cubs could already determine at least some of the forest things that were harmless and some that were not, else they would not have come to me when they heard and scented the bear. Acutely aware as I was of the intelligence of the wolf, I was yet gratifyingly surprised by the wit and wisdom they displayed, while at the same time I could not help wondering how they knew that a bear was a formidable and dangerous enemy. Later I was to learn the answer to this question, but that night I was admiringly curious over the intelligence displayed by Matta and Wa as fond parents might be over unexpectedly good marks brought home from school by their offspring.

Such an analogy was apt. The cubs were indeed at school, the academy of life that they would continue to attend as long as they survived, an "institute" whose curriculum espoused the principles laid down by Aristotle, more than two thousand years ago, for the guidance of human learning, namely: that the purpose of education is to teach an individual how to live and not to teach him or her how to earn a living. A seeming contradiction, until one realizes that if an organism truly knows how to live, the getting of a living will naturally follow. Alas that modern man should be so intent on earning and so inept at living!

For these reasons Matta and Wa were enclosed within their pen that night, and I was rather ineffectually attempting to act as both mentor and protector.

Returning to the tent after the inspection of the fence, I called the pups to me by emitting a soft *whoof* and squatting down in front of the canvas doorway, a practice adopted some weeks earlier that sought to copy the calm "come here" sound made by an adult wolf to its young. To my ears the note was all wrong, but the cubs responded to it, especially when I reduced my height, bringing myself closer to their physical level.

Reassured, all vestiges of earlier tension were gone when the pups bounded through the entrance and raced away to play their games and to hunt real or imagined beetles and moles while I once again entered the tent, added yellow pyrethrum powder to the smoldering can that was suspended by a string from the ridgepole, and then lay down on the sleeping bag, my head propped up on a pillow brought from the house. There, relaxed but feeling itchy from the mosquito bites I had gathered, I contemplated the night, trying to listen to every bushland sound and to separate the smells that even with the tang of pyrethrum filled the tent. I had done this many, many times in the past, but now I was trying to relate sound, sight, and smell in wolf terms.

Through the open doorway I noticed the moon moving slowly but noticeably toward the west, arcing slightly higher as it traveled, its glowing halo creating the illusion of two lunar orbs. On the ground splashes of yellowish light played around the edges of amorphous, charcoal shadows that lay as though brushed on the canvas of a mural painting, so still was the night.

CHAPTER FOUR

A little more than a month after Matta and Wa spent their first night with me in the rendezvous within the maples, I took them and Tundra for what I was to term their initiation into forest life. It was now August 15.

I rose at 4:30 in the morning, breakfasted, then prepared food for the cubs and a bone for Tundra, taking it to the rendezvous.

True dawn was still about half an hour away when the cubs, Tundra, and I left the farmhouse, where we had all foregathered for a few moments while Joan packed a haversack with my lunch and some beef bones for the other members of the party.

Walking from house to maples I couldn't help dawdling a little to admire the predawn with its thick and sluggish mists rising from the ground, in places heavy and almost billowing, in others spotty and lacelike, depending on the amount of surface moisture remaining in particular locations. Overhead, the sky was pale, and only a few of the brighter stars still shone; of the moon there was no sign.

In the east, the direction in which we were going to travel later on, an aquamarine glow backdropped the evergreens, revealing their ragged tops in silhouette. The signs proclaimed that this was going to be a still, hot day once the sun reached its noon zenith, but that the first two or three hours of daylight would be fresh and damp underfoot, with abundant mist in the lowlands, conditions that I always enjoyed and that would be particularly welcome today because they would introduce Matta and Wa to a combination of topography and weather that they had not yet encountered.

The forest has so many different moods that though I have been compiling a list of them for more than twenty years, the end is nowhere in sight; and I am certain that the task is beyond the limits of my span on earth. For me, this is a small hobby, something that I can work at when I feel like it or ignore when I don't. But for a hunting animal, the mood of the environment is of vital importance because it affects the conditions in which it will hunt and the habits and availability of its prey. Humans, who count the passage of time in days, weeks, months, and years, often fail to realize that no one day is exactly like another and that a twenty-four-hour period in the wilderness is not simply a matter of night and day, of black and white, as it were, but is divided into a great many shades, or "mini-periods," each of which is as motile as the second hand of a watch, one melding into another under the influence of sun, moon, stars, tides, and atmospheric conditions, to say nothing about the composition of each part of the physical wilderness itself.

Just as a person's mood can alter his or her countenance, posture, walk, and mannerisms, so does the wilderness change, but with far greater speed and variation. In daylight, clouds can come to cast their shadows on the land; wind, from a tiny breeze to a full gale, can alter both cloud conditions and the movement of the forest vegetation. Rain, snow, accumulations of moisture on the ground; heat sucking up the wet from lake, river, and pond; trees falling, either because they are old and dead, or because they have been dropped by beaver or been struck by lightning; atmospheric electricity that is constantly reaching earth from space; the movement of animals . . . these and many, many more variables alter the daylight wilderness from hour to hour, even from moment to moment. It is the same during darkness, or during the periods between dawn and day, or dusk and night.

A wild animal, especially a hunting animal who must constantly travel long distances through the bushland in order to keep itself fed, must not only know its territory, it must also understand the moods of the wilderness and the effect that these have on the environment.

Life is a little simpler for the grazers, particularly those smaller ones who inhabit a relatively modest piece of forest, scrubland, or prairie; food is usually easily procurable, almost always within reach, and it is not difficult to get to know an acre or two of habitat. But for an animal like the wolf, who ranges one hundred miles or more during a ten-day to two-week period, the task is far more complex.

For these reasons I felt that the time had come to broaden the scope of learning for Matta and Wa, who were now two and a half months old and had grown to respectable proportions during the last month. Wa was a husky thirty-four-pounder; his sister was twenty-three pounds two ounces. The cubs were strong and healthy and eager for the lessons of life, and although I was really looking forward to this "school outing," I was also worried about it, fearful lest the pups scamper too far afield and get themselves into trouble. For at that time not even Tundra could run herd on both of them at once, and I wasn't sure whether they would obey my growled order to stay, or my *whoof* command to follow—also used to call them to me—if they became single-mindedly excited over some scent or sound.

My greatest disadvantage was my inability to keep up with the canines, all of whom could walk faster than I could run, despite the fact that I am an agile person and quick on my feet. I could, of course, put on a sudden burst of speed that was calculated to allow me to reach the walkers if they got too far ahead of me, but the trouble with this notion was that as soon as I started to run, Tundra and the cubs joined in the spirit of the thing and did likewise, leaving me even farther behind.

To complicate matters further, I could not train them to an ordinary whistle for fear they might later respond to such a sound made by one human hunter to another and thus put themselves in jeopardy. But it was still too early, I felt, to teach them to answer to an ultrasonic whistle. In any event, I could not be sure that they would accept such an alien note even when they were older, but I was fairly certain that the high frequency would, at this unsure stage of their lives, have the opposite effect, making them afraid and more likely to run away.

For the hundredth or more time since becoming their foster father, I realized how difficult it is for a human to raise such fast, agile animals and how simple is the task, by comparison, when this is undertaken by their own kind. In situations such as the one in which I was likely to find myself soon, an adult wolf could overtake Matta and Wa without half trying, but, what was more, pack discipline, constantly enforced, would prevent the cubs from running ahead of the adults or from detouring on some errand of their own.

One might have expected Tundra to control the cubs in this way, and he did, to a limited extent, but he was not a wolf. Though of lupine stock, his breed has lost many of the traits of the wild dogs during centuries of domestication. Wolves are always extremely cautious; rarely do they charge into a situation without having first examined it thoroughly. Perhaps they lose a number of meals in this way, but they survive longer because they do not run headlong into danger. A dog, on the other hand, even a malamute, tends to behave much as an inexperienced cub might do, retaining all the "childish" impetuosity but lacking the caution that tempers this brashness and is likely to rush in at the first sound or scent that interests it. Then, too, a dog will hunt when it is not hungry, even within minutes of having eaten, obeying the ancient urges of the chaser whenever an opportunity presents itself.

It is evident to me that "three squares a day" can only appease the empty stomach, while the mind of the hunter is not satisfied until the entire animal is engaged in stalking, chasing, and bringing down its own food. Nowhere is this better illustrated than in the behavior of a captive raccoon, which animal, though fed abundantly, never ceases to try to earn its own living.

It is for this reason that the raccoon acquired a reputation for washing its food, when, in fact, it is only going through the motions of hunting in its water pot, into which it has previously dumped its bread, or corn, or whatever. In the wild the raccoon does not wash its food. It is an omnivorous animal that hunts as much in the forest as it does beside pond, lake, or river, and it would be ridiculous to expect it to rush in search of water after it had captured a frog, or found a berry in a forested area that is perhaps several miles from the nearest source of water. Within the confines of a cage, however, kept supplied with food but gripped by its innate urge to hunt and search, a raccoon has only one logical place in which to work out its frustrations: the water container. Elsewhere in its prison, every boring inch of which it knows intimately, there are few places where it might expect to find natural food. The floor is flat and featureless, the walls usually made of bars or wire mesh, and because accumulated debris is invariably removed by the human jailer, nowhere except in the mysterious depth of the water container can the captive employ his ever-questing paws.

Domestic cats are also similarly confused, and many a pet owner has been horrified to find that his or her beloved puss has brought home a bird as a toy or has captured a mouse and brought it into kitchen or living room, where it deliberately releases its slightly crippled victim and, if allowed, spends a considerable amount of time playing with it, even after it is dead. Once again, humans have jumped to unjustified conclusions; many people believe that cats are cruel creatures who deliberately torture their victims. Nothing can be further from the truth, but try telling that to your neighbor after your tabby just mangled her pet canary!

Even man himself has not escaped from the inherent urges that grip the wild hunter. He consciously believes that he earns his living as carpenter, doctor, accountant, or what-have-you, yet he appears unable to resist the urge to go out and kill something with his very own hands, telling himself that he isn't doing it because he wants to kill but rather because the act of hunting allows him to spend some time communing with nature. Bosh! The civilized "sport" hunter goes out to seek a victim because he cannot control the ancient urge to earn his daily bread the hard way, and it seems to me that the more routine and boring his occupation, the more he wants to "wash his food" or "play cat-and-mouse."

Be that as it may, Tundra, while most helpful in controlling the cubs in or around the house, could not himself be trusted in the forest, being likely to dash away in pursuit of almost anything, particularly a bear if he so much as caught a whiff of one. Often he killed a groundhog, hare, or mouse and brought his trophies home for our admiration, then mouthed them and tossed them around until their bodies resembled nothing so much as a partly filled hot water bottle gone cold. Joan, even after she understood the reason for the dog's actions, was always somewhat horrified by them, and I, too, felt distress at such—to a human mind—needless killing. But there was nothing that could be done about it except to restrict Tundra's opportunity within reasonable limits (reasonable to me, that is, never to him). To attempt to eradicate the hunter from an animal designed by nature to secure its food in this way was impossible, and a task that I would not have attempted even had it been possible.

For these reasons, then, I was apprehensive on my first forest outing with the "pack," but soon after we crossed the fifteen-acre clearing that separated us from a long, meandering rock ridge that in turn led to a small lake some two miles to the northeast, I became so interested in the reactions of the cubs that I forgot to worry.

The farm was located in a natural valley within an area of Precambrian granite that stretches for miles in all directions. Once, a billion years ago, the rocks that dominated the landscape were part of a mountain range that extended across what is now southern Ontario, ran through southern Quebec and Labrador, and ended at the shores of the Atlantic, a part of what is now known as the Canadian Shield. How this mountain range disappeared under the cataclysmic attacks of nature does not greatly concern this account, but the shape of the land after the last ice age bulldozed its way through does have relevance, for as such it was to become the amphitheater of life arising out of devastation.

On either side of the 350 acres that comprised the farm boundary lay swamps that were virtually impassable to inexperienced humans during the frost-free season. These were muskeg lands, for the most part, the haven of beaver and water birds, through which threaded a number of spotty game trails made by animals such as wolf, fox, and deer, who used as stepping-stones the thick clusters of swamp grass that grew there in abundance. A man could negotiate these trails if he was careful and knew the country, but there were not too many of us who had acquired this knowledge; as a result North Star Farm, under my ownership, became a cork in a wilderness bottle, keeping out the thoughtless and destructive humans who might be tempted to pass through it in order to gain the higher land beyond, country not otherwise accessible by road or waterway. In this regard, Tundra also helped to discourage such intruders.

From the air, the land looked sparse and thinly treed, which it was, when compared to some of the huge, dense forest tracts in other parts of North America, but from the ground one discovered country that offered a nice blend of forest and grass-land interspersed with areas of rock outcrop, some covered by toppings of moss in which were mixed small shrubs—such as blueberry bushes—fungi, and wild flowers, while an occa-sional pine or spruce managed to find roothold and sustenance in deep pockets of soil.

To the west the land was fairly flat, and here was found the most soupy swamp; to the north one encountered a mixture of forest, rock, and occasional swamps, while to the east a series of rock ridges allowed progress through country that was studded with beaver ponds whose convenient dams formed bridges lead-ing to virtually virgin stands of mixed trees. The southern bound-ary was delineated by a narrow gravel road that ended at the farm gates at a point that marked the center of the property.

Beyond the extreme northern boundary thousands of acres offered themselves to the flora and fauna of the land and gave me endless hours of pleasure during my almost equally endless wanderings. I knew this wilderness like an urban dweller knows his own neighborhood, perhaps more intimately, because I used it more. Tundra also knew it, better than I did, for his infallible sense of direction allowed him to travel through it without need to study the back trail. Now it was the turn of Matta and Wa to explore this rather special section of wilderness, and I found myself excited for them, infinitely interested in their reactions to the many things that they began to encounter within minutes of entering the forests that grew thickly on either side of the ridge.

From the flat land, this East Ridge, as I had named it, rose gently for about twenty feet; leveled off on its spine, furnishing a three-foot-wide pathway; then sloped downward again. On either side stood tall trees of thick girth, forming a dense mixed forest containing no less than fourteen different species, the most predominant being the white spruce. Some of these at-tained a height of up to 150 feet and a girth of three to four feet. In dense clusters, as though wishing to keep to themselves, grew eastern cedars, *Thuja occidentalis*, which supplied browse for deer in winter and shelter all year round for snowshoe hares and birds. Big hemlocks, tall, straight trees that can reach up for good light, grew in solitary splendor in some of the more open areas or hobnobbed with the spruces. The deciduous or broad-leaved trees, such as maples, elms, poplars, birches, and oaks, rooted themselves wherever they could find space, some of them succeeding in reaching giant proportions, others failing to make the grade and becoming stunted or dying, those cadavers that yet stood furnishing lodging for many insects that in turn offered sustenance to a variety of birds, chief among them being the woodpeckers. Here lived the great "cock of the north," or pileated woodpecker, crow-sized, resplendent in black and white plumage with a red cockade (shared by both sexes), the male additionally adorned by a scarlet "moustache."

As might be expected, the ubiquitous red squirrel was present in disciplined numbers, each redback jealously guarding its small territory from its rivals and sometimes filling the forest with its shrill, spiteful cry. At the foot of every large spruce was to be found a mound of cone scales, some of them four feet high and six feet wide, marking each big evergreen as a squirrel "supermarket" and proclaiming that generations of these solitary rodents had labored long hours during many autumns to harvest the small seeds contained in each cone.

The East Ridge area was also a favorite of the porcupines, which bristly types I hoped we would not encounter this day. Tundra knew all about them, avoiding them carefully ever since he had incautiously thrust his nose against one that I had been forced to shoot when it took up winter residence in our evaporator house. The dog got two quills stuck in his nose, and from that moment on lost all interest in "quill pigs." It was my hope that if any of these animals crossed our path today, Tundra's avoidance of them would warn the cubs to stay clear. Yet, I was at the same time anxious to meet one, under the right circumstances, because sooner or later Matta and Wa were going to have to learn that *Eretizon dorsatum* was not an animal to be disposed of casually.

Wolves kill and eat porcupines, but they do so only after observing, as cubs, how the adult pack members tackle the spiky creatures. Even so, expert wolves can make mistakes during an attack; when they do, results are often fatal and invariably painful.

Wolves killed during predator control programs have, on dissection, been found with quills embedded in the linings of throat and stomach, such quills evidently causing no ill effects, for the dissected specimens were otherwise perfectly healthy and well fed. But if a wolf gets a full frontal smash from a porcupine's stubby, quill-studded tail, the barbs sink deeply into its mouth, tongue, gums, and face, causing fearsome injuries and usually condemning the wolf to a slow and agonizing death, the result of both infection and starvation.

When a wolf attacks a porcupine, the event becomes a contest between agility and endurance. The porcupine's defense when it is caught in the open and unable to seek refuge in a tree or rocky den is to stand its ground, tucking its head between its stiffened front legs while presenting its rear to the enemy. In a world where all other animals that are forced to stand at bay invariably seek to face their foes, the porcupine's stance is unique and appears foolish, until one takes stock of the animal's offensive technique.

The rodent's teeth and claws, while eminently suited for eating shrubs, tearing off tree bark, and climbing, are of no use as weapons, but its quills, especially the shorter, heavier ones on the tail, more than make up for its lack of tooth and claw. In combat, the porcupine's main weapon is its powerful, clublike tail, while its body quills serve rather like armor, protecting all but the rodent's nose and its belly. The tail is lifted several inches off the ground during an emergency and is flailed from side to side. One smash of this war club is enough to incapacitate even the most powerful predator.

In order to keep its tail constantly presented toward the adversary, the porcupine holds its back legs loose and swivels rapidly on its stiffened front legs, using them as a pivot and altering the position of its rear in accordance with the movements of its enemy. Meanwhile, it protects its vulnerable nose by tucking it down between its front legs, its rather bulging eyes being endowed with enough peripheral vision to allow the animal to see "out of the back of its head," as it were.

A wolf daring and experienced enough to tackle this otherwise slow and docile rodent knows that it must tire its prey before it can hope to dart in, grab the defenseless nose, shake

71

mightily so as to break the neck, and then, even as the porcupine is dying, toss the body into the air in the hope that it will land on its back and so expose the quill-free underbelly. The wolf may have to pick it up again and continue tossing it until its victim eventually lands in the desired position. When the dead animal is upside down, the wolf opens the stomach and eats it from the outside in, avoiding most, but clearly not all, of the quills.

To acquire the successful, killing nose-hold, however, the wolf must remain constantly on the alert and must call upon its entire stock of experience and agility, making lightning-swift feints, leaping out of the way of the lethal tail, circling around and around the porcupine, always seeking an opening while trying to wear it down. If the wolf is very hungry and persistent, and the porcupine is very husky, such a contest can go on for an hour or more before the wolf gets its meal. Sometimes the battle ends in a sort of stalemate, when the wolf gives up and walks away and the porcupine scurries for shelter in the nearest tree. Often a wolf succeeds; less frequently, but by no means rarely, the porcupine connects with its bristly club and ends the fight then and there.

Many people believe that the porcupine is almost immune from attack by predators, but this is far from the case. Apart from wolves, such animals as the cougar, lynx, bobcat, coyote, fox, fisher, and wolverine seek to feed on its flesh, the predators of canine origin generally employing the same tactics, while the cats seek to smash the nose with a swift paw, and the fisher and wolverine, infinitely fast animals, try to tip the prey over and rip open its stomach.

It almost goes without saying that experience is the predator's key to porcupine hunting, even after a young hunter has learned some of the techniques by observation. No matter how keenly observant the cub may have been, it must in the end put its learning to the test in the field of battle, no doubt trying and failing and giving up a number of times before it achieves its first success, provided, of course, that it does not walk into a tail smash.

Thinking ahead, I knew that sooner or later Matta and Wa would encounter this extremely dangerous antagonist. When that happened, I wanted them to know the peril that faced them. Ideally, I hoped, they might be able to learn how to kill this quarry effectively when the time came. But as matters developed, this was not yet to be.

Soon after we climbed the ridge, Tundra began to lead the way, becoming almost oblivious of my presence, as he so often did when prowling the wild places. But the cubs, to my delight and relief, remained near me. I had underestimated them, even though I should have known better.

As yet they were too inexperienced and insecure to move far from me; their well-developed sense of caution exercised more influence on them than all the tempting smells, sounds, and sights that they were encountering. But they were greatly excited, obviously delighted, even if not yet ready to explore new territory on their own.

This timorous conduct caused Tundra to modify his own behavior. I am sure that he had expected the cubs to follow him, but when they didn't, and he looked up and noticed that he was more or less alone, he came back and joined us, sniffing at the things that interested the cubs, pouncing at an occasional mouse, or acting as if he really thought that this was so much kid stuff but that he would humor his wards and show them how it was done.

Little by little Matta and Wa moved ahead of me until, about an hour after we started walking the ridge, they were some thirty feet away. I had been waiting for this.

I stopped suddenly, wheeled around, taking care to make as much noise as possible, and *whoofed* loudly. Matta, the chicken, led her brother on the dash back to the security offered by my person. Tundra stood and looked at all of us, as astonished as a dog can become. When the cubs stood beside me, tails droopy in the alarm posture, I started moving downslope, but when they made to follow, I turned and growled at them. They hesitated, undecided. I growled again, more fiercely, and they dropped to the ground, lying there, noses on paws, Wa just a little ahead of his sister, and watching my every move. Tundra remained where he had halted earlier, undoubtedly wondering about what was going on, for he had not heard, seen, or scented anything that merited so much caution.

I turned away from the cubs and walked downslope, reached the bottom, looked back. They had stayed. Now I grinned at them and *whoofed* softly, and at once the twins jumped up and scampered down to where I waited. I squatted, fondled both for a moment or two, and spoke to them gently, then I rose and climbed the ridge just in time to meet Tundra as he came to see if he could discover the cause of such odd behavior.

As we carried on with our walk, the canines acting much as before, I found myself marveling at the intelligence of the wolves, realizing that, at least at this stage, they were most receptive to training and quick to learn. During the next couple of hours I called them to me on some half-dozen occasions, each time ordering them to stay by growling, getting them used to my imitation of wolf orders.

When we came to the end of the ridge, at a place where it leveled off to join a comparatively rolling landscape of sparsely covered granite in the middle of which was situated the small, round lake, Tundra stiffened suddenly, then took off at speed, the cubs following him as fast as they could go. In vain did I *whoof* and call!

I had been only half a dozen paces behind the bunched-up trio, watching them as we approached a gentle rise the other side of which, I knew, led to the north shore of the lake. From their position low on the ground none of the three canines could possibly see the water, but I, standing higher, could just do so. At one moment the dog and the wolves were ambling along casually, sniffing and listening and looking, at the next their ears pricked forward, their tails rose, and they exhibited all the mannerisms of the hunting wolf. I looked toward Tundra just as he was taking off, his ears and tail and the tenseness of his body showing that he had been alerted by something well worth going after. Though I was displeased by the dog's undisciplined behavior and worried about the cubs who followed him, I was yet greatly intrigued by the simultaneous reactions of the trio. It was clear that both Matta and Wa, as well as the dog, had heard or scented the same thing at the same time. Running after them, I fervently hoped that it wasn't a bear!

Tundra, almost a blur of brown gray movement, was heading directly toward a thick clump of alders growing on the lakeshore; the cubs were also aimed toward it, Wa several yards ahead of his sister.

I had just reached the top of the slope when Tundra dove into the alders. Matta and Wa were trying to lengthen their stride and were about halfway to the target area when the dog emerged, only seconds after entering the cover, carrying in his jaws the wriggling body of a muskrat. Once clear of the scrubby trees, Tundra shook his head sharply once. I was about one hundred feet away by this time, the cubs half that distance. I stopped, watching, noting immediately that the rat's neck had been broken by the dog's shake and that the brown rodent was even then gripped by the death dance. In another moment the prey hung limp in Tundra's jaws.

He ran toward the cubs as they sped toward him. Now he stopped, holding the prize; he appeared to be waiting for Matta and Wa. When they got to him, Matta went to the left and Wa to the right; both immediately reached up to the dog's mouth and closed their own, smaller jaws on the ends of the rat's body that hung down on either side of his muzzle. I expected the dog to resist, perhaps even to show anger, but instead he released the rat and stepped back, watching intently as Matta and Wa staged an instant tug of war with the unfortunate victim.

Wa, being the bigger and stronger, began to drag his sister, backing up and increasing his reverse speed as he gained ground. Matta let go suddenly, and the male tumbled over backward. Before he could regain his feet, the bitch charged him, grabbed the rat, and pulled it out of his mouth.

Wa growled in anger, a young growl perhaps but full of menace just the same. Back on all fours, he ran at Matta, who now growled in reply. A fight was in the making.

Furiously, Wa hit his sister with his chest, snapping at the rat's head as he did so. Matta lost her grip of the prize as she fell and rolled over, yipped once, a shrill cry of outrage, then got good and mad and scrambled up, mouthing wolf curses as she returned to the fray.

Tundra moved forward quickly, and because Wa happened to be nearest, he grabbed the cub by the scruff and started to shake him. The male let go of the rat as though it had suddenly developed a nasty taste. He shrieked in anguish. At the sound, Tundra dropped him and Wa tumbled down a short slope several times, still yelling; his sister, patiently anxious to avoid Tundra's attention, tucked her tail between her legs and sped toward me, ki-yiing almost as loudly as her erstwhile rival. Wa, meanwhile, had picked himself up and was bringing up the rear. Expecting them, I was already in the crouch position, arms open wide to receive them.

While they pushed themselves eagerly into my waiting embrace and soaked up my soothing noises and petting, Tundra, having broken up the firht and regained his legitimate spoils, tossed the rat around a few times, "killing" it all over again, shaking it until it looked as though every joint in its body was dislocated; then he lost interest, dropping the dreadful-looking cadaver on a moss-covered rock. I walked the twins toward it, and their differences already forgotten, they started a new tug-of-war, now behaving more calmly, turning the struggle into a game.

None of the three was hungry; this I knew positively. Tundra killed because he could not deny his urge to hunt; the cubs responded for the same reason, but also because at this, their time of learning, young wolves are seemingly programmed to hunt at every available opportunity, hungry or not, in this way gaining the experience and skills that will prepare them for the life of the adult. Later, I knew, when they attained maturity, they would hunt seriously only when hungry, though they might occasionally be tempted to make a pass or two at some slow-moving animal if chance put one across their path.

(I once observed two large timber wolves initiate an attack on an old male raccoon they caught in the open. The 'coon, unable to escape, hunched his shoulders, bared his teeth, and offered to fight. The wolves, sleek and well fed, circled him a number of times, occasionally making a quick grab for his neck or body, but as the raccoon turned quickly to meet the attack, they backed off. After no more than a few minutes the wolves gave up, walking away, stopping a couple of times to turn and look over their shoulders as the 'coon ran toward a tree, into which he climbed speedily. Had they been hungry, the raccoon would have been killed at once.)

Going to a convenient boulder nearby, I sat down, filled my pipe, lit it, and watched the game that Matta and Wa were playing. Tundra, as though such childish things were suddenly beneath his dignity, came to sit beside me, but continued to observe the cubs intently, his ears standing at attention. It was now almost noon, the sun full and hot, the sky a clear, deep azure. In the distance, two turkey vultures glided with the supreme ease always displayed by their kind; a number of birds flitted from tree to tree, some of them singing lustily.

Part of my mind noted these things, another part continued to attend to the cubs, but most of my faculties were busy examining the nearly incredible sensorial demonstration that I had witnessed earlier.

I was not surprised by Tundra's ability to sense the presence of the muskrat, nor even by the similar acuteness displayed by the cubs; I had witnessed many such astounding feats demonstrated by a variety of other wild hunters on numerous occasions. But what motivated me at that moment was a consuming desire to understand more fully the extent, source, and mechanics of the mysterious senses that allow animals to probe their environment so deeply and accurately, and with such reflexive speed.

Stated simply, it is a matter of action and reaction, of stimulus and response, but it is so evident that animals are able to detect influences that are quite beyond man's sensory powers, I have long concluded that humans, for all their marvelous reason and inventiveness, long ago lost contact with the real world, with the *whole environment*. We have become good "plumbers," inspired tinkerers, able to dissect a body and to trace the pathways of blood, opine on the state of liver and heart, chart a few of the functions of the brain; we can count the stars, set our feet down on the moon, and reach even farther with mechanical extensions of ourselves. We are very clever. But what do we *really* know of ourselves and of the world to which we belong, the ambient so readily perceived by the so-called lesser animals?

Platonists would argue that the only real world worth considering is the mind, that philosophy is *the* thing; but to me, though I greatly value the mind and its ability to philosophize, this concept fails in that it does not take into account the whole being and the influences exerted upon it by the whole environment. It's rather like claiming that only the aboveground portions of a tree are real and that the roots and the soil and all that this contains for the nourishment of the entire plant are of little account.

Man has too often come to conclusions based upon *his* observation of the world, ignoring the perceptive powers of the animals that share it with him. In this way it has been generally decided that wolves and dogs and most other mammals are color-blind. They may be, in our terms, but if color does not play a role in their lives, why then, I often wonder, are animals so colorful and so well camouflaged? I have not yet come across a satisfactory explanation of this phenomenon, examples of which are legion: the deer fawn, born clothed in woodsy colors with white spots, making it virtually impossible to see the little animal as it crouches immobile in a sun-dappled forest glade; the snowshoe hare, who each autumn trades his brown and gray and white fur for an almost pure white overcoat that causes it to blend into a snowscape; the chipmunk, with its pale stripes, to name but some camouflage combinations.

Indeed, nature is most careful to dress an animal so that it will blend with its habitat; we find that desert animals, in contrast to their kin of the same species that inhabit forested country, are usually pale colored, drab; young cougars are born spotted, rather like the deer fawn, then lose their spots as they become larger and better able to care for themselves; some northern wolves and some caribou are white, and so on.

Of course, it can be argued that white and black are not colors, but even accepting this, there are still enough true colors left in nature to cause me to wonder about this color-blind theory.

After pondering these mysteries for a while, I rose and paced the distance between the edge of the alders, inside of which the rat had been hiding, and the place where Tundra and the cubs had first detected it: seventy-five yards. At this distance the canines had heard or scented the rat, for, of a surety, they had been unable to see it. I, having the vantage of height, had been deaf, blind, and scentless. And Tundra made it look so ridiculously easy!

It was nearing five o'clock when we entered the home clearing that afternoon. We were not in sight of the house yet, but we had only just stepped out of the concealing forest when Tundra came to attention and the cubs became afraid, edging so close to me that they interfered with my walking. I stopped. Tundra halted also, staring intently toward the unseen house for some moments, then he galloped ahead, tail curled tightly.

His behavior, and that of Matta and Wa, suggested that something out of the usual was taking place at home. I guessed that we had visitors and was once again impressed by the sensory awareness of the trio. Because Joan and I were anxious to conceal the fact that we had two wolves living with us and had thus determined to raise them in secret, I picked up one

78

cub under each arm, entered the forest, and detoured so as to come out behind the evaporator house, on the west side of our dwelling. Once within the shelter of the trees, I put the cubs down again, and they, still keeping very close to me, trotted along, showing less anxiety but nevertheless displaying nervousness.

Our reason for hiding the cubs from our neighbors stemmed from the fact that we lived in a farm community among a rural people who were very much biased against the wolf. I knew that if word got out that North Star Farm was harboring two of the animals, a great fuss would be made. It was even possible that some of the locals would decide to shoot the pups.

So I was as anxious as Matta and Wa to avoid visitors at that moment. I led the cubs to the saphouse, leaving them inside it and closing the door behind me.

Walking upslope to the house, I sighted an alien vehicle, a pickup truck that I recognized as belonging to neighbor-friends who lived three miles away. As was the practice in our community, they often dropped in for a chat and a cup of coffee, with perhaps some "growlies" (a snack) thrown in.

Tundra and the cubs had no doubt scented the strange vehicle.

CHAPTER FIVE

Matta and Wa were great smilers, as are all members of the dog family, but the cubs led me to observe something that had hitherto escaped my notice: Each smiled and grinned in different, highly individual fashion, reflecting their personalities in the ways in which they moved their lips and held their mouths, as well as in the accompanying twinkle in their eyes. It was no big discovery, but I was annoyed with myself for not having noticed it long before, especially when, on reflection, I realized that Tundra also smiled and grinned in an individualistic way and that all my other dogs had done likewise—even as people do.

Wa possessed a strong sense of humor and seemed destined to run through life with an almost permanent, impish grin creasing his lips. This would give way to a broad smile if he was particularly pleased with himself, such as on those occasions when, as a two-month-old, he would purloin something from us humans in order to coax us to chase him, knowing full well that we couldn't catch him unless he allowed us to do so.

Matta, though more sober and often seen wearing a serious expression as she poked and sniffed at her world in seeming anticipation of calamity, also smiled and grinned frequently during her more quiet and confident moments, but her grin was more sedate than Wa's, a sort of inner thing, like the Mona Lisa's.

At two months of age the personalities of both cubs appeared to be well entrenched. Wa, as he had shown from the start, was an easygoing, happy-go-lucky, adventurous sort of wolf. Matta was considerably more serious, high-strung, and especially cautious.

Both were extremely intelligent, even precocious, like most young wolves. They were quick to learn and blessed with exceptional memory. They were little more than six weeks old when they answered to their names, knew where their food was kept in the kitchen, recognized our voices and even the way that we walked, and had adapted to using a sandbox as a toilet. In the last case, they learned by association rather than by training. When preparing the box, which was to be placed in one corner of the kitchen near their rug and nesting chamber, I mixed in with the sand some small samples of their own wastes. When all was ready, each pup was placed in turn on top of the sand.

It happened that Matta was the first to be introduced to the box. She had been fed, cleaned up by Tundra, and allowed to scamper about the kitchen for a few minutes to stimulate her urges. Then I put her in the container; initially, she reacted predictably, getting ready to panic. But before she had time to scramble out and run for the nearest cover, her nose detected the hidden samples and she forgot her fear. Becoming interested in the sand, she dug in it in several places, then circled ritualistically as a preliminary to the act of half-squatting and doing her business. When done, she turned, sniffed as though to make sure that she really *had* answered the call, and then stepped out, sauntering toward Tundra, who was lying down, waiting for Wa to finish eating so that he could be licked clean.

A little while later Wa was placed in the sand; he behaved similarly to his sister, except that he showed no fear and did not produce solid waste the first time around. He had the advantage, of course, because apart from the stale samples, he also encountered his sister's recent scent as an inducement. He, too, circled a few times, but he didn't squat as Matta had done. Instead he flexed his back legs slightly as he stood on all fours, then he wobbled a little as he piddled, a beatific smile wreathing his features. Finished, he evidently felt that it was his duty to investigate the container quite thoroughly, in the process of which inspection he dug up quite a lot of sand, parts of the samples, and even managed to put both his front paws into his sister's waste. While Tundra cleaned him up, I cleaned the rug.

From that time on, neither cub soiled the floor or their bedding except during moments of intense excitement or great fear; on such occasions they could not control the small but steady leaks that escaped their bladders. Thanks to their ability to reason, the sandbox was a great success, its only disadvantage being that Tundra felt that he, too, should be able to use it. He did, once, soaking the sand, the box, the wall and a considerable area of blanket and kitchen floor. After that, until the cubs were old enough to spend most of their time outside in the rendezvous or inside the evaporator house, we had to keep a weather eye on the dog, whose speed of action was prodigious. It was rather unfair, really, because he couldn't understand why the cubs were allowed to use the box and he was not.

In the wild, wolf pups at first soil inside the den, but their solid wastes are cleaned up by their mother, who ingests them; fluid waste, naturally, soaks into the earth floor. When the pups are old enough to leave the den for short trips, they void outdoors more often than not, though some soiling is still done inside. But once they have gained strength and confidence and are spending most of their time outside, they usually use those places patronized by the adult pack members.

Soon after this stage in their lives the pups are led away from the den and introduced to a suitable piece of country where they will spend the rest of the summer. Such rendezvous areas are evidently selected for their strategic advantages. Ideally, they should be off the beaten track, fairly open, but dressed with shrubs and grasses and small trees, with perhaps some rocks or boulders, while at the same time located either within a forest or at least having one boundary closely adjacent to heavy timber. Such an area allows the cubs to run about, play, do a bit of practice hunting. The shrubs and small trees give them shelter from the sun and places in which to lie concealed when resting; the nearby forest offers deep cover if, when alone, the cubs are threatened by some enemy and must escape from the rendezvous.

About two miles north of the farm, in a flat, fairly open place that was entirely surrounded by dense, mixed forest, was a rendezvous that was used annually by one of the wolf packs whose territory included the eastern part of our land. Here, some fifty feet from the more open section of the nursery, I found what I can only call a wolf toilet, a rock uplift some thirty feet long by about fifteen feet wide that had a fairly flat top that rose perhaps eight or nine feet above the forest floor. Tundra led me to it in early autumn eighteen months before Matta and Wa came into our care. I had never seen anything quite like it, despite all my wanderings through the wilderness and my keen interest in wolves. The top of this small ridge was literally covered in wolf feces, some of it fresh enough to tell me that it had been deposited there that year, much of it old and fibrous, reduced by time and the elements. Clearly, the place had been used for a good number of seasons, as had the rendezvous, for when I searched this carefully to see if I could find any scats, but failed to discover a single one, I turned up innumerable pieces of bone leftovers, some recent, others quite old, having that gray, striated appearance characteristic of bones exposed to the weather for a long time. Additionally, a number of well-defined trails led in and out of the area, and many of the saplings and bushes were scarred by the teeth of the cubs.

Toilet Hill, as I immediately christened it, was evidently used only during the time that the rendezvous was occupied, such intelligence being obtained from a study of the scats that littered it.

From late spring to late autumn, the wolf feeds quite well, as a rule, there being available a good supply of smaller prey animals such as mice, moles, raccoons, beavers, groundhogs, and others that offer "snacks" during those times when big game animals, being fleeter of foot and unrestricted by deep snows, avoid the hunter. Also at this time, the wolf will eat moderate quantities of vegetable matter, such as tender grasses and berries (though these constitute a minor part of its diet). Under such conditions, wolf scats contain larger amounts of waste, rather like those deposited by dogs that are regularly fed.

In winter, when the wolf must go from feast to famine, often existing on leftover scraps or on nothing at all for periods of ten days and more, the animal's magnificent digestive system extracts every last bit of protein from its food. This is reflected in its scats, which are then composed of little more than fur and chips of bone bound together by mucus and perhaps a few shreds of sinew. I cannot pretend that I examined every single one of the scats found on the hill, but I looked carefully at many of them; in any event, winter scats are most distinctive and easy to identify at a glance, since they resemble nothing more than white gray oblongs of rough appearance when fresh; when old, such scats expand to about three times their normal diameter and fluff out, so that if inquisitive people like myself take two twigs and poke at them, they disintegrate, turning into mounds of brittle fur that release the quite small chips of bone (average size about a quarter of an inch).

As Joan and I recorded the progress made by the cubs, and while discussing their personalities, habits, and peculiarities, we found ourselves using terms and concepts usually applied to the development of human infants. Joan used these naturally, unselfconsciously; I was a little more cautious and deliberate, being well aware that I was indulging in a practice considered almost sinful by many biologists, who eschew the use of anthropomorphic sentiments when describing animals.

Such purists contend that anthropomorphism confuses the issue. During my own biological studies I also absorbed this bias, but after stumbling over complicated, nearly meaningless sentences crammed with the jargon of the profession, and when, what is more, I began to discover during extensive field research that animals are not so awfully far removed from people inasmuch as the basic necessities of living are concerned, I rebelled against this doctrine. I felt then, as I still do, that apart from the similarities in the nature of animal and man, clarity of communication is far more important than dogma. I concede that if used solely as the basis for communication between biologists, such jargon *may* be excusable, but even in this context I cling to the idea that simplicity is best and that analogy is useful. The opponents of anthropomorphism claim that the use of such terms as *bed*, *smile*, *anger*, *love*, humanize animals when they are applied to them. But when I say that Matta and Wa smiled or used the toilet or went to bed or were happy or sad or afraid, I am merely stating facts in words that anybody can readily understand and relate to. I am most definitely *not* saying that Matta and Wa behaved like humans. To the contrary, what I am at least implying is that humans often behave like animals in these regards.

All beings inhabiting this planet owe their origins to the same natural world. As children of nature (of God, if you will) humans still retain animal (mammalian) characteristics, however submerged within our subconscious these may be. It is no coincidence that many people recognize extensions of themselves in the behavior and personalities of their pets and other animals. How often have I heard someone observing an animal exclaim in amazement, "He's so *human*!" And why not? We are, after all, so *animal*. And I use the word in admiration, not denigration.

Wolves, despite their bad press, are admirable beings. Their social life is orderly, practical, and extraordinarily free from strife. Their young are nurtured gently and are cared for by all members of the pack. They are highly intelligent, magnificently quick-witted, and inordinately responsive to their environment. And they are completely honest.

There can be no doubt that we looked upon Matta and Wa and Tundra as members of our household, our family; in turn, they looked upon us as members of their pack. Such was their influence on us that by the time Matta and Wa were three months old, I used to refer to our ménage as the North Star Pack; jokingly, at first, then seriously and with a sense of pride in that we had been admitted into such an exclusive society. In this sense we did not think of ourselves as two humans and three canines, but rather as five beings unified in a rather marvelous way, each understanding and respecting the other and capable of communicating across the barriers of language and species.

Had the cubs been fully exposed to the world of modern man, they would have lost much of their beautifully unsophisticated nature and might even have perished altogether. By the same token, had we been forced to live in their world on their terms, we could not have survived. But the farm became a halfway house, a place where human and wolf could live together without either species suffering as a result, each being able to adjust to the modified environment of the other. Withal, this was achieved without conscious intent; it just happened after Joan and I determined that the cubs should be raised as close to the wild as possible so that one day they might return to their own world.

For these reasons, when I decided to spend the first few nights with them in their rendezvous, I did so in the awareness that I could not take on the characteristics of an adult wolf, nor sleep like one, nor even eat like one (though I suppose this might just have been possible). I was effecting a compromise: I could keep them from harm, I could reassure them when they were afraid, I could seek to learn more about their natures; but I would do it in relative comfort, using the tent as shelter, the sleeping bag for warmth, the pyrethrum to keep away the mosquitoes that plagued me but had relatively little effect on the cubs. No doubt they could have managed on their own by then, but I could not submerge my human tendency to worry. So I chose to fence in their rendezvous instead of exposing them to the freedoms and the dangers that would normally be encountered by wild pups when the adults of their pack are away hunting.

The bear incident was a case in point. Confined behind the wire, the pups could not escape, but they had enough sense to come to me for protection. In the wild, by that age, they could easily have avoided the bear, which would have soon recognized the fact and abandoned the hunt, going away to seek food more easily obtained. My presence scared the bear, and as far as I know, he did not return during the entire time that Matta and Wa lived in the fenced rendezvous. Five days later, when I was satisfied that the cubs had become acclimatized to this new phase in their education, I allowed Tundra to take over from me, feeling no anxiety.

The big dog was quite capable of leaping the wire had the bear returned. He would have done so at the first whiff of the marauder, whom he would have chased away or caused to tree in panic when it found that it could not outdistance its fleet and agile tormentor. (One of the quirks of ursine nature is the animal's tendency to run under such circumstances.) Motivated by hunger, it will dare the wrath of a pack of wolves, but will turn tail and flee if unexpectedly attacked by even a small dog. It is a matter of aggression versus caution. Wolves, provided their cubs are not threatened, do not, in my experience, go after an adult bear when they meet one during their travels; they are aware that this animal is powerfully dangerous and, nearly impervious as it is to damage from their teeth, is just about impossible to kill—but wolves will certainly attack a cub if its mother is not nearby.

(Dogs, on the other hand, being frustrated hunters and made foolhardy by domestication, are ever ready to tackle anything on either four legs or two. We call this courage. In reality it is misguided aggression brought about by ignorance. Such magnificent rashness is admirable to us humans; it is the stuff of heroes, but it is not calculated to increase the life-span of a dog. Fortunately, because a powerful, wild predator is taken aback by such impudence, it becomes cautious, electing to run away, much as a man will prudently avoid stepping in front of a moving automobile. But when a bear, or one of the big cats, decides to stand its ground, poor Fido is liable to become mincemeat. My old friend Yukon almost lost his life during such a confrontation, and many a hunting dog has been torn apart before the gaze of its master.)

When I introduced Matta and Wa to the rendezvous, they had already passed through their first and second learning stages, having sharpened all their faculties to a greater or lesser degree, and had lost some of the nervousness displayed earlier when confronted with new situations. Now, too, they used their reasoning powers when confronted by the unknown, assessing each separate experience with uncanny accuracy. They were still cautious, a trait they would retain for the rest of their lives, but the pull of curiosity so inherent in all young creatures caused them to explore every single smell, sight, or sound that they encountered, even if they did so with many misgivings and were ever ready to escape at the first sign of danger.

Perhaps the most noteworthy facet of their education thus far was the way in which they had responded to, and accepted, the scruff punishment, which caused them to modify their behavior so as to minimize considerably its application by Tundra or myself. The dog and I were tolerant, but there had been some occasions, such as Wa's unwitting challenge to Tundra's authority during the door incident, when discipline needed to be enforced. Now a severe look from either one of us was sufficient to interrupt any serious mischief within moments of its start; they knew just how far they could go, and no matter what particular bit of devilment they might be tempted to initiate, both of them kept a wary eye on the two whom they already recognized as the dominant males of the pack.

The scruff punishment is painless and harmless, but it instills acute emotional discomfort because it causes its recipient to feel completely helpless when lifted off its feet and shaken violently. The meaning is indelibly imprinted on a wolf pup when it is handled in this way by its mother. Once is usually enough for the young cub to learn, sometimes two or three such demonstrations are needed to completely impress recalcitrant offenders. It is an unusually effective and humane form of discipline (and it works equally well on dogs), which in adulthood is replaced by the scruff *bite*, an important ritual of pack hierarchy.

In the latter case it is only a token bite that is administered to a subordinate's scruff by a dominant animal following real or fancied provocation, and quite often as an expression of affection, as between a male and his mate. On other occasions it may be a sign of friendly tolerance that yet carries a mild warning, telling the subordinate not to presume too greatly. Frequently, delivered with some serious snarling, it can be interpreted as the human equivalent of a severe reprimand, to be followed if necessary by some rough handling. Almost invariably it is given after a status fight, when the dominant pack member (male or female) reinforces its victory by scruff biting and the subordinate meekly accepts it as a sign of surrender. I often used it on Yukon and Tundra in an affectionate manner, and on the cubs, in this case gripping the scruff lightly while talking in a friendly tone and shaking gently from side to side. As an act of censure, I would grip tightly, without shaking, and accompany the act with some stern talk. But when it was necessary to use it as a form of punishment, my hand would gather up as much loose skin and fur as possible, grip tightly, and shake violently half a dozen times, turning the ritual into scruff punishment. I have never attempted to discipline an adult, wild wolf in this way—and I don't think I would greatly care to try it—but adult dogs, being, as I have said, somewhat neotenous because of domestication, respond to such punishment much as wolf puppies do.

I had been anxious to ensure that Matta and Wa learn to understand and to respect the implications of the ritual, so I was considerably pleased when they responded so well to it.

During one of our short walks together Wa's rashness got him into trouble with an old, somewhat irascible raccoon, who had reserved for himself an apartment inside the trunk of a big, downed maple. For three years One Ear had occupied these quarters during spring, summer, and fall at those times when his rambles did not take him too far away from its location.

He was a big fellow, battle-scarred, his right ear chewed off at some time, probably by another male during a fight over a female. He had turned up at our feeder one evening, there to sit like some hairy, miniature Buddha ingesting the goodies that were always set out for our forest friends morning and evening. The feeder in question, one of several strategically located around the farm house, was fastened to the kitchen windowsill; it consisted of a two-foot-by-three-foot tray connected to the ground by a leaning pole that acted as a walkway. During the day it contained seed and peanut bits for the birds and squirrels and, of course, for Scruffy and his ilk; after supper, table scraps and a fresh supply of seeds and nuts were put out for our many raccoon friends and for the flying squirrels, who always enjoyed a nice bit of protein when they could get it and who alternated between chewing leftover bones and stuffing themselves on seeds.

One Ear was a total stranger when he first showed up, but being aged and wise, he knew a good thing when he saw it. From that evening onward he appeared with regular punctuality soon after the feeder had been restocked. In no time, he allowed himself to be fed by hand, accepting tidbits such as marshmallows and sandwiches of peanut butter and honey with a sort of regal condescension.

One Ear was far from amused when a bumptious male wolf pup entered his recumbent log one morning and within this sanctum performed some unspeakable act almost under his pugilistic nose. My attention had wandered to Matta, who was attempting to crawl down a groundhog burrow, so I was not aware that Wa had trespassed until I heard One Ear's growl and Wa's scream of utter terror. I knew what had taken place before I completed the turn that would point me toward the raccoon's fortress.

Sure enough, I was in time to observe the appearance of one hysterical wolf cub whose legs were moving exceedingly fast but whose body seemed to emerge in slow motion; a few seconds later the reason for this anomaly became evident. Holding fast to Wa's ruler-straight tail was One Ear, who, despite his most strenuous efforts, was being pulled out of his redoubt by the screaming cub.

I was about to step across the two or three yards that separated me from the scene of the action when Matta did the unexpected. Emitting as deep a growl as she was capable of, she charged, taking the raccoon from the rear and delivering a series of fast snaps to his bulging bottom. Her teeth could not possibly penetrate One Ear's fur, but her attack caused him to let go of Wa's tail in order to turn swiftly, stare in unbelief at this second intruder, and then, hunching his shoulders, going into a fighting crouch and baring his not inconsiderable armament, he charged the little bitch. Meanwhile, Wa was hightailing it for the rendezvous yowling incessantly.

Little Matta, now that she had committed herself, stood her ground, but before any further skirmishes could take place, I reached the combatants. One Ear was booted unceremoniously in the rump, whereupon, essaying one vengeful snap at my right Kodiak boot, he dived back into his now somewhat odoriferous log. As she was rashly about to follow her fleeing enemy, I grabbed Matta by the scruff and lifted her to safety. We were only halfway back to the rendezvous when Tundra came leaping into the woods, tail curled, ears pricked forward, the glint of battle in his eye. Evidently Joan had head Wa's laments—she couldn't very well help hearing them—and had let Tundra off his chain, following him as fast as she could go.

Inasmuch as Tundra did not stop to comfort Wa, as one would have expected, I concluded that he had heard One Ear's growls, and perhaps Matta's, and had not tarried, for if there was one thing that Tundra wanted to taste more than Scruffy, it was One Ear.

When all the parties came together and Wa, comforted in Joan's arms, became silent, I explained the situation to my wife as I checked the cub's tail. The raccoon's teeth had torn the skin a little, but that was all; it was nothing to worry about. However, as I was examining him, I realized that either he had had a bowel movement in the log and thus aroused One Ear's ire on two counts or he had been unable to control himself and had fired a salvo while the raccoon's teeth were clamped to his tail. In any event, he was in a rather disgusting condition, and a goodly amount of the waste that plastered his nether regions had transferred itself to Joan's white blouse, a fact that she noticed only when my gaze was directed toward her person and my nose signaled that all was not well. Wa, terrified and screaming, had aroused all that was good and kind and maternal in Joan; Wa, almost unscathed and plastered in manure, was able instantly to trigger a series of almost opposite reactions in my wife. She did stoop so as not to drop him from too high, but his return to the ground was rapid and unceremonious. As Joan turned to run home, already beginning to unbutton her blouse, she called over her shoulder, "You *filthy* little pig!" But an hour later all was forgiven, and Wa, thanks once again to Tundra, was clean enough to receive a thorough sponging with baby shampoo and warm water, an act of kindness and cleanliness that our wolf objected to more than to the tail chomping he had received.

Matta, for the first time in her young life, was the heroine of the hour. The praise, endearments, and petting she received from Joan, in addition to the surreptitious pieces of my supper steak that she was fed, more than rewarded her for what I suspected was an instinctive act, a sort of premature self-defense reaction. But I did not utter such a base thought aloud.

A week later Wa walked himself and his sister into trouble of another kind. The result of this escapade created an even greater outcry from both cubs; but it ended with positive results.

On this occasion I led the cubs away from the evaporator house early one morning and then allowed them to select our route, doing so partly because I wanted them to exercise freedom of choice and partly out of curiosity, wishing to see what they would do and what direction they would take.

Initially each wolf was intent on pursuing its own affairs, Wa going one way, Matta another, but neither of them running too far ahead on their own. At the end of half an hour we were still within the edge of the northern part of the maple woods and only about a quarter of a mile from the house. But at this point Wa suddenly elected to follow a definite course, though his reasons for doing so were never to become apparent to me.

He was sniffing at the entrance to a chipmunk burrow, while Matta was pawing apart a cluster of fungi that grew on a rotting branch, when he stopped, lifted his head, and stared toward the east, ears pricked forward and tail held high. Looking in the same direction, I failed to detect anything out of the ordinary. Through the thinning maples the small, eastern clearing was visible; beyond it, the mixed forest that led to the East Ridge basked quietly in the new sun. I listened carefully, but only the sound of a soft breeze coursing through the treetops was audible to my ears.

Wa moved forward, stepping out almost daintily, lifting each leg high and placing his paws with care. Matta abandoned her task to stare at him, then she ran ahead of me and joined her brother, maintaining her usual walking pace and lagging just behind him. I followed.

It was clear that Wa was now intent on some definite errand. He continued moving eastward, his pace constant, his senses oblivious to those local inducements through which we were passing. Only Matta looked up when a blue jay launched itself out of a high branch, swooped low over the clearing, and flapped away into the trees on the other side. Wa kept his gaze fixed ahead, as though he were following a compass direction. The pace he was setting allowed me to keep up with both cubs by walking only a little faster than usual, the distance between us remaining a constant twenty to twenty-five strides. A short time later it became evident that Wa would take us directly to the ridge.

In due course we came within sight of one of my own trails where this converged with a game track only yards away from the spot where I usually ascended the rise. Wa increased his pace slightly; soon he was climbing the mossy slope, Matta close to his heels.

When we all gained the top, Wa led south instead of north, a direction along which I had never taken him. He still had about him that purposeful bearing so often displayed by a dog who leaves home intent on going directly from *A* to *B* and stopping not to wet or sniff. But the reason for such deliberate travel was not at all evident. I knew that if we continued to follow the ridge southward for another quarter of a mile, we would arrive at an old, largely overgrown homestead clearing in the center of which lay the remains of a log cabin built there, according to local history, by the first owner of the farm, who had come here from England in 1861. All that was left of the building were a few rotting pieces of hand-squared log and some pathetic, broken relics discarded by the former occupants: bits of china, rusty pieces of an old woodstove, and so on, showing here and there among the grasses and stone rubble that lay within a depression where the dug-out basement had been. On the western lip of the hollow grew a tangle of once-cultivated lilac bushes now gone wild and untidy, some of them mere dead sticks, others alive but tall and rangy, in season showing but scant blooms.

Wa did not know of the existence of this place, yet ten minutes after climbing the ridge he led us directly to the untidy clearing and aimed himself straight as an arrow at the clump of lilacs, his sister, as before, dogging him. Thinking that no harm could come to them here, I stopped at the edge of the trees and let them cross the intervening seventy-five yards on their own. But because I was extremely interested in Wa's reasons, if indeed he had any, for heading in this direction, I lifted the field glasses and scanned the area ahead, focusing first on the lilacs, afterward sweeping the more open ground all the way to the forest on the other side, a matter of two hundred yards. Apart from a few birds and a number of insects, I saw nothing that could have accounted for Wa's singular behavior. The cubs reached the lilacs, and Wa went into them and led the way to the depression beyond. I started walking, but was only halfway to the lilac bushes when the agonized screams of both pups galvanized me into a full run, my stomach contracting with fear.

Running around the lilacs, I literally jumped into the hollow to discover both cubs blundering around in frantic circles as they pawed at their muzzles.

The porcupine was even then climbing sluggishly up the bank, heading toward the lilac bushes, the only refuge around the place, his club of a tail lashing jerkily from side to side, his muttering voice, like the grumble of a toothless, aged man, audible above the yelping of the pups. I grabbed for Matta first because she happened to stumble toward me, but when I saw that only one yellow quill was stuck fast at the very end of her nose, I let her go while I went to check Wa. He avoided me at first, made too frantic by the burning quills to realize that rescue was at hand. Matta, meanwhile, was following me, crying pitifully. Again I turned to her, held her head with my left hand, and grasped the quill firmly between thumb and forefinger of my right. I gave a quick, sharp pull. The quill, buried in her flesh to a depth of a quarter of an inch, came out with that rasping feel with which I was personally familiar; a gout of carmine blood seeped out. Matta stilled her screams, whimpering softly instead.

I managed to grab Wa a few moments later and was much relieved to see that though he had collected three quills, only one was properly embedded. Two dangled loosely from the top of his nose, like badly placed *banderillas* in the back of a *Muira* bull; the bad one was in his cheek, only two inches below his right eye; it appeared to have penetrated to a depth of half an inch. I pulled out the two loose barbs and tried to extricate the deep one, but it kept slipping through my finger, pouching Wa's cheek at each jerk. The cub, naturally, shrieked the louder every time I pulled. In the end I bent down, put my face close to his, holding his head still with both hands, and grasped the end of the quill between my front teeth. The serrated point let go in response to the yank that I gave, and the usual red goutlet blossomed on Wa's face. He gave a great shriek when the thing came out, but the immediate relief that followed transformed the cry into a whimper. Since my own flesh had been similarly punctured several times in the past, I knew exactly how my wards felt.

I called them to me, climbing the opposite edge of the hollow, where I sat and cradled them both, stroking them and speaking soothingly. They became quiet; soon they stopped shivering.

While this was going on, the porcupine, after attaining the highest point possible, clung to a spindly lilac trunk about seven feet from the ground and stared at us in myopic apprehension. The creature did not feel safe so close to the enemy; it would have much preferred a tall tree, it seemed to say with its husky, muttering voice.

When first Wa and then Matta recovered most of their equanimity, and bearing in mind the need to drive home the lesson, I got up and sought to lead them toward the lilacs, intending to growl warningly when we got close. I didn't have to. Neither cub would allow itself to be led anywhere near the porcupine, and when I carried them back down into the hollow, then set them on their feet, they scrambled hastily up the bank and started to run toward the distant trees, causing me to chase after them and to call until they at last stopped and waited for me a good hundred yards away. The lesson had been well and truly learned. Henceforth, they avoided even the scent of old porcupine droppings, and when, that winter, I was forced to execute one of the prickly fellows whom I discovered one morning breakfasting on the bark of one of our healthiest and most spectacular elm trees, the wolves, now almost full grown, would not come near the cadaver; neither would Tundra.

Homeward bound after the scare, Matta and Wa were subdued, following close to my heels as we retraced our route. I gave long and serious consideration to Wa's inexplicable behavior, tempted to believe that the young wolf was able to scent the porcupine from a distance of more than a mile but not daring to entirely accept such an incredible conclusion. Yet no other presented itself for scrutiny, unless the cub had been initially motivated by some different odor or sound and was drawn to the hollow only after getting closer to it and catching the porcupine's scent. I gave up trying to solve the puzzle in the end. It was to remain unsolved.

Matta and Wa had been exceedingly fortunate to escape so lightly from an encounter with a porcupine. Perhaps their agility contributed to their narrow escape, but luck, it seemed to me, was the main agent of their deliverance. The barbs removed from their faces were the shorter, thicker quills from the porcupine's tail, which evidently had brushed lightly against both cubs at the same time. I was prompted to this conclusion by the fact that if one had been harpooned before the other, the unscathed cub would have backed away when its sibling screamed in agony. I shuddered to think what would have happened if one or both pups had taken a full smash in the face from the lethal tail. Nevertheless, since the fracas had ended so well, I was glad that the incident had taken place. It was an excellent lesson for the cubs.

"I just don't care what you say, Mister, Tundra is *not* second in importance in *this* family, unless *you're* third!"

Joan delivered herself of this rather convoluted sentence one evening in late August after she had read my notes on the development of the young wolves. On this occasion I had described the hierarchy of the North Star Pack, noting clinically and without the least nuance of chauvinism that, insofar as the wolves and the dog were concerned, our pack status had developed in this order: I was the alpha male, the leader; Tundra was the beta male, second in command; the cubs, not yet having resolved their own hierarchical positions, shared third place, while Joan occupied a sort of female beta position that was more or less junior to Tundra's. My notes concluded:

> Being the only adult female member of the "pack" and having been blessed with a gentle and loving nature, Joan occupies a rather unusual position within the order of dominance. From close observation of the three canines, one must conclude that the senior female is regarded as an equal by all three, yet deserves and receives the full respect of all and the protection of the beta male, who is extremely agressive toward strangers who might approach her when the alpha male is absent. Even during the latter's presence, Tundra always places himself beside Joan under such conditions and does not remove his gaze from a visitor until he is personally satisfied that the newcomer intends no harm to her. When, as often happens, Joan sheds a tear or two out of sympathy for some person or thing—she is easily moved—all three canines rush to her and seek to comfort her, sensing her sadness instantly. Thus one must conclude that she occupies what could be termed an honorary beta position within the pack, a being to be cared for at all times, to be loved often, but one who will not readily be obeyed unless her command happens to coincide with the intentions of dog and wolves.

As I said, I had been scrupulously clinical; I had made it, at least in my view, abundantly clear that it was the canines that decided the order of status, not I. I was justifiably surprised, therefore, when Joan, with blood in her eye, looked up from the conclusion of my notes and fired her verbal salvo. I didn't answer right away, needing time to think of a politically persuasive reply.

"Well, my love, you know that you are always first in *my* book, and you know that they (Tundra and the cubs) really love you. I don't quite see why you're objecting."

"No, you wouldn't. Men never do! You're as bad as they are."

I had her there, and I jumped in quickly.

"Hold it! Matta's a girl, too, you know. She has voted with Tundra and Wa. Me, I didn't vote."

"You're impossible—*all* of you! But I guess I'm stuck with you . . . but just don't go thinking that you and those *beasts* can outvote *me*!"

Upon receiving my hasty assurance that we wouldn't dream of doing any such thing, Joan's equanimity was restored, and she got up to go and have a game with the wolflings. I can't swear to it, but I think she deliberately ignored Tundra, who was lying at my feet with his head resting against my outstretched leg.

CHAPTER SIX

The summer was fading gracefully, celebrating its retirement with the more gentle colors that presage the robust hues of ripe autumn. The open places were carpeted with browns and fawns and embroidered with patches of fresh green against which the distant tamaracks stood tall and as yellow as spring butter. Within the mixed timberlands bordering the larch swamp the oaks bore traces of copper, the poplars and birches displayed lemony hues, and the red maples wore a scattering of crimson leaves that fluttered gently, like small flags preceding the final burst of color still to come.

The sugar maples were splendid. Orange and scarlet mixed with fading green adorned the patriarchal trees the tops of which blended one with the other to form an undulating, kaleidoscopic mass further embellished by a clear, powder blue sky. The whole panorama announced almost brazenly that the wilderness was even now engaged in preparing for winter.

Carrying the field glasses and a portable tape recorder, I stopped to admire the shades of September, greeting them with wonder and delight and marveling, as I always do when meeting each new seasonal transition, at the subtle ways with which Creation manages to introduce change without ever duplicating its shades and patterns. Then I was struck by a new awareness. I realized that while the scene that stretched on all sides of me to the limits of vision was translated by my human senses into beauty and tranquility, its meaning to the inhabitants of the wilderness was remarkably different.

To Matta and Wa this altering land would probably offer at least as much interest, but its beauty would have no meaning. Their attention would be taken by the changes noted in the environment: the differences in temperature and daylight, the emerging physical landscape, the changing patterns of behavior exhibited by the animals that dwelt here, the ones that would remain to face the cold and the ones that would leave, migrating each at its appointed time according to the dictates of daylight and weather and its response to ancient genetic codings that would be activated during the next five or six weeks. To the wolves this was a completely changed wilderness now, as it was to the other animals and birds that used the land. Like all the young ones that had been given life since last spring, Matta and Wa had never before experienced these particular conditions; the land now offered them another opportunity to further develop techniques necessary for their survival in the wild. By the end of winter and with the arrival of spring—a season that the cubs had been too young to absorb—Matta and Wa would have come full circle. They would have gained knowledge encompassing an entire year after meeting and getting to know the wilderness during all its transitions. But their time of learning would not be over; it would never be over. Until the last gasp there is not one single organism that can afford to stop learning. Wild animals are, I believe, instinctively aware of this and are forever seeking, always trying to improve their hunting and survival techniques.

Such endless striving is necessary because of the constant changes that take place in a wild environment. These go beyond seasonal differences; indeed, an animal must get to know two environments at the same time: the day world and the night world. Of these, the night habitat is perhaps the more complex in that it is so heavily influenced by the phases of the moon, which, unlike the relatively constant sun, waxes and wanes as it lightens or darkens the forest, at the same time exerting its strange pull upon the organisms of this planet. Humans, most of whom (at any rate in the Western world) have practically no knowledge of the night wilderness, are unaware of the radical differences that become evident with the setting of the sun.

Relying as we do on our eyes for guidance, we become blind and awkward in the forest dark; even if we have a flashlight to light our path, our awareness is limited to the narrow cone that guides our feet as we stumble through a penumbral land that has become mysterious and is often frightening.

Matta and Wa needed to know this black world as intimately as they did the one that was dominated by the sun. They must experience and recognize the innumerable moods of their environment, acquire close knowledge of each game trail, watercourse, valley, and rise while pitting their wits against those of the species that they hunted. In the end, they would at best acquire a degree of experience that would allow them to survive perhaps only marginally, for such factors as disease and adverse weather conditions frequently combine to offer a glut today and a famine tomorrow. Only the keen and the careful can hope to survive in the wild.

It was late afternoon. I wanted to try to record some of the wolf howls that, since noon, had issued forlornly and at intervals from several areas of the wilderness surrounding the farm.

Three packs of timber wolves made periodic appearances in our neighborhood, but the one I had named the West Pack, which often used the part of our property that included the tamarack swamp, arrived more regularly than the others, and by now its members were perfectly well aware that I meant them no harm. The alpha male of this pack was a big, brindled-gray old-timer, whom I had first met four years earlier during a winter outing five miles from home. He had been on his own then and had stopped to stare at me when I emerged into a forest opening while he stood on top of a minor rock scarp. Since then we had met often; sometimes he had been accompanied by his pack, often he was alone. I called him Lobo. His group contained between five and seven wolves, fluctuating from year to year for reasons unknown, but probably because some were trapped locally and others, the young wolves, either moved on to form new packs or became victims of disease or starvation.

Because of our familiarity with each other, I thought I would stand a better chance of getting near to members of the West Pack in order to capture their voices. If lucky, I intended to play these back to Matta and Wa, who, surprisingly, had not yet started to howl. I hoped the recorded calls would stimulate their inherent urge to answer.

Wild pups start howling at a very early age, certainly by the time they are three months old; but they have the pack to learn from. Our cubs only had Tundra, and he, for some reason, howled seldom, which is uncharacteristic of the malamute. Lacking a satisfactory example, Matta and Wa had not yet begun to vocalize, though they were mouthy enough in other respects and had perfected their ability to scream when in trouble. I had tried to get them going by imitating wolf howls, but my efforts were to no avail, and even I recognized that my voice lacked the lupine timbre and power.

By the time I emerged from the maples and stopped in the clearing to admire the scenery, our resident flock of chickadees found me. They arrived, seemingly out of nowhere, like a small explosion of soft feathers, calling as they came. I had been standing beside a hawthorn, and this was suddenly packed with the black and white little birds, but the leaders of the flock, perhaps half a dozen, landed on my person, squatting on my hat, shoulders, and one arm, the boss bird actually fluttering within inches of my face.

They had come for their usual handout of sunflower seeds mixed with crushed peanuts, a pocketful of which I invariably carried during my wanderings in the bush. Interestingly, the birds always showed up when I was accompanied by Tundra, but since the wolves arrived, they only came when I was alone. I presumed that this was more because of our numbers than because they felt fear of the wolves.

I got a handful of feed and held it out in my open palm; the boss bird landed immediately, taking his time about selecting just the right seed or bit of peanut while his underlings waited impatiently, voicing their delicate little song but somehow making it sound peevish. The first bird found what it was looking for and flitted away to sit on some branch and eat its prize. Now the second-in-comand of the pecking order alighted on my hand and went through the same routine, and so on until some eight or ten birds had taken a turn. By now, impatient to get going, I scattered seed on the ground and walked away, leaving the chickadees to their own devices.

For all their smallness, these interesting and exceptionally tough birds are remarkably intelligent and quickwitted. Once they are given cause to trust a human, they show absolutely no fear.

We had started feeding them a number of years earlier, first putting the seeds in the usual feeding stations. Then, one morning when I was late filling the feeders, three of the bolder birds landed on me, and one of these, the dominant member of the flock, hopped down into the seed container I was carrying and began to help himself. When it finished, I scooped out a handful of seeds and held it out to the others. One bird immediately landed on my hand. From then on, whenever I was walking through the wilderness and around the farm, I had a constant escort of chickadees that I hand-fed at intervals during my travels. There were times when they almost became a nuisance, but their presence was always so cheerful and friendly that even when I was in a hurry, I would pause briefly to feed them, then scatter seed on the ground or in the snow. Some of them even landed on my pipe while it was clenched between my teeth, occasionally getting a hotfoot when they sought to perch on its bowl. One day, curious, I filled my mouth with seed and opened it wide, to become quite startled when a bird flew at my face, set its small but sharp claws firmly into my lower lip, and proceeded to stick its head inside my mouth and to take a seed. From then on I only did this on those occasions when I wanted to show off for a visitor, because the feel of those curved little claws on one's lip, while basically painless, produced a most strange sensation.

By that September afternoon I was, of course, quite used to the chickadees, but I was still as intrigued as ever by their trust and confidence, characteristics shared by most animals once they learn that man can be a friend rather than an enemy. Again and again during the last twenty years I have met similar examples of trust among a wide variety of wild animals, my only contribution to these relationships being my interest in, and my concern for, the wild things with whom I have shared the forest and the sea and the plains. In some cases, admittedly, I have gone out of my way to win the confidence of some particular animal or bird, but in most instances the mere fact that I felt no aggression and that I walked easily and in reasonable quiet through their domain caused the wild ones to take me on trust. The lesson I learned from this, stated simply, is that man is almost invariably the aggressor, but if he is able to rid himself of the urge to kill and manages instead to be at peace with himself (I mean *really* at peace, totally relaxed *inside*) and with his surroundings, the animals of the wilderness respond to him.

Had I needed proof of this, my next encounter that afternoon, soon after I left the clearing and entered the mixed woods, would have supplied it. Inside a part of the forest where lowland cedars mixed with second-growth poplars over a floor topped by thick sphagnum moss, I caught a fleeting movement out of the corner of my eye; turning my head, I found myself being observed by one of last spring's deer fawns, now quite large and beginning to exchange its summer coat for the thick, hollow-haired winter dress that, often two inches thick, offers excellent protection against the cold. This one, born the previous May within the maples, still showed traces of its birth spots along the back and partway down the flanks; these blazes, now almost gray, would disappear with the full development of the winter hair.

I first saw the fawn when it was about three weeks old, a spindly-legged little fellow (it was a buck), whose mother, accustomed to Joan and me, didn't panic when I invaded the nursery. As a result, the fawn continued sucking from its mother and became so tame that even when Tundra accompanied us—on his lead—the young buck didn't run.

On the one hand I was pleased by the animal's trust, on the other I was concerned, worried in case it became equally trusting during the hunting season, when it would most certainly die. By the same token, I had enough experience of the species to know that animals are well able to distinguish friend from enemy; that is, they recognize those people who have won their trust, but usually avoid strangers, who are detected as such by the way they move, smell, and talk—different people have different, individual odors, though human noses cannot detect them unless such scents are strong.

Soon after leaving the deer, I encountered another old friend, One Ear, who was humping along to meet me with a gleam in his eye, put there by the prospect of peanuts, a supply of which, unshelled, I carried in another pocket—a habit that even now, as I sit before a typewriter in town, still persists, causing all of my topcoats to rattle strangely when I walk.

About One Ear I had no concerns. He'd lived long and was

wise and quick enough to escape or, if need be, hold his own against his enemies. I once saw him put the run on a neighbor's dog, a smallish mongrel who invaded the farm one day when Tundra and I were walking through the maples. The stranger was lucky that our malamute was on his lead, else he would have been more roughly handled. As it was, he sniffed One Ear inside his maple fortress and rashly stuck his nose in it. One Ear came out fighting mad, and although the dog retreated, he wasn't quick enough to avoid the slashing teeth of the raccoon, which clamped tightly on his nose. Yowling in agony, the visitor shook his head, dislodging his attacker. Once free, he streaked for home, ki-yiing as he went.

Today One Ear came in peace, sniffing and listening as I spoke to him. I stopped, took out a few peanuts, and, bending, held one out to him. He accepted it with his usual gentleness, taking it daintily between his front cutting teeth while extending an open paw and cupping my hand with it. Holding the prize in his mouth, he retreated a few steps, sat on his wide behind, thereby exposing a bulging gray and black belly only sparsely covered in fur, and took the peanut out of his mouth with both hands; now he rolled it back and forth between his palms, fingers spread wide, then he brought the nut to the side of his jaws, thrust it in, and, still holding one end between his palms, proceeded to husk the nut, expertly spitting out the shell and bits of the red, inner skin while he masticated the kernel. I tossed some more peanuts to him and left.

Heading toward the tamaracks at a slower pace, listening for the wolf howls, which had now been absent for some little time, I remembered my reaction to this part of our property when I first encountered it soon after buying the farm. It offered excellent shelter to the animals and birds and was rugged enough to discourage the trepassers who, despite my wrathful vigilance, occasionally managed to sneak in during the hunting season. When Tundra joined us as a puppy, Joan and I had decided that we would make this place out of bounds to him, or as out of bounds as possible, for on those occasions that he got away from us, there was no way of controlling his movements. But we never took him for walks there and only visited the area ourselves on more rare occasions. This was sanctuary, a place where dogs and humans should not trespass—this did not include me, of course! But I had an excuse, I needed to come here to study the life of this place, which, now and then, tempted Joan strongly enough to cause her to play Eve to this particular apple when I wasn't around. Joan being Joan, however, I always knew when she had sneaked in on her own; her guilt was as apparent as Times Square on New Year's Eve.

I could not stop the wild predators from entering here—and would not have done so had this been possible. It was as much their sanctuary as it was that of the lesser ones. It was also their larder, I well knew, but this was ever the way of nature. I had no wish to upset the balance, even if I worried about folk like One Ear and the young buck whitetail. But I consoled myself at such times with the knowledge that prey animals are not always the losers in the contest of life; the keener, stronger ones learn to survive, and their sensory equipment is no less effective than that of the hunters.

One day, I knew, Matta and Wa would themselves come here and seek to hunt. It was their right; I would not forbid them; yet I fervently hoped that they would not kill One Ear or any of our other friends that sought shelter within the area. In this sense I was perfectly aware that I was exhibiting a most unscientific approach, but I have never been able to separate my emotions from my academic discipline; I could not be clinically detached, and I didn't want to be, preferring to suffer the consequent emotional drain.

Our wolves had to be raised properly, taught to survive, encouraged to hunt and to gain experience before they were allowed to go it alone. To this end, I was in the forbidden land today, tape recorder at the ready, seeking Lobo's pack. But now the wolves were silent. Time passed as I threaded my way through the labyrinthine forest, eventually emerging on the edge of the swampland. There I found wolf tracks, recent ones, but the silence persisted. It was late evening before I heard a wolf howl issuing from some distance ahead. Others followed, also faint; I activated the recorder, turning the volume to full.

The light was fading rapidly by the time I was forced to give up. I had only a few rather distant howls on tape. I hoped they would do the trick.

When I was halfway back to the clearing, but still more than a mile from home, I heard numerous howls coming from the eastern part of our property, from East Ridge, it seemed to me. They were too faint to record, and I became exasperated.

If I had gone that way, instead of heading west, I would have gotten some really good recordings!

I was still inside the forest when the last rays of the sun faded entirely. It was not yet full dark, but the walking became awkward, and I was thankful when the trees ended and the clearing began. Ten minutes later I entered the house, to be greeted profusely by Tundra and the wolves, and sternly by my wife. Once again I was late for supper, I realized. What I didn't realize was that this was a special occasion.

"You're totally impossible. You really are! You know that? What day is today?" Joan was quite stern, for her.

I hadn't written in the wolf log for several days, leaving this chore to Joan lately because I was busy with other affairs, so I had no idea what the date was. I shrugged, about to tell her so, but she forestalled me.

"It's your birthday, you great oaf!"

Joan was big on such things. I'd forgotten all about the day when, onboard a British passenger vessel in Spanish territorial waters, I had emerged into an unsuspecting world in the middle of a Bay of Biscay storm that had caused my unfortunate mother to accelerate things.

I suppose I looked sheepish when my wife reminded me of the event.

"Well, supper's spoiled . . . again! I've a mind not to give you your present—or the cake."

Joan's lips gave her away; she tried hard, but when I grinned hugely, she could not help but smile also.

After we had eaten an excellent dinner at a fashionable hour, my wife produced a cake top-heavy with more candles than I cared to count. Then she gave me my present, a new pair of snowshoes. After I had unwrapped these (she was a firm believer that *all* presents must be wrapped, no matter what their shape), she gave me, on behalf of Matta and Wa, what was in effect a second present.

It seems that in my absence the wolves had howled on their own. Evidently they had heard the wild ones and responded; their voices set Tundra off, and the three rendered the concerto that I had heard and had attributed to a pack in the area of East Ridge. Before the evening was over, stimulated this time by the faint howls on the recorder, the canine songsters performed for my benefit their version of "Happy Birthday."

Ten days after the cubs howled for the first time, I was strolling toward the evaporator house only minutes ahead of the rising sun. It was going to be a glorious day; there had been a heavy frost during the night, and now the bushes and grasses were glittering with milky rime. The autumnal colors had intensified and were practically at their peak, and the day before, a large flock of Canada geese had passed low over our house. Matta and Wa had tipped the scales at thirty-two pounds five ounces and forty-seven pounds, respectively, on their last weigh-in on the morning of my birthday, September 12, at which time I decided not to put them through any more antics with the scales, which they were beginning to dislike intensely.

The cubs were three and a half months old on that day, healthy, active, inquisitive, and, if possible, more intelligent than ever. Wa continued to be the bigger of the two and remained placid; Matta was not quite as highstrung as before, but it was clear that she would always be the more nervous of the two. At this time, they spent all their nights in the evaporator house with Tundra, his presence being required because the wolves had not yet settled their social status and were liable to scrap at the slightest excuse. We were afraid that they might seriously injure one another if left alone, but with Tundra there to break up the fights when these became too serious—as one or another of the adult members of a wild pack would do under the same circumstances—we felt no concern for them when they were led from the house and settled for the night.

We were still feeding them twice a day, morning and evening, and it was for this reason that I was trudging to the sap house, carrying a mixture of Olac, milk, and cereal Pablum, in which was mixed some chopped, cooked liver; I also carried a side dish of two small bones. For the peace maker I had a large bone; he didn't need it, but it seemed unfair to feed the cubs and leave him out of it.

Naturally, the three heard me even before I closed the house door, and then *I* was hearing *them*, for they were howling plaintively, no doubt because they were eager to receive their accustomed meal.

Soon I would have to cut out the morning feed and later on, perhaps by winter, it would be time to feed them one large meal every second or third day, at irregular intervals. This was necessary in order to keep them hungry and thus give an edge to their senses and also to accustom them to the feast-famine way of life that would be theirs when they were set free. Joan and I didn't like the idea of doing this, but we consoled ourselves in the knowledge that had the cubs been raised by a wild pack, they would long ago have experienced such a feeding pattern.

At the sap house, I was mobbed as usual by the trio, though such greetings were nothing more than demonstrations of cupboard love. Tundra, as beta male, received his bone first; then, one tin plate in each hand, I bent and put both containers on the floor at the same time, treating the cubs equally. The remaining two bones I held onto, for afterward. As the wolves lapped up their thick formula, they seemed to me to be doing so more hurriedly than ususal, exhibiting symptoms of restlessness. Perhaps they should be taken for a good long walk?

I determined to lead them into the north forest, taking them by way of East Ridge, but I thought that I would leave the dog at home on this occasion, allowing myself a better opportunity to observe the cubs without the distracting need to keep an eye on Tundra as well. When they finished their platefuls, I gave them the bones, called Tundra, who had already demolished his tidbit, and led him out of the evaporator house. At home, I told Joan what I intended to do and asked her to make sure that the dog did not get out of the house while we were away, for he would certainly follow us.

"I'll have breakfast when we get back," I told my wife, who was holding the dog by the collar as I left home.

When I returned to them, I found that Matta and Wa had abandoned their bones.

And I noticed that they had been chewing at the doorway, tearing some large splinters from it, as though they had been trying to get out. Obviously, they needed a good run.

The sun was tipping the trees as we walked toward it escorted by some pathetic howls from the malamute, who, having found his voice on my birthday, was evidently going to use it now each time he felt slighted. The cubs replied a few times, but as soon as we entered the forest, they forgot all about Tundra as the scents and sounds of the wilderness gripped their interest. Within a few minutes Wa pounced suddenly and slapped both big paws in unison at the crisp grasses; shuffling his feet forward jerkily, but keeping the pads against the ground, he put his nose down and pressed and sniffed at the same time. He came up holding a vole in his mouth. The little animal was already dead, but was still twitching feebly as it was bolted down whole. Matta was about to go see what her brother was doing when a red squirrel burst hurriedly out of a mass of deadfall branches. It had evidently been caught in the open and had sought temporary shelter under the downed spruce, coming out when Matta's attention veered toward Wa. The redback streaked for a nearby tree with Matta hot in pursuit; for a few seconds it was touch-and-go, but the squirrel got to the tree, scurried around its bole, and ran numbly up the trunk to the safety of one of the topmost branches. There it sat and cursed all of us.

The cubs were evidently learning more quickly than I had thought. Catching a vole and almost catching a squirrel were no mean feats at their age, but they had a long way to go yet before they would be ready to tackle bigger game.

For no particular reason, I aimed toward Toilet Hill, letting the wolves range ahead as they wished. Most of the time they stayed twenty or thirty feet in front, sometimes they detoured downslope, exploring some scent or other on either flank of the ridge, but whenever they felt unsure, they returned to my side on their own accord. In this way we came to the end of the ridge and began to cross the opening that led to Toilet Hill. The cubs quickly caught the scent of the place and became immediately interested in it. They ran ahead, leaving me to start picking my way into the clearing. Wa was leading, as usual; Matta was about five yards in the rear.

Without warning, and certainly without making any sound that I could hear, the shaggy bulk of a big black bear appeared only feet away from Wa. Despite the panic that I felt at the instant of seeing the great carnivore, I remember thinking that the bear must have scented the cubs and had headed for them intent on bringing one of them down. I yelled. Matta wheeled about like a well-trained horse and dashed toward me at full run; Wa, obviously confused and in panic, turned away, running at an angle along the clearing toward its opposite end, where heavy timber grew in profusion. The bear didn't hesitate; it may have glanced briefly in my direction, but now it swung to its right and took after Wa. Its speed was frightening.

My next moves were reflexive. Stooping, I grabbed Matta,

lifting her off the ground. As I straightened, I was already running after the bear and Wa, yelling as I went, hoping to distract the bear and to cause Wa to swing wide and return to me. What I would have done if the cub had turned and brought his pursuer with him is more than I can say now; my only weapon was a six-inch bush knife, puny armament with which to face a five-hundred-pound creature that was clearly intent on having a good meal of wolf pup. But Wa kept on going. By the time I reached the trees, I could no longer hear the sounds of the chase.

I knew I could not hope to catch up with them, even without the added weight of Matta, but I kept on running, yelling as often as my laboring lungs would allow, while feeling great despair. With awful clarity I visualized Wa being torn to pieces by the big predator.

Finding myself in a part of the forest where large spruces dominated the land and kept lesser trees from growing in their shade, I halted for breath and to listen, still hoping to hear some sounds of the chase ahead. I had hardly stopped when the noise of a heavy body running at speed through the undergrowth made me wheel around, the hair on the back of my neck prickling. I fully expected to see the bear.

Instead I saw Tundra. He was running flat out, his belly almost touching the grasses and shrubs as he came. I didn't know how he happened to be here, and I didn't much care, my relief was so great. As he passed me without so much as checking his stride or deigning to glance in my direction, I yelled at the top of my lungs.

"Get-him-Tundra!"

Wa wasn't safe yet, but now he had a chance. There was no doubt about Tundra's intention. He must have scented the bear while he was still running along East Ridge, and now he was on a hot scent, aroused and committed to the chase. I prayed he would catch up to his quarry before Wa was destroyed.

I stood undecided, still holding a very nervous and subdued Matta and trying to work out the next move. Moments later, having now elected to continue in the general direction of the triple chase, I heard the sound of crackling underbrush coming from my left. Turning quickly, I was in time to see Wa appear between the boles of the spruces, running toward me for all he

110

was worth. He reached me a few moments later, and I picked him up.

Was the bear still following him? Holding one cub under each arm, I began to retrace my steps, listening for the sound of a heavy body moving toward us. There was only silence.

Back in the small clearing, I put the cubs down and began to walk briskly for home, only slightly worried about Tundra. The dog had chased so many bears during the years that he had been with us, and treed half a dozen to my knowledge, that he was now an expert at the sport. If they ran, he chased; if they turned at bay, he circled them, darting in to snap and leaping clear before they could take a swipe at him. A few minutes of this and a bear was ready to run again, or if there happened to be a convenient tree handy, it would climb it, moving with amazing speed and ease.

More collected now that the excitement was over and both cubs were dutifully walking beside me, I had time to wonder about Tundra's sudden and fortuitous appearance. I thought I knew the answer, because I knew the dog so well: He must have gotten away from Joan and immediately tracked us, arriving in the nick of time. Presently I heard Joan call, and I replied to her. When she emerged, looking worried, I hastened to assure her that everything was all right, and as we walked home, she told me what had happened.

Trying to make up to Tundra for being left at home, she led him by the collar, intending to take him for a short walk down the road. As soon as she opened the door, he gave a lunge and ran off. She followed at a more leisurely pace, angry with the dog. But when she learned from me what had occurred, Tundra suddenly became a hero; then she began to worry about him and was almost on the point of getting cross with me when I refused to go looking for him. I pointed out that I couldn't hope to catch up with him; in any event, by now I had no idea where he and the bear would be. In *finale* I delivered my last line:

"And anyway, I'm starving to death. I haven't had my breakfast yet, remember?"

I could always appeal to Joan's motherly instincts! The discussion ended forthwith, and we made good time getting back. Not long afterward I became engrossed with eggs and bacon and toast and lots of coffee.

An hour and a half later Tundra came home. He was soaking wet, coated liberally with swamp mud, reeking like a manure pile, and happy as a clam journeying through soft ooze. He was *not* scolded for his escapade.

CHAPTER SEVEN

It was still dark when Tundra came upstairs to wake me by slapping one big paw on my chest and then sticking his nose into the junction between my neck and my chin, a method he had evolved when only half grown and that he continued to use because it produced such immediate action. The bedside clock said it was 4 A.M., but I responded to the dog because he had never yet called me without good reason. Joan was fast asleep in her own bed; so as not to disturb her, I got up more quickly than I would otherwise have done.

At first I thought that the dog needed to go outside to relieve himself, for the basement window was now closed at night on account of the colder weather, but when I went downstairs, hastily clad in warm pants, a wool sweater, and heavy socks, Tundra was so evidently restless and anxious to get out that he communicated his urgency to me. For the past couple of weeks he had been sleeping either in the house or outside, fastened to the front porch by a long chain. This change in nocturnal arrangements was introduced when Matta and Wa appeared to come to terms in the matter of pack status, evidently content to accept equal social position within the North Star Pack in preference to their continued bickering. Because I did not want the cubs to become too accustomed to Tundra's presence for fear that they would form a permanent attachment to him that would interfere later with their release, I altered the arrangements, allowing them to sleep in the evaporator house on their own.

As I slipped on a pair of boots, Tundra went to the front door and scratched it with his foot, an action normally forbidden and resorted to by the dog only under conditions that he considered to be urgent. With that, I grabbed a flashlight, put him on his lead, and took him outside, wondering if perhaps a bear was around.

Tundra immediately turned and began dragging me toward the sap house, his mien signaling that something untoward was occurring either in the distant building or in its vicinity. I started to run, an easy exercise when pulled by a hundred-pound dog, but when halfway there, with my legs scissoring too fast for comfort, I leaned back on the leash and slowed him down. It was at this moment that I heard the angry snarls and growls coming from inside the evaporator building, telling me that Matta and Wa were having a serious fight. I released Tundra, letting him streak away on his own, and I ran as fast as I could.

Tundra aimed for the back door; I went toward the side entrance, wanting to be first inside the building in order to see what was going on before the dog got mixed up in the fight. The cubs were now over four months old and, Wa especially, powerful enough to contemplate a fight with Tundra while gripped by the inherent desire to prove their status. I switched on the five-cell as I opened the door, entered quickly, and closed it behind me. The growls had subsided, but a series of vicious snarls continued unabated.

The evaporator house was fifty feet long by twenty feet wide, divided into three sections. The first, outside of which Tundra was waiting, contained a large store of firewood to feed the evaporator firebox, which occupied the central portion of the building. The last part was given over to the sugar room, a place where the newly boiled syrup was stored in large holding tanks and where a small taffy evaporator stove stood in a corner. Matta and Wa were in this section of the long shed. The light quickly found them.

Wa was straddling Matta; his head was down, his lips peeled back to show all his teeth, a continuous snarl issuing from his mouth; Matta lay on her side, head on the ground. Her eyes avoided Wa, but her lips were also pulled back in the snarl,

114

and the noise she was making was only a little less ferocious than her brother's. Even at first glance I noticed the blood; Wa's cheek and muzzle were coated with it, so was his chest. Matta showed red on a number of places on her body, especially on her right hind leg, near the thigh.

I was concerned, of course, but I was also pleased. It was quite obvious that Wa had trounced his sister and that she, for the first time, accepted her defeat, her entire stance signaling submission.

For a few seconds longer Wa continued to lean over his prostrate sister and to show his teeth while snarling viciously, then, knowing me instantly despite the fact that I hadn't spoken and that he couldn't see me because of the light, he stepped over her and ran up to me. Matta picked herself up, shook her fur into place, thereby spattering some blood in our direction, and came limping toward me as well. I felt a little concerned. Would Wa turn on her again?

The male surprised me by reaching across my thigh (I was now squatting) and licking Matta's face, just as though the recent, fierce contest had not taken place. Better and better, I thought as I stood up to go light the kerosene lantern that hung on a long wire from the hip roof. By its light I turned to see each wolf licking the other's injuries, perhaps solicitously, but probably because they were enjoying the taste of each other's gore. At this moment a succession of loud scrapes captured the attention of all of us. Tundra had relinquished his vigil by the back door and had come to the side entrance, scratching at it with his paw, demanding to be let in. I opened the door, and he bounded inside, tail tightly curled, hackles raised, and ears pricked forward. I thought it was just as well that I had kept him outside, for his demeanor signaled hostile intentions; if the fight had still been in progress, I am sure he would have waded into the fray. Anything might have happened then.

When the three canines settled down, I was able to examine the cubs. Matta had two fairly deep bites on her back leg and several slashes on her left flank and hip; Wa had collected a bitten foot and he had a small hole in his left ear. The injuries were not serious, but they did require some first aid, even if the wolves would have been just as content to lick themselves well—as they would have done if they had been members of a wild pack. It was fortunate that the cubs had not yet developed their permanent teeth, which would have done more damage, but the needle-sharp primary canines were nasty enough weapons in a fight.

With peace restored and sunrise some three hours distant, I elected to lead my three pack subordinates to the house, to treat the injured while coffee was brewing and then, after settling each canine with a bone and having a much-needed cup of coffee, to return to bed for a couple of hours. It was a decorous procession that proceeded in single file from evaporator shed to residence, but my plans were slightly disrupted when we entered the house to find Joan not only awake but up and fully dressed, about to emerge into the dark and cold morning to see what was going on. Her keen eyes missed not one flake of blood on the bodies of her darlings, and her already furrowed brow became deeply lined. Advancing swiftly, like some stately clipper ship in full sail, she dropped to her haunches and opened wide her arms, an invitation that Wa, Matta, and Tundra accepted instantly. At one moment there she was, in tears, arms as wide as they could go; in the next instant she was flat on her back, Matta standing on her abdomen and chest, Wa pushing his wet nose into her right cheek, while Tundra, one enormous paw settled firmly on top of her head, licked the right side of her face with slobbering affection. The tears still trickled out of her eyes, but her laughter prevented her words of protest from emerging intelligibly.

In due course, I knew, the melee would become disentangled. I wanted coffee, so I left them and walked into the kitchen to get the brew started. Five minutes later I heard Joan murmur to herself as she inspected the cubs, her voice alternating between inarticulate laments and expressions of comfort. Later she reminded me that she had protested when I decided to allow the cubs to sleep alone in the sap house. She sat on the living room floor, one arm around each cub, who stood flanking her. Tundra was lying down nearby, chin resting on one of her legs.

"I *told* you they shouldn't be left alone! Now see what's happened; they're *all chewed up!*"

"Yes," I agreed cravenly (although in truth they were not), "but it's all over with now. They've settled the matter. Wa is top dog."

This comment did nothing to appease my wife's concern.

"There you go, taking his part right away! He could have killed poor little Matta. You're a nasty, bullying *brute*!"

The last part of her utterance was directed at Wa, who was grinning widely. But I noticed that Joan's arm was not removed from the "brute's" shoulders. It was now time to treat the injuries.

"Are you going to sit there and let 'em bleed to death?" I asked.

Joan forgot about her scolding. She rose and went to get the first-aid box, which was placed in my hands without another word.

Ten minutes later harmony was restored. Matta's cuts were swabbed with permanganate of potash, her bitten leg was dusted with sulpha powder. Wa, on close examination, needed little attention. The ear was powdered with sulpha, the paw was left alone; he'd soon put that to rights with his tongue.

Coffee was made and we drank the hot brew while our three wards made disgusting sounds as they gnawed large bones on the living room rug under the approving gaze of my wife. Now I told Joan why I was so sure that the status contest was over.

It would serve no useful purpose to attempt fully to document each of the actions and reactions with which wolves, and dogs, reveal to each other their acceptance of the hierarchical slot into which they have been placed by a more dominant pack member. But a more curtailed description of the signals employed by canines in this and other situations will be useful, if only because it will allow dog owners to understand the body language of their pets better.

There are five basic postures adopted by a canid to signal these moods: relaxation, attention, aggression, fear, and playfulness. When relaxed, the animal's entire body is visibly at ease, whether it is standing, sitting, or lying down. In this loose posture, its ears are erect (noticeable even in dogs that have floppy ears, such as hounds, though in such cases most of the ear still hangs down while only the upper part rises). When in a playful or alert mood, the ears stiffen noticeably and are moved forward, this action being first initiated when something captures the canine's attention. From the upright ear to the aggressive and playful ear, there is a noticeable change in the forward angle, especially at the tip, which now curves forward. When the animal is afraid, or is showing submission, the ears

117

are moved progressively backward, according to the degree of fear or submission being signaled. Intense fear or submission will cause the ears to be placed so far back that they lie at the same angle as the animal's back.

Simultaneously, the tail signals attitude: relaxed, the tail hangs loosely to more or less form an inverted V with the rump; alert or attentive behavior causes the tail to rise visibly, but not yet to curve over the hips (except for sled dogs, who have a greater curl to their tails); to signal aggression, or while engaged in play, the tail is carried higher, more stiffly, and now its tip is definitely over the hips, or haunches. Fear and submission, however, cause the tail to drop; the farther the fall, the greater the fear, or submission, until in extremes the tail is tucked between the legs and actually presses against the stomach. In the final stages of submission the animal first crouches, then lies on its side, tail tucked tightly against the stomach. The back leg not against the ground is now lifted, exposing the inguinal region.

An aggressive canine raises its hackles along the neck and shoulders and along the lower back, from the tail root to a spot approximately corresponding with the position of the kidneys. Fear and submission will cause the hackles to rise, but not as noticeably as in the aggressive state. After a while the hackles subside but do not become completely flattened as in the relaxed state.

In unison with the actions of ears, tail, and hackles, the animal's entire body adopts different postures that clearly signify its attitude. The attentive or aroused canid usually lifts one front leg, curving it backward as though ready to initiate the first step preceding forward movement. Aroused to aggression, the leg is usually set down as the entire body is thrust forward; now the forequarters are lowered slightly and the opposite front leg is flexed, like a runner waiting for the starter's pistol. During displays of fear, or submission, both front paws are placed side by side on the ground, and the animal leans backward, reversing the aggressive angle; in extremes of fear or submission, the body appears to be pulling backward against an unseen leash.

When a dog or wolf is playful, that is, is trying to get another animal (or a human) to play with it, its forequarters drop noticeably, and one of its front legs rises and paws at air usually repeatedly, this accompanied by a swiftly wagging tail.

During all this, the lips are either held in a grin (playful), kept together in a serious expression (relaxed or attentive), peeled back into an obvious snarl that reveals all the teeth (aggressive), or held in a half snarl as the head rises (fearful-submissive). In final submission, the lips are puckered, as though the animal is trying to whistle.

In addition to all the other signs, the eyes of a wolf or dog invariably signal its attitude and mood. At attention, the eyes gaze toward the cause of the alert; aggression will focus the gaze unwinkingly on an opponent (or postman?). Fear and submission cause the gaze to be pointedly averted, while during play-soliciting the animal will look toward the object of its attentions obliquely rather than directly, like a person wearing reading glasses might do when trying to look at a distance over the top of the rims. Neutrality is signaled by avoidance of eye-to-eye contact while the body is held in the attentive stance, with perhaps a slight raising of the hackles.

After a fight, the losing animal, apart from signaling in the ways outlined, will hold its head back while lying on its side, offering its vulnerable throat to its opponent or to its master. This is the final surrender, putting the subordinate at the mercy of the dominant animal. One might wonder why a dominant wolf does not immediately tear the throat out of its opponent at such times. The fact is that nature has implanted inhibitory mechanisms in the more powerful predators that prevent them from destroying their own kind in most instances. Precisely how these work is unknown; the fact remains that when a wolf is defeated during a one-to-one encounter and finally offers its throat, the winner does not take advantage of the offer, usually ending the status contest by straddling its recumbent opponent, growling, and showing its teeth and perhaps initiating a painless scruff bite before it walks away, legs stiff and tail erect.

All of these interactions took place during the fight between Matta and Wa. When I shone the light on the pair, Matta had evidently just offered her throat and Wa was intent on rein-forcing his dominance by continuing to growl and to show his teeth. Matta was also growling, but doing so in a more subdued way, partly in submission and partly as a warning that she *would* fight again if Wa attempted to seize her throat, which

119

is perhaps one of the reasons why the winners of such a contest refrain from seeking a death hold, being satisfied to end the contest while they are ahead, without exposing themselves to further, unnecessary risks. But that is only a guess on my part.

Later that day Joan prevailed upon me to allow Tundra to stay with the cubs at night again, but this became a needless precaution. Wa had truly emerged as the dominant wolf. He knew it, and so did Matta, who from then on always kept her place as punctiliously as Wa refrained from abusing his station. The North Star Pack, as of this time—the end of the first week of October—ranked as follows: myself, alpha male; Tundra, beta male; Wa now occupied third place, Matta fourth. Joan was still considered an equal with special status—by all of us! My wife, of course, argued about this. But it didn't change matters.

Not long after the wolves resolved their status differences, I sought to photograph them again, hoping that perhaps by now they might have lost their inordinate fear of the camera, which instrument had caused both of them to panic when I thoughtlessly attempted to take their pictures about a month after they came to live with us.

At first I had been too busy to worry about taking photographs of our wards, but when they were five weeks old and scampering over the kitchen floor, I thought it time to begin a picture record. Instead of allowing them to become gradually accustomed to the odor and shape of the camera, and to my relationship with it, I squatted in the living room doorway, focused on both cubs as they were playing with Tundra, and then called them. Matta looked up first, saw the glaring, Cyclopean eye and the black metal that obscured half my face and immediately ran for cover; Wa, slower to react, stared a moment or two before seeking refuge under the kitchen table. In vain after that did I try to coax them to accept the instrument; the smell of it, or of any other piece of photographic equipment, was enough to make them panic, causing me reluctantly to abandon my efforts.

For the last two months I had been careful to keep the camera out of their way. Now I thought it appropriate to try again, believing that their new-found confidence would eliminate their fear. But it was not to be.

They were outside at the time, with Tundra and Joan, but as soon as I opened the front door and emerged with the 35-mm Pentax hanging from my neck, both wolves started to run for the evaporator house, tails tightly tucked between their legs. For two days after that they would not approach the house, yet they showed no fear of me when I divested myself of the camera.

There was no doubt now that the camera had become imprinted on their minds as a thing to be feared. As the future was to show, they never did lose this fear, though by using a 500-mm telephoto lens I did manage to sneak a few shots of them when they were almost fully grown.

It was a disappointment, but entirely my own fault. I failed to take into account the lupine temperament, with its attendant caution and long memory, being lulled into my folly by the fact that I had long made a practice of photographing the many wildings that came into our care, none of which ever exhibited fear of the photographic equipment.

Reconstructing my actions and how these would have appeared to the cubs the first time I tried to take their picture, I understood the reason for their fear. Wolves are extremely observant animals, who use their fine intellect to interpret all the signals encountered in their environment. They have an inherent ability to read "sign," even at a very early age, and are quite capable of actually recognizing human features, though I had not considered this last trait until after the incident with the camera.

It seemed to me that what I had done was, first of all, take the cubs by surprise, then alter my features, changing my face with the Pentax. To them I became an alien thing, probably tainted with an odor that was equally strange to their noses. In order to test this concept, I made some experiments over a period of time. The first was simple. I bought some cigars and approached Matta and Wa holding one in my mouth. They reacted, showing momentary caution, but soon identified me; the cigar, after all, was not much different from the pipe and offered a similar scent; they had become used to my pipe ever since I first handled them. Next I tied a scarf around my face, over my mouth. They immediately registered fear and ran under the chesterfield. My last experiment took place when I asked Joan to alter my face with some of her makeup. With mascara she drew lines on my cheeks and forehead; she applied great globs of lipstick to my lips, extending their line past the normal, then, as an afterthought, she further bedecked me with a wig that she had bought the-Lord-knows-for-what-reason and had worn but once. This was blonde and rather shaggy. Glancing in the bedroom mirror when she was done, I hardly recognized myself.

Tundra and the two volves were downstairs in the living room, lying relaxed in various locations. As soon as I presented myself at the bottom of the staircase, all hell broke loose. Matta actually ki-yied as she ran for the chesterfield; Wa thumped into the wall in his haste to flee to the kitchen, and Tundra launched one deep, dark growl as he came for me with all his teeth gleaming evilly, leaving no doubt as to his intentions. Indeed, I whipped the wig off my head and told him to settle down, stopping him only a yard away from my legs. That ended the experiments. As far as I am concerned, wolves are able to recognize the features of a human; so are dogs.

Heeding this, and their reaction to strange objects, I allowed them later to get acquainted with the regurgitation helmet that Joan made for me, and we were both careful thereafter to look and to behave as ourselves when the wolves were around— not that either one of us was given to the habit of altering our features in bizarre ways!

Although we were intitially the losers because we didn't have a whole series of pictures of the gowing cubs, we gained in the long run. The incident with the camera caused me to appreciate more fully the intellect of the wolf and to respect the animal's ability to interpret its surroundings and to retain an excellent memory of those things that are likely to affect its life.

I had been aware before this that wolves have a retentive memory, but now I realized that this played an extremely important role in the development of the cubs, teaching them to distinguish between "good and bad" at a very early age.

The recent status struggle reminded me of the importance of memory. The hierarchical rituals of wolves are many and complex, including the behavior patterns already outlined, in addition to many others. Pack discipline is maintained largely because of good memory. Remembering their social standing and taking care not to trespass beyond its limits, wolves maintain an orderly society remarkably free from strife, which allows all members of a pack to concentrate on the difficulties of survival.

In addition to this, memory of the lessons learned as cubs during the tutelage of their parents and of other pack adults, as well as from personal experience, gives them a much better chance of surviving later on. In this regard, pups first learn to be cautious because, like all extremely young organisms, they feel insecure; such inherent caution is reinforced by the adults of the pack to such an extent that as the cubs grow older, this desirable trait becomes an integral part of their nature, continuously sharpened by the promptings of memory and experience. The same is also largely true of domestic dogs, but here the lack of parental teaching and the secure, assured life in a human abode combine to make many dogs incautious to the point of folly.

This is well illustrated by the fact that some dogs never learn to stay away from porcupines. Time and again these foolish ones will rush blindly into the quills of a porcupine whenever they meet one, despite previous, agonizing experiences, while wolves, and some other dogs, learn to avoid the prickly animals, or to attack them cautiously when anger drives them to take this risk. None of my sled dogs ever needed more than the one experience to teach them that the docile vegetarian with the forest of barbs is a dangerous opponent; neither did Matta and Wa.

I believe that all of the higher animals have a better memory than humans credit them with, such belief being encouraged by experiences too numerous to list, though a few may be worthy of mention.

I once raised a young beaver, taking care of him from late spring until autumn, then releasing him.* When I returned the following spring and called his name, Paddy came out of the water and waddled up to me, clearly remembering our association. The chickadees furnished me with another example of memory. Before buying the farm, we owned seventy-five acres of wild land some four miles away, and because of the many

*R. D. Lawrence, *Paddy: A Naturalist's Story of an Orphan Beaver* (New York: Alfred A. Knopf, 1977).

123

chores at the farm, more than a year went by before I returned to the first property. As soon as I stepped out of the car, the local chickadees, which we had been hand-feeding, arrived and landed on me, seeking seeds.

Having had a great deal to do with a large number of raccoons over the years, I know that these animals retain good memory of the events that take place before they den up for the winter. Come spring, they know where to seek food, they remember that I will feed them, they recall my voice. Red, gray, and flying squirrels have similar powers of recall, so do cougar and killer whales, to name but some of the animals that have given me proof of memory.

The elephant is universally credited with having excellent recall and is almost always held as an example in this regard. This animal certainly has a good memory, but it is by no means an exception. Comparisons are always odious and rather hard to prove, but I am tempted to believe that wolves, because they must work harder in order to earn a living and are not nearly so powerful as pachyderms, probably need to have better memories than the big African vegetarians.

Humans, inordinately conceited as we are, tend to downgrade the intellect of "the lower orders," not stopping to consider that animals can only survive if they are able to reason. It is hard to conceive of reason without memory, which, together with observation and deduction, lead to experience and survival.

CHAPTER EIGHT

On November 14, despite intentions to the contrary, it became necessary to weigh the wolves once more. The reason for this was an infestation of intestinal roundworms in both cubs and in Tundra, no doubt first picked up by the wolves when they fed on whole prey that they caught, for even the small animals—the only kind they had captured thus far—are hosts to a large number of such worms.

Roundworms, or nematodes, are, as their name implies, cylindrical in shape, with unsegmented bodies. No less than twenty-four different species have been reported to infest wolves, though many of them rarely occur in Canada. Some of these creatures seem to do little harm. Some are small, perhaps no more than an inch long. But there are veritable giants among the class, including one, the kidney worm, that grows up to forty inches in length within the cavities of the kidneys. None is beneficial to the host, and a number of species are extremely harmful.

The ones I had to deal with were what might be termed the standard kind, *Toxocara canis*. They became evident in the feces of all three patients. Matta carried the worst infestation; her scats were packed with the creatures, which were almost two inches long; obscene, yellowish white, jerkily moving pests that clustered all around the emerging stool. Joan noticed them first. After she attended to the spasms caused by a departing breakfast, she drew the fact to my attention and was almost ill anew when I picked up a couple of sticks and started fishing some of the beasts out of their hiding places, placing them carefully on a bit of bark. I wanted to view them under the microscope, though my wife was adamant about refusing to give them house room. But I had to know what kind they were so I could treat them with the right stuff, didn't I? In any event, the worms entered the house and were duly inspected, and the proper medicine was procured.

It now became necessary to weigh the cubs, for the medication was prescribed by weight, so much for each seven pounds of dog (or wolf, in this case). While Joan entertained Wa and Tundra outside, I coaxed Matta inside and picked her up, stroking her and talking gently all the while because wolves do not like being picked up off their feet, relying as they do for food and safety on their pedal agility. Holding Matta, I stepped on the scales, weighing both of us at the same time. When I put her down, I deducted my weight from hers. She scaled fifty pounds eleven ounces. I repeated the procedure with Wa, learning that he weighed sixty pounds nine ounces. I also discovered that his second set of teeth were fully developed and quite capable of hurting abominably, even when he didn't bite hard; he only mouthed my elbow affectionately, but it felt as though I'd shut a heavy door on my arm.

Wa's new teeth began to displace his old ones on November 3; Matta's were not fully developed on the day of the (positively!) last weigh-in, and she didn't seek to practice with them on my person; perhaps her gums were still sore.

In view of the fact that I was going to have to stuff a whole lot of enormous pills down their throats with my naked fingers, I thought it would be wise to take them for a long walk on an empty stomach, to get them tired out—if such a thing were possible—and then shove the pills down, after which they could eat. Tundra, I knew, would be no problem; he had been wormed several times already; he didn't like it, but he didn't try to take my arm off. I wished I could feel as sure about the wolves.

Worms or no, the wolves were in excellent condition, clear-eyed and energetic, with sleek, shiny fur. Now they were truly wolves; they had lost all their puppy charm and acquired instead

126

a kind of wild dignity that was impressive to behold. Perhaps their only unattractive features were the great big feet that didn't quite seem to go with their bodies; but they would grow into these in a few more weeks.

Wa continued to be placid and mischievous, always willing to romp with his sister, or with Tundra and me, and getting pretty rough at times. Joan he treated with gentleness, but he loved to pick up one of her hands in his big mouth, set his teeth gently, and walk along beside her. My wife enjoyed this until the moment when Wa began to salivate all over her hand, at which point she would coax him into letting go and then, treacherously, pretend to be fondling him as she rubbed off the drool on his fur.

One of the things that Wa enjoyed doing most of all was ambushing me. He would lie in wait, perhaps in the evaporator house or concealed behind a bush and, when my back was turned, would charge at speed. The first time he did this, hearing the clatter of his ungentle paws, I turned and made the mistake of trying to dodge his hurtling body at the last minute, thinking to fool him. The result was that his carefully worked-out move, which was to swerve clear of me inches before a collision, was aborted by my move, and he hit full tilt, knocking me down. He got me on the right thigh with his shoulder, and in addition to an instant and agonizing pain, my leg was incapacitated for several minutes. As I tried hard to see the funny side of the action, which Joan thought was hilarious, while massaging my crippled limb, Wa considered that this would be a good moment to grab my other leg and pull it. Attempting to foil his lunge, I moved the target. He missed the solid, but his teeth caught the pants cuff, on which he clamped down hard. He began to pull, and he actually moved me bodily about a yard before the jeans tore out of his mouth. By now, hurt or not, I made myself stand, and when he came in for another mock attack, I grabbed his scruff and shook hard, twice. That settled him. Tail tucked between his legs, ears flattened, whining, he ran to Joan, who immediately cuddled the savage beast and kissed his head, the while calling *me* names.

Matta was not a playful wolf now. She was much too formal and stately for such frivolity. She preened herself regularly, spending much time in licking her fur and then arranging herself so that she always looked her best. She would unbend occa-

127

sionally to play a bit with Tundra, but when he, a bit carried away by her charms, sought to become too familiar, she would turn on him with a high-pitched yap and snap at him, more than once drawing blood from ear or nose. Poor old Tundra couldn't understand her. He didn't know that she wasn't yet of breeding age and that, in any event, had she been, his blind, unpracticed rushes would have been repelled in similar fashion until such time as *she* was good and ready. But Tundra was a gentleman, nevertheless. Whereas he would have thrashed Wa, or tried to, and killed any other male dog that dared to snap at him, he only looked hurt when Matta nipped a corner of his ear, shaking his head with a puzzled expression in his eyes.

Wa would also try to make up to his sister in the same way, but his attempts were prompted by sheer bravado and additionally hindered by a great deal of anatomical ignorance. Matta, once she realized that it wasn't status behavior that caused him to take such liberties, treated him as she did Tundra, her brother responding like the dog. She acknowledged herself subservient to Tundra and Wa in most things, but she sure knew her rights in that one respect!

Of course my wife thought that the two males were being rude and impertinent, and there were times when she became so incensed with Tundra or Wa that she would actually punch one or the other. This was always a mistake. Invariably she hurt her hand on the tough bodies of the "rude" ones, and they, believing that her little taps were invitations to play, would romp all around her, not touching her in any way but causing her to stay rooted in one place for fear that she would be hit by a wildly careering body.

I said Matta was not playful; what I really meant was that she didn't play with me or with the two males very often, but there were times when she would have a great game on her own with a stick, or some other hard object, such as my flashlight on one occasion, or the legs of my typing chair, which bear the marks of her teeth to this day. Then she would be as puppyish as ever, growling, pawing, chewing. If the object of her game was a stick, she would toss it, chase it, stalk it, and ambush it, killing it many times over, until it was reduced to small chunks of wood all covered in slobber and filled with teeth marks. If either of the males sought to participate in the game, she would stop playing, surrendering her stick and

128

sauntering away disdainfully. Being a female, she was pre-cocious, as are all females of all mammalian species, and in-tellectually ahead of Wa, for all that she was physically smaller. In nature, this is a planned design; the female generally bears most of the responsibility for perpetuating the breed. Males, even wolf males, are usually more carefree and "childish" for a longer period, though, unlike most other animals except man, wolf males, once they reach full adulthood, are ready to take on pack responsibilities, even helping to raise and educate the young.

Now that the wolves were five and a half months old these differences in sex were becoming quite apparent, particularly when they went hunting without Tundra; during such occasions Matta often took the lead, and Wa was content to follow, a reversal of the status order; but if Matta caught anything larger than a mouse, such as a groundhog or, very occasionally, a snowshoe hare, Wa would exert his dominance and take the biggest share, despite his sister's snarls and growls. When hunting "little stuff," each wolf went his or her own way, but if Tundra was with them, they both followed his lead.

I began to take them into the forest more and more frequently without the dog, allowing them to outdistance me whenever they chose and encouraging them to become independent. Oc-casionally they would leave me altogether, not returning until the small hours of the morning, then going directly to curl up inside the evaporator house and to sleep for the rest of the day. At dusk they usually emerged, trotting up to the house in quest of food. Tundra always knew when they were back, and he never failed to awaken me. In the same way, whether he was inside the house or outside on his chain, he would alert us the moment that Matta and Wa left their quarters in the evening.

Their hunting forays to this point were not particularly suc-cessful; we could always gauge their failures by the extent of their hunger and by careful examination of their scats: Invari-ably, their stools would contain the fur of the animals they had eaten. Mice and voles predominated; occasionally I would find squirrel fur, now and then the pelage of a groundhog, more rarely the fur of a snowshoe hare. Twice when they had been gone most of the night, I found grouse feathers in Matta's scats, but whether she managed to pull down the birds herself or had merely found the leavings of fox or hawk and eaten them, was impossible to say.

These forays were obviously responsible for the infestation of roundworms, but, apart from doctoring them while they were in our care, there was nothing more that could be done. In the wild they would become permanent hosts of these creatures, which were only one of the risks attendant with freedom. I avoided discussing such things with Joan, and I didn't allow myself to dwell at any length on the many other parasites and diseases to which they would be exposed once they returned to the wild.

Even without worrying about them under such circumstances, the temptation to keep Matta and Wa, to turn them into pets, was ever present, something we had to guard against continuously. Repeatedly, watching Matta and Wa, or during our walks, the little voice in my mind would whisper, "Why not keep them?"

The answer was twofold. No matter how great the temptation, we could not possibly keep all the wild ones that came into our care without starting a zoo, which was something I could not begin to contemplate. To me, even now, the concept of taking wild animals and confining them in pens or cages, depriving them of freedom of choice, was abhorrent, no matter how well housed and cared for the animals might be. A prison may be lined with velvet and offer every amenity and comfort and convenience, yet it is still a prison. Then again, with wolves, which can certainly be tamed if obtained when very young, as we had obtained Matta and Wa, the greatest problem is public opinion. People fear wolves; no matter how mistaken this fear may be, it is real. People are also fascinated by them, as they are by horror movies and gruesome fairy tales; some, the careless, thoughtless ones, are disposed to take liberties with tame wolves.

Once it became known that we were keeping wolves, two dangers would immediately arise: Some of our neighbors, being farmers and trappers, would protest, seeking to have them destroyed, perhaps even sneaking in to shoot them; others would come to visit, to see the "freak show," and might well take liberties that could result in a bite. It is socially tolerable if a dog, minding its business on its home ground, bites a stranger who either trespasses or who, visiting, unwittingly provokes

130

the animal. But let a tame wolf bite a visitor, even if the animal has been severely provoked, and it becomes headline news.

So, for these reasons, we committed ourselves to raising Matta and Wa as wild as was possible under the circumstances, determined on releasing them when they were old enough to earn their own living in the wilderness. Equally, we decided to raise them in secret. Nobody should know that North Star Farm housed two wolves.

Up to the day that they were to be dosed with worm medicine, neither wolf had seen any of our friends and neighbors, or been seen by them. At first it was difficult to keep them concealed. Often they were in the house on the arrival of neighbors, and I had to pick them up and rush them down to the basement, exaggerating my anxiety with deliberate intent, in this way telling Matta and Wa that strange humans were to be avoided. Inevitably, once they were in the cellar, we worried in case they started to whine or yap, but they never did.

When they were old enough to stay in the evaporator house, it was easier to keep them concealed, but we worried about them nevertheless each time that visitors arrived; and I am quite sure that some of our friends must have wondered why I always disappeared for a while on their arrival, departing, then returning hurriedly after all the doors of the big shed were locked, just in case some strolling visitor became inquisitive and entered the building unbidden.

The risks were appreciably reduced as the cubs grew older, and now, at five months, they exhibited the cautious, secretive traits of their kind, mistrusting new things in their domain and taking care not to show themselves if strangers were present. We had been treated to several examples of this caution during the last four or five weeks when unexpected visitors arrived as I was walking the cubs through the maples. Before the vehicle carrying friends or neighbors even came into view, the cubs showed concern and started to head for the sap house. Naturally, I encouraged them, running toward the building in what I hoped was a distraught manner. Invariably, the wolves got inside before I reached the door.

Without any promptings from me, both cubs showed a natural distrust of things mechanical if these made noise, such as the car and the tractor. They would not approach the machine shed and always detoured around the car if this was parked near the house. Music, whether on the radio or from the stereo, left them unmoved, but caused no visible distress; yet they disliked voices coming out of the radio and positively hated listening to the news—not that I blamed them much!

After their November weigh-in, while entering the figures in the wolf log, I noted that Wa had gained a total of fifty-eight pounds nine ounces and Matta forty-eight pounds fifteen ounces since June 8, in a matter of five months and six days. I wondered how tall and how long they were. On the premise that they were going to be considerably disturbed today in any event, I decided to measure them. For this, with Joan's assistance, I used a length of string, this being less alien than the metal measuring tape. Wa was 51 inches long; his tail comprised 15 inches of the total. Matta was 47 inches long and had a tail that measured 14½ inches. Height from shoulder to ground: Wa, 29 inches; Matta, 26 inches.

After this last indignity, which they accepted calmly enough, I dressed for the bush and led the two wolves away from the house, telling Joan we would be back by supper time and ignoring Tundra's loud protests. Snow had fallen two weeks earlier, accumulating to a depth of three inches in the open places but drifting to a depth of seven or eight inches in some locations. The afternoon was partly cloudy, but not too cold, the mercury standing at 15 degrees Fahrenheit. It didn't look as though it would snow today.

Entering the maples, where the ground was covered with their old tracks, Matta pushed ahead almost immediately, nose down to the trail that led almost due north of the farm into an area of mixed timber that grew on top of Precambrian granite, some of which upthrust itself above the soil to create moss-covered openings that rolled like static ocean waves. We had traveled this route three days ago, and I presumed that Matta was drawn to it by traces of her and Wa's scent, still discernible to her keen nose.

Wa trotted behind his sister at first, then changed his mind, stopping and waiting for me to catch up and loping along beside me. I understood from his behavior that Matta was not following a hot scent of any kind, otherwise he would have remained immediately behind her. Half an hour later we crossed over the farm's northern boundary and entered government wilderness land that stretched for many miles to the north, east, and west, a region where few men ventured, except, perhaps, for occasional parties of deer hunters during the shooting season. This was to open the next day, the fifteenth, which meant that I was going to keep the wolves at home for the next two weeks, just in case.

The terrain changed radically and suddenly soon after we crossed into it, first of all presenting a series of granite bluffs honeycombed by small caves wrought by ancient rock slides.

The area afforded shelter to porcupines, and it didn't take Matta long to find one. This was a large male who was pressed tightly into a shallow, downward-sloping shelter. Both wolves stopped about two feet from the porcupine's winter den, alert and eager, but definitely cautious. Stooping, I was able to see the porcupine change directions, moving so as to aim his tail toward the intruders, then to begin lashing the thick, quill-studded club. It was amazing how such a large animal (it probably weighed a good thirty pounds) could squeeze its bulk into such a confined space and no less interesting to hear the dry, scraping sounds made by the quills when they rubbed against the stone.

A month earlier the cubs would have avoided this place as soon as they scented the occupant; today, though they showed considerable respect for the creature, they were also interested in it, instinctively studying the situation for advantage. After a few minutes during which Matta approached a little closer but jumped back swiftly when the porcupine accelerated the tempo of its tail, the wolves lost interest. It was evident that both of them decided that there would be no profit, only danger, in seeking to kill the prickly vegetarian. Wa turned away first, moving into a narrow cleft that threaded through the area of bluffs; Matta, devoting one last look to the tantalizing quarry, about-faced, trotting so as to catch up to, then pass, her brother. I followed at leisure.

Around three o'clock, after the wolves had taken me on a variety of wide detours that included three frozen-over beaver ponds but placed us only about three miles from the farm, I judged it appropriate to stop and have one of the two sandwiches that Joan had prepared for me. The cubs had caught a number of mice—I wasn't sure how many, because they ate them so quickly, like a hungry person might eat a canapé at a party—

133

but they nevertheless eyed my sandwich, shaming me into sharing some of it with them, which sacrifice was not altogether altruistic on my part since it kept them beside me while I rested.

Soon after we got going again and within moments of starting, Matta found a hot scent. It was made by a deer, its tracks clear in the snow, its passage through here evidently recent, judging from Matta's excitement; now Wa became acutely alert.

Wolves and all other predators do not hunt by visual tracking; they follow tracks because they contain the scent of the animal that made them. If the odor is old, they lose interest after no more than a cursory sniff or two; if it is relatively recent, they will probably follow for a time, giving up when a new scent or a sudden sound offers more interest. But if the spoor is fresh, a hot trail, they put their noses down and lope away at a deceptively swift gait that from a distance looks as though they aren't going much faster than a good walk; this lope, in fact, covers the ground at a rate of six or seven miles an hour.

The wolves soon outdistanced me, disappearing into heavy timber on the other side of which, I knew, lay a large swamp and two quite big beaver ponds, also frozen solid. Feeling sure that they were still too young and inexperienced to pull down a full-grown deer (this one was an adult, its tracks told me), I let them go ahead, for this was good training. They would probably return when they realized that their quarry had the edge on them; and if they didn't come back when I was ready to go home, I would leave them, certain that they would turn up at the farm during the night or early the next morning. Nevertheless, curious, I continued along the trail, which was easy to follow now that the prints of the wolves were added to the deer tracks.

Maintaining a steady pace, I soon realized that the chase was proceeding along a relatively straight course and that Wa had taken the lead from his sister; he was running to the right of the deer tracks. Matta ran along the trail, a little behind her brother. I started to feel uneasy. It seemed that the wolves were being most persistent, and from what I could discern of the deer trail, it looked like the quarry had lengthened its stride, in places taking long leaps.

It was begging the question, of course, but I wasn't yet emotionally ready to accept the killing of a deer by Matta and

Wa. Once more I was the victim of myself, part of me clinically interested in the chase, the other emotionally disturbed by the possibility of a kill.

An estimated three miles away from the place where the chase began, the tracks told me that Matta and Wa were catching up to the deer and that the quarry was either almost exhausted or there was something physically wrong with it. The animal was leaving a staggering trail, evidently unable to keep to a straight course. It was leaping more often, obviously aware of its pursuers, but the distance between jumps was shorter, and several times it had stumbled to its knees. I was now certain that the wolves would close with the quarry. And I became distressed, feeling a great sorrow for the unfortunate deer. I had succeeded in raising Matta and Wa as wild wolves, but faced by incontestable proof of my success, I could only feel deep concern for the animal that they were hunting.

I didn't see or hear the kill, but twenty or thirty minutes later I heard the wolves eating, the unmistakable sounds of ripping flesh smothered occasionally by a warning growl. Soon afterward, breasting a slight rise that led to small forest opening, I saw the wolves. Matta lay on one side of the outstretched deer, working on one of the front legs; Wa lay on the other side, feeding off one of the haunches. I stopped, not really wanting to approach closer. But I had to. I wanted to see, if possible, how the kill had been made; I also wanted to check the condition of the deer. It still seemed strange that the young wolves should have been able to effect this kill with such relative ease.

As I stood undecided, first Matta, then Wa, raised their heads and looked at me intently for some seconds, then returned to their food. How would they react to my presence at their kill? There was only one way to find out. And it would allow me to test, once and for all, my vaunted alpha status.

Walking at a normal pace while gazing directly at the deer, I moved nearer, paused, still careful not to look at either wolf, then walked all the way to the front of the animal, nearest to Matta. She looked up and growled, showing her teeth. I fastened my eyes on her yellow orbs and growled right back, moving closer. At once she avoided my gaze, dropping her head to the feast, continuing to growl but not so threateningly.

How she was able to growl and eat at the same time I didn't pretend to guess.

Squatting and growling intermittently I reached out confidently and took hold of one of the deer's ears. Wa growled now. I treated him to one of of my best and deepest growls, gave him a direct and fierce stare, and he, too, dropped his head. I really *was* alpha!

It took but a moment to see that the whitetail's throat had been torn out, leaving a gaping wound from which a vast amount of blood had poured. It was also easy to deduce that Wa had done this thing, for his head, neck, and chest were plastered in gore, in contrast to Matta who, apart from modest splashes of blood on her muzzle and chest, almost certainly acquired as she was feeding, was remarkably free of red stains.

I pretended to eat of the kill, lowering my head until my mouth was barely an inch from the deer's neck, growling and making intermittent eating noises, or the best imitation of such that I could muster. Wa had been engaged in chewing through the sinews, muscles, and bone that joined the back haunch to the pelvis; when the last strand parted, he picked up the entire leg in his mouth and moved some distance away, there to lie down and to hold his prize with one great paw while he proceeded to eat in a dedicated way. I continued to pretend.

A short time later, Matta also gnawed away the leg she had been working on and she, too, rose and took it away, copying Wa's behavior. This left me in sole, but temporary, possession of the carcass, the uppermost side of which, being now shorn of two of its legs, offered few clues.

All that was certain thus far was that Wa had evidently gripped the throat and made the kill, but, apart from the severed limbs, I could find no other marks on the side of the carcass that faced me. I decided to turn the animal over.

Gripping the remaining legs, one in each hand, as I squatted on the other side, by the backbone, I heaved, turning the whitetail from one side to the other. The animal was in good, autumnal condition, fat and sleek and healthy looking. Now I could see deep bites on the remaining back leg, suggesting that one or the other of the wolves had fastened its teeth on it and probably brought the deer down. Perhaps Matta attacked there and Wa had seized the throat when the quarry fell to the ground.

Then I noticed a small, older, but yet recent, injury just

behind the shoulder, high up, but below the spine. The edges of the wound had darkened, and lymph still oozed from the center of an opening the size of a shirt button. I had seen too many bullet holes not to recognize this one. A .22-caliber lead bullet had done this, probably at extreme range. With a penknife I probed and soon encountered the leaden mass. I cut into the hide and muscle, making an X incision and peeling back the four Vs of the cut. About three-quarters of an inch deep and nestled against a fractured rib bone was the misshapen bullet. This accounted for the kill; the unfortunate young buck was badly crippled after being shot by some unscrupulous and inexpert hunter who had sought to steal a march on the hunting season.

A .22 bullet at close range, expertly aimed, will certainly kill a deer, but the chances of knocking the animal down with the shot are remote, for the projectile does not have enough shocking power. Usually in such cases, the quarry runs so far into the bush that the hunter is unlikely to retrieve the game, leaving it for the scavengers. All too frequently, as had happened in the present case, the animal is wounded and is condemned to hours, perhaps days, of agony, before it either dies or is mercifully killed by wolves. The wound I was examining looked to be about twenty-four hours old, so this poor beast endured considerable agony before Matta and Wa got onto its trail and finally killed it.

Many a time have I found evidence of similar butchery resulting after inexperienced or irresponsible hunters have fired indiscriminately using weapons designed solely for small game. Once I found a moose that had been gutshot in this way. The animal was still alive when I discovered it lying inside a deep stand of spruces in northern British Columbia. It was a bull, still adorned by a magnificent rack. It had evidently managed to keep the wolves at bay until I arrived; the wolf tracks and urine stains were profuse in the immediate area. That bull had suffered the tortures of the damned; its stomach was rotten, smelling like a cesspool, but it still lived. I shot it through the head and left it for the wolves. More than twenty years later I still feel anger when I recall that poor beast. And there are those who claim that the wolf is a ruthless, cruel killer! I was infinitely glad that Matta and Wa had taken out this animal.

They had at least ended its suffering. Then, too, they had

gained invaluable experience, doing so on their own, without any prompting from me. Now that they had made this kill, they would know how to proceed later, when their survival would depend on their abilities.

The sky had cleared completely soon after my sandwich stop, and now, looking up, I realized that it was late and that the sun was low in the west. I wasn't wearing a watch, but I guessed it was close to five o'clock. Should I start back and leave the wolves, or should I wait until they were ready to come with me? Not relishing a return trip through the darkness without a flashlight, I was tempted to leave, but my curiosity overcame caution. I wanted to observe the wolves.

Belatedly, it occurred to me that I would not now be able to give them their worm pills, which were supposed to be administered on an empty stomach. Well, there was always tomorrow, or the next day; the worms would certainly wait, and they weren't likely to cause problems during the interval. I found myself a seat on a moss-covered rock after first brushing the snow off it, then draping it with a couple of evergreen bows.

There I squatted, watching Matta and Wa as they positively gorged themselves. It was almost full dark by the time they showed themselves ready to return home with me. In the interim they had eaten, rested, eaten, rested, and then slept for about forty-five minutes. At last, rising and stretching and walking stiffly to the deer carcass, they sniffed it cursorily, yawned, scratched a bit, peed each in his and her selected places, and, after Wa scratched up a storm of snow with alternate hind feet, padded over to me.

I let them lead the way, but kept calling them when they ranged too far ahead, in this way using them as guides within the blackness of the forest. I was chilled to the bone by the time we set off, but walking fast enough to more or less keep up with the wolves soon warmed me. The clean blanket of snow on the ground reflected enough crepuscular light to allow me to pick my way over and around obstructions.

Nevertheless, since we had to cover an estimated seven miles in order to get home, it was nearly ten o'clock by the time that my worried wife and jubilant dog were able to welcome us back.

I went to bed that night worrying about the damned worm pills.

The wolves were kept inside the evaporator house all the next day, the doors closed to ensure that they would still be there when pill time rolled around. Probably because they were too full and sluggish after their big meal of yesterday, neither of them howled in protest until after Joan and I had finished our supper, but when Tundra popped up from the basement, looked toward the kitchen window, and let loose with a long, wild howl, we knew the wolves were calling; we hadn't heard them across the distance and over the cackling emerging from the radio at news time, but the dog's keen ears picked up their voices. I went to fetch them.

Soon afterward Matta and Wa were inside the house, restless and jealous of Tundra, who had already had his pills and had eaten a good supper an hour earlier. Traces of his repast evidently clung to his mouth, causing first Matta and then Wa to lick at his chops expectantly, no doubt hoping that he would regurgitate for them. Those days were done, as far as Tundra was concerned; he selfishly hung on to his meal, for which egotistical action he received lavish praise from Joan.

The oval worm capsules, gelatine coated and shocking red in color, were about the size of olives, rubbery to the touch and filled with exceptionally bitter contents. I know; I sampled one of them, breaking it open and taking a small sip, thinking that if I could mix it with hamburger, the stuff might be introduced into the wolves that way. But nothing edible could possibly have disguised *that* taste!

Wa was selected for the first try. His dose called for nine capsules, while Matta was to eat eight. Being the less excitable of the two, I thought the male wolf might, by example, show his sister that this operation was not really all that dreadful. Watched intently by Tundra and Matta, assisted by Joan, who consented to hold the red bombs, but refused to handle Wa because she was certain that he was going to use his good, new teeth, I made the wolf sit on his haunches by pushing down on his hips; then I straddled him, all the time speaking softly and, I hoped, reassuringly, and reached for the first capsule. Holding Wa's head with one hand, the pill between thumb and middle finger of the other, I poked my index finger at the join of the wolf's lips and thrust it into his mouth, praying that I was back far enough to reach the naked gum behind his last molar. I was, and I introduced the capsule by sort of popping it out from between thumb and middle finger. As soon as the index finger encountered it, I pushed the thing down Wa's gullet. He swallowed. He had to, the red tidbit had been thrust past the point of no return. But Wa, though quite evidently puzzled by my strange behavior, remained calm, appearing to derive some pleasure from the feel of my knees against his body and enjoying the rubbing that I gave his head and throat after he swallowed the first antiworm depth-charge. What he didn't know, however, was that the reason behind the throat rub was to make sure that the medicine went all the way down.

I tried again, with the same result. And yet again, with a sense of triumph. Wa remained placid, but continued to hold a speculative gaze. The fourth capsule went down as easily as the others. Now for the fifth. I became clumsy, managing to get my index finger between Wa's last two molars, the upper and the lower. Naturally, he chomped. I take pride in my stoic acceptance of the mangling, never faltering as I popped the capsule into the mouth and pushed it down with an agonized index finger. When I removed my digit from his jaws, Wa smacked his lips appreciatively, as though he had really enjoyed the fifth potion. Looking at my finger, I understood his enjoyment; blood bubbled out from a jagged wound that was half an inch long located on the fleshy tip of the index.

Since the harm was done already, I thought I might as well take advantage of the savory blood. From then on Wa actually opened his mouth to receive the other four capsules, and he was quite disappointed when the quota was reached.

I released the male wolf and turned to Matta; she volunteered herself forward, eager to sniff and lick my bleeding digit. She even sat down quickly. But when I tried to pop the pill, she shot out from between my legs like greased lightning, causing me to drop the capsule. It rolled toward her as she stood glaring at me. The movement caught her eye, and she lowered her head to sniff, then stuck her tongue out to lick. A second later she ingested the damned thing of her own accord!

I had found an easy way to get wolves to swallow large capsules. All that needs to be done is for the "doctor" to cut his finger, or some other part of his anatomy, coat the capsules with fresh, warm blood, and let the wolf do the rest. Matta wanted more when I was done and Tundra and Wa were becoming nuisances as they pressed close, seeking their share of the new, succulent tidbits.

CHAPTER NINE

Christmas, despite being the glad season, presents problems for those who would raise two wolves in secret. In our case, these started to crop up on December 24, when neighbors came to call, sample a tot, eat some goodies, and go on to the next place. It was all warm and comforting and neighborly and enjoyable, but...

By now almost seven months old, Matta and Wa had some definite ideas of their own about how to spend their time, though happily they preferred evening, night, and early morning for prowling around. Nevertheless, they were quite likely to appear outside the house in daylight. Big, rangy, gray, and positively wolfish, they were not the sort of canines normally welcomed by those people who lived in the area of North Star Farm. As a result, Joan and I found ourselves in constant tension every time we were visited. Why didn't we lock them in? Joan suggested this on December 23 because we knew what was to come, but I firmly vetoed the idea on two major counts: The wolves wouldn't like it and were liable to damage their teeth and mouths trying to chew their way out; in addition, the wolves were very likely to howl their protests at being so treated, thus surely giving the game away. As I said to Joan, we could hardly expect Matta and Wa to be raised wild, to be encouraged to seek independence, and then be locked up suddenly without complaining. Joan continued to press the point until I put up a final argument.

"You know, you're taking a typically human attitude. Human parents, it seems to me, spend endless time trying to prepare their children for independence. But what happens when the kids grow up and start trying to exercise this carefully nurtured independence? Mother and Father are horrified! The kids are now ungrateful, irresponsible, and just too damned independent!"

Joan, prepared to argue when I began, started nodding her head, remembering, as she later admitted, the great argument that she had had from her own parents when, at twenty-one, she elected to leave home and set up housekeeping in a Winnipeg apartment.

So we entertained our neighbors to the best of our ability while keeping our eyes and ears open for the wolves. And though I kept telling myself not to worry, that Matta and Wa were too canny to emerge into view when we had visitors (for they could hear the alien cars and trucks long before these entered the yard), I couldn't help fretting. But I flatter myself that we pulled it off, though perhaps some of our local friends may have wondered why I kept getting up and going to the kitchen window to look outside. Matta and Wa, naturally, didn't so much as show the tip of one black, shiny nose; they had too much sense for that.

We were nevertheless glad when Christmas receded into the immediate past and Boxing Day dawned clear and sunny, the outdoors beautifully decorated. The ground was covered with more than a foot of snow, and since there had been a fresh fall on Christmas night, the landscape was innocent of tracks and footprints.

Tundra sounded his usual "Here come the wolves" warning at around 3 A.M.; I sat up, listened for a few moments, and then went back to sleep; but when the dog awakened me again at sunrise, I got up, sensing that Matta and Wa were outside. And so they were, waiting on the porch. Our second Christmas began.

The wolves and Tundra were treated to as much raw beaver meat as they could eat, this food coming our way courtesy of a trapper neighbor, who saved the carcasses for Tundra, or so he thought. Leaving the trio to ingest enormous quantities of the red meat, we humans sat down to our own breakfast, watching the jays and chickadees as they came and went to and from the window feeder. Afterward I let Tundra and the wolves play in the yard while Joan and I dressed for 10-degree-below-zero weather. Outside, nosed and pawed at by the wolves and the dog, we strapped on snowshoes, I said the magic word *walk*, and we all trooped away, heading toward the flatlands that sprawled northeast of the farm.

Well filled with beaver meat, the four-legged ones gave only cursory attention to the scents and sounds of the wilderness, though they were ever ready to initiate a half-hearted chase if some careless, or particularly daring, squirrel lingered unsafely in their path. In between such sporadic rushes, the three stayed fairly close to us, sometimes too close, for they all liked to follow in our snowshoe trails in those places where the snow had drifted deep and hindered their progress. As we opened up the way, one or the other of them would step on the back of our shnowshoes, causing some ungainly stumbles.

The sun was halfway to its noon zenith when we entered the rocky area north of East Ridge. The terrain here dropped fairly suddenly, ending at the shores of a large beaver pond that was linked by means of a series of dams and spillways to four others. From the highland two snow-covered, conical beaver houses projected above the ice, for the main pond was so large that it was able to accommodate two different families. At the top of each lodge the snow was yellow and melted, revealing the ends of a number of untidy sticks that sprouted from the mounds at all angles; these conditions were caused by the warm air rising through the breathing hole of each lodge, which stained and melted the snow.*

---

*The word *hole* does not adequately explain the ventilation system built into a beaver lodge, but no single word readily describes this. A lodge is built solid, that is, beaver pile branch on branch, forming an oval mound of desired height, then, starting below the water level, they literally carve out their entrance tunnels, usually two, and their living chamber. The outside of this little fortress is covered with mud, stones, rotting vegetation, and anything else that will add to the solid, impregnable walls, but the center of the mound is unplastered. The trellis of sticks, piled helter-skelter, rather like what happens if a box of wooden matches is dumped out to form a pile on the table, allows fresh air to enter and stale air to emerge, but effectively keeps out enemies and light. One cannot see down into a lodge chamber by attempting to look through this central, unplastered section, but, like air, sound is also conducted through the interstices of the piled sticks, allowing a listener to hear the beaver down below, or allowing a beaver to hear what's going on above.

144

The big pond was shaped something like a gourd, the narrow neck of which began opposite where we were standing and was about one-quarter of a mile wide. We crossed this over the ice and climbed the opposite granite slope, presently emerging below a rocky tor that had a flat top on which grew a solitary white pine. This giant of a tree somehow sustained its growth on the limited soil available—probably because it had snaked roots deep down into the rock itself, beginning with slim, almost silken threads that, as they grew, put pressure on the fissures they had entered, enlarging them and allowing additional moisture to seep down; when the water froze, the ice exerted more pressure, widening the cracks and furnishing more space for the probing roots.

We were about a hundred yards away from the base of the rocky hillock when all three canines raced ahead. As they got close to the granite face, four ravens wafted themselves upward and went to perch in the branches of the pine, cawing and cooing and generally cursing us roundly for having disturbed them. I didn't need to get to the wolves and Tundra to know that the big ebon marauders had been eating some leftover carrion; they would not have been there in a bunch otherwise.

Sure enough, when Joan and I reached the scene, each canine had appropriated a piece of gnawed deer bone. Scattered around, some on top of the snow where the ravens had left them, others underneath the white mantle, were the remains of the wild wolf kill. There wasn't much left, but, having dispossessed the ravens, our three companions were going to make sure that they had their share of the find, despite the fact that they were not hungry.

We had covered approximately four miles of country to get here, and since Joan was not as accustomed to snowshoeing as I was, she voted to allow the wolves and the dog to chew the bones while we found a place in the sun from where we could sit and watch. This proposal met with my approval; I was anxious to see what the ravens would do now that their bonanza had been so unceremoniously usurped. I was certain that they wouldn't accept the loss tamely.

Tundra was quite accustomed to the highly intelligent black scoundrels; he knew how to deal with them. But I didn't think that Matta and Wa had yet experienced close contact with *Corvus corax*, who is, in my considered opinion, the toughest and most intelligent of all the birds in the northland. In the Yukon Territory I have seen them flying nonchalantly, high in the air, when the ground temperature was down to 60 degrees below zero. I have watched them land at a wolf kill while the big predators were busy feeding, the birds biding their time as they strutted through the snow, then darting in to grab some morsel right under the nose of a big timber wolf, who, wise to the ways of the ebon robbers, would essay one swift snap and be content to continue eating when it missed the target.

When everybody else is seeking shelter from the biting cold of the north, it is not unusual to see a raven fly straight down, as though intent on dashing out its brains against the ground, level off a few feet before collision, apply brakes at the last moment, and plop itself into the snow. Seconds later the glossy black head will emerge, followed by the neck and, at last, by the shoulders. Now the wings flap, like a domestic chicken essaying a flight; the snow spatters upward, but it has hardly had time to settle before the raven is off, running with all its body buried in snow; propelled as much by its hidden but flapping wings as by its pumping feet, it will career along for distances of fifty yards or more, the strange and disembodied inky head sticking up a few inches above the snow. When the run is over, the raven will take a snow bath in the same way that sane birds take a dust bath. Much refreshed, it will flap madly again for a few moments and then climb skyward chortling loudly as though wanting to share its pleasure with all the more craven beings of the northland.

When I was last in the Yukon, about the time that I received the news from Florida telling me of the Largo wolf, I watched a raven remove the metal lid from one of our garbage cans. I was writing, but I became suddenly disturbed by a steady, tinny banging. When it didn't stop, I got up and looked out of the window. The sound occurred each time a big raven closed its beak on the edge of the garbage can lid and lifted it with a jerk, then let it fall, making the clang. I had built an off-the-ground, wooden-slatted cage for the garbage containers in order to keep the northern dogs out of the cans; but I hadn't reckoned with the ravens. Interested, but not believing that the robber baron could really remove the lid, I stayed to watch. Unfortunately I didn't time the feat, but I would estimate that it took the bird about two minutes to get the lid off.

That bird had technique! It could not physically lift the lid high enough to remove it in one go, but by lifting and dropping the thing, it gradually bounced it off. Having achieved its purpose, the raven hopped onto the edge of the garbage can, gripped tightly with its sturdy feet, dipped forward and downward until only its back and tail showed, and then rose again, carrying in its great beak a half-full grocery bag containing table scraps.

Holding the prize, the bandit paused a moment, perhaps to recover its breath, then rose into the air. When it was some ten feet above my driveway, it opened its beak. Bombs away! The bag burst, scattering its contents all over the place. Now the raider descended and found a tidbit, in this case the remnants of a chicken breast. With that, it flew into one of our lodgepole pines and began to devour its spoils. In the meantime, half a dozen of its eagle-eyed relatives appeared, each from a different direction. Almost regretfully, I went outside to break up the party; I didn't want all the garbage scattered over the driveway. But every one of the latecomers left with a prize in its beak, the last one taking off with a waxed cardboard container that had held honey.

Now, as though gathering for a quick tactical meeting, three of the birds swooped off their perches and landed on the same branch as the fourth member of the gang. Immediately, amid a great deal of bobbing and bowing, untidy crests fully erect, the quartet began to chatter, mixing deep caws with an entire range of glottal variations that ranged from coos and gurgles to slurred squawks. Finished, they all launched themselves out of the tree in near unison, split up in the air, and planed down, each raven landing in a different place, undoubtedly under the premise that it is a good deal more difficult to keep an eye on four scattered individuals than on a grouping of the same number.

Tundra wasn't about to be fooled. He had jousted with these brigands often in the past, and been bested every time. By now, like the wild wolves, he knew it was useless to charge at any one of them; not only would the target bird escape, but while he was charging, one of the others would dart in and grab the prize. As soon as they landed, Tundra lifted one massive paw and plopped it deliberately on the bone he was chewing, sparing the birds but a short, darting glance.

The cubs had yet to learn this particular lesson. One bird, the one I presumed to be the leader and who was certainly the biggest and toughest looking, strutted with stiff gait toward Matta, walking easily on top of snow that had become crusted during the time that the wolves had spent here eating the white-tail. Matta immediately raised her head, ears pricked all the way forward, lips peeled back in a silent snarl. The raven changed direction slightly, now angling toward a point a few feet to one side of the bitch. When the bird was about a yard away, Matta charged, leaping swiftly and fluidly, going from a prone position to a fast run in one movement. But when her gleaming teeth closed shut, all they got was air, the snap of ivory on ivory ringing loud. The object of her anger was already six or seven feet up by the time she collected herself sufficiently to jump for the raven, rearing on her hind legs. But by then the big bird had risen another six feet and was circling around.

While this action was taking place, Raven Two flapped quickly from its position just outside the area of the kill and grabbed Matta's bone, taking off with the prize immediately. Matta turned sharply, took a run at the airborne robber, and thought better of it, returning to dig in the hard snow and to uncover a new bone.

Meanwhile, the remaining birds were individually concentrating on Wa and Tundra. The one that was advancing on the dog, evidently an old hand, was soon able to judge that Tundra was not to be coaxed into a charge. It hopped a few feet into the air and reversed direction, no doubt to see if its buddy needed help; this bird was repeating the technique employed by the first raider, but Wa didn't wait for it to get close. Angry, growling like a tiger, he leaped up and dashed full bore at the raven, thus allowing its companion to make off with the bone.

Twice more did Matta try to kill the ravens, and each time she returned unsuccessful to find her tidbit stolen. After the third time she gave up in obvious disgust, leaving the scene of her defeat and coming to lie down beside Joan. Wa proved himself a little quicker in the uptake in this instance. He lost one more bone, but the third one that he dug up was quickly protected by a big paw. He may have taken his cue from Tundra, or he may have figured it all out for himself. However it was, he, like the dog, now ignored the ravens. The birds, finding that the game was over, started a free-for-all, each

148

raven attempting to corner all the profits. As far as I could make out, the ones that got away with bones hid them somewhere in the forest, then returned to seek more.

Despite the sunshine, Joan and I were soon ready to stand up and move about, feeling the chill particularly in hands and feet and seat. When the aerial circus ended, we walked around the rock upthrust, studying the messages left in the snow. From the signs, I deduced that six wolves comprised the pack that had killed the deer, and because this was part of his territory, I felt confident in guessing that old Lobo's bunch was responsible for the kill. Four of the hunters had followed the deer out of the forest; two others had evidently detoured around the rocky hill and confronted the fleeing animal at the site of the kill, the tracks, coming from two directions and converging on the deer, seeming to agree with those casual observers who claim that wolves will deliberately team up and haze their prey into the jaws of an ambushing party.

This quite widely held belief is in error. Wolves are chasers where big game is concerned. They will pick up a fresh scent, put their noses to it, and attempt to run down the prey. Sometimes the land causes the pack to split up, some running directly behind the quarry, others, happening to be off to one side, detouring around deadfalls, heavy brush, or, as in the case of the kill site I was examining, around rock outcrops. More often than not, the pack comes together after the detour without running down the prey and continues to chase if there still appears to be a chance of effecting a kill. At other times, as had evidently been the case here, luck puts the splinter group in a strategic position to charge the prey, either stopping the animal then and there or slowing it up long enough for the rest of the pack to catch up. In such fortuitous circumstances it might be fairly said that the prey animal was ambushed; but this is accidental rather than deliberate.

The greatest problem faced by those who seek to study the hunting techniques of wolves stems from the difficulties encountered during field observation. Both hunter and hunted are fast, unpredictable animals ranging through country that is more often than not heavily wooded and inhospitable to man. Another stumbling block is the individualistic behavior of wolf packs as well as the condition, experience, and intelligence of the quarry. Then, too, the terrain that causes difficulties for the human observer imposes certain disciplines on the hunter and on the hunted; techniques may have to be modified when the physical land alters, which it does constantly, sometimes within half a mile or less.

Taking such things into account, it is little wonder that a satisfyingly clear picture does not emerge and that most mammalogists must rely on brief sightings on foot or on distant sightings taken from an aircraft *or* on lucky views of a hunt from some advantageous location. From these three kinds of observation something of a picture has emerged, but there is much work yet to be done before anyone can write with authority on the hunting behavior of all wolves.

I have spent almost half a lifetime studying these fascinating animals and have read the writings of others similarly occupied. Yet I find it impossible to describe with any degree of certitude all of the ways by which wolves earn their living in the wilderness. At best one can give the known facts and advance logical theories.

There is, I believe, sufficient evidence with which to deny the claims that wolves deliberately seek to trap their prey, but the matter is not nearly so positive when seeking to classify the different approaches taken by different packs hunting different types of big game in different territories.

Wolves use the large ungulates as staple food, especially during winter. These include bison, musk-ox, moose, elk, deer, caribou, bighorn and Dall sheep, and mountain goat. Of these, the bison and musk-ox, being now relatively scarce, form part of the diet of few packs. The next largest prey species is the moose, which feeds many packs in Canada, in some parts of the northern U.S.A., and in Alaska. Next, because of territorial abundance, are two species of deer: the mule deer (*Odocoileus hemionus*) and the whitetail deer (*Odocoileus virginianus*); the former, in the northern part of its range, is a predominantly western species, whereas the latter is distributed throughout most of the United States and Canada, except in the far north. Before they were exterminated from the prairie regions, wolves also fed on antelope, but today, though the odd timber wolf *may* find its way onto the plains, it would be the exception, unlikely to pose a threat to the fleet-footed pronghorn.

Apart from the big game species, wolves, being opportunists, will take small game, birds, and, in agricultural country, cattle, sheep, and even horses. In some parts of its range, such as in Ontario, beaver is an important constituent in the diet of the wolf between spring and winter, while raccoon, fox, porcupine, and in fact practically every other kind of small game are taken when opportunity presents itself.

Obviously, the techniques for hunting big, swift animals such as moose and deer are quite different from those employed to capture small animals. In the former case the wolves usually seek to run their prey, tiring it until they can get alongside the quarry and pull it down. In the latter case, the hunting is usually done on an individual basis, either as a pack is moving through an area at a leisurely pace, spread out, or by lone hunters, or by small numbers of wolves, perhaps two or three. At these times a wolf will hunt like a dog, stalking, trying to sneak up on its quarry; or it may scent and pinpoint an unwary animal, as Tundra did with the muskrat, and simply dash in and seize the prey. Birds, such as grouse, are stalked, occasionally killed in midflight, when the wolf leaps up to snatch the escaping bird out of the air. I believe it is fair to say that wolves will take anything they can get whenever they can get it.

These strong, efficient hunters spend many hungry days, going from feast to famine on a quite regualr basis. From personal observation backed up by the experience of others, I can say that wolves lose more big game animals than they kill. Figures from various sources indicate that wolves manage to kill only about 10 percent of the big game animals that they chase, whereas human hunters appear to kill between 22.4 and 38.5 percent of the animals that they hunt.

The wolf has a large stomach and can pack away twenty or more pounds of meat at a sitting, at times consuming prodigious amounts during a twenty-four-hour period when it eats, rests, eats, rests, again and again, until the prey animal is stripped clean. By the same token, the wolf can go without eating for two weeks or more without collapsing from starvation (in one documented case in Russia, a wolf went seventeen days without food in winter and, though thin, was still in good health when it was finally shot, though it had been lightly wounded more than two weeks earlier). Wolves will eat carrion, including bits of hide, harness leather, the gut of snowshoes (I can personally attest to the last two), and anything else likely to offer an ounce of protein.

The noted American mammalogist, Adolph Murie, summed it up nicely when he said: "It is hard to know how 'nip and tuck' the relationships are between the two species (predator and prey). A predator's ability to catch its prey must balance with the prey's ability to escape." If this were not the case, either the wolves would kill all the prey and themselves become extinct, or the prey would avoid all wolves, which would then die off; in this case the prey animals would overpopulate and eventually eat themselves into extinction by destroying available vegetation.

It is extremely doubtful that Matta and Wa would have been able to run down the deer they had killed if it had not been wounded. Moose, deer, elk, and caribou can run faster than wolves. To balance the odds, wolves can run for greater periods of time and are thus able to wear down their quarry on occasion. With smaller ungulates, such as deer, if the wolves catch up to it, the animal is almost certainly doomed, but with the bigger prey animals, such as moose, if the quarry turns at bay, the wolves will rarely attack, if it is healthy. I have seen a bull moose munching water plants at the edge of a slough with total unconcern while wolves hovered nearby, hoping to stampede the giant into running. Equally, I have seen a cow moose guarding her calf and keeping eight big timber wolves away from it. In this case the wolves got tired of waiting and left to seek easier prey. It is the sick, the old, and the inexperienced ungulates that the wolves kill most frequently, running them down and attacking while the animals are still seeking to escape.

Matta and Wa, when on their own, would not have an easy time of it in the wilderness; they might not even survive beyond their second or third year. Yet, despite this, I felt we owed it to them to let them go. But I did want to equip them as best I could for the hard life of the wild hunter. And I felt most inadequate in this respect as I studied the scene of the deer kill; I knew so little about the hunting techniques of the wolves!

Looking at our cubs, I considered it indeed fortunate that they were inherently well equipped for the life ahead. Each had demonstrated time and again that they were superbly intelligent and that their senses were finely attuned. So far, it seemed to me, they had already learned many techniques on their own, or by observing Tundra. I felt confident that they would eventually graduate summa cum laude, despite me.

152

Recently, during those occasions when he sought to ambush me, Wa had developed a new trick reserved for the times when I discovered him and pretended to run away. He would then chase me, catching up quickly. But whereas at first he simply tried to grab my leg or arm with his teeth (playfully, but hard enough that I wanted to avoid it if possible), he now tried to curl his nearside front leg around mine, at the same time lunging with his shoulder against my limb. The first time he did this, he brought me down with a crash, tripping me as neatly as a wrestler might do. I had observed the same trait in Yukon and Tundra, and although I have never actually seen hunting wolves resort to this technique, its results are so effective that logic suggests that at times the wild wolves may well use the method to bring down their quarry. Matta didn't indulge in such games with me, so I never discovered if she had also learned to employ the same gambit.

In this respect, I had already learned that each wolf, while sharing many similar hunting traits, was also given to developing little individual tricks. Matta would hunt mice in the open places by jumping quite high and coming down on all fours, her idea being, I judged, to shock the quarry into movement, when she would immediately strike with her front paws. Wa invariably walked along, batting at the ground with alternate paws, seeking, no doubt, to achieve the same results in his own way.

When downwind of prey, both wolves could immediately follow the effuvium to its source, being able to pick up an odor under ideal conditions from as much as a mile away. (Wolves have been known to detect a scent that was four miles from them.) But upwind scents, by and large, would go undetected. In such a situation I have actually seen a groundhog sitting still as a statue outside its burrow only one hundred yards away while the wolves and Tundra walked right past it when the wind was blowing from the canines toward the quarry.

Often, evidently responding to some sound that I could not hear, but lacking a scent to go with it because the wind was in the wrong direction, the wolves would leap up, all four legs leaving the ground at the same time, while they literally swept their heads around to try to get the scent. But although Matta did this repeatedly during such situations, Wa contented himself with no more than three leaps, after which he would quarter the ground like a well-trained bird dog. Sometimes one or the other would pick up a scent and race away after it. As often as not they would both fail and abandon the hunt unless the sound persisted, at which point they would track by ear.

Like all wolves, they had excellent sight for movement but could miss an obvious object altogether if it was absolutely still, the way they failed to see the groundhog. I would sometimes stand upwind of the cubs, remaining perfectly still, wait until their backs were turned, and then call out once. They would swing toward my voice and scan the country, almost invariably failing to see me, but, knowing that I was nearby, they always searched, each selecting its own route as they quartered the ground, drawing closer and closer. Eventually one or the other would notice the slight movement of my breathing, or I might betray myself by some minute twitch that they would spot instantly.

A number of years ago I developed my own little technique for measuring the canine IQ. The results of this quite simple test are noted on a scale from one to ten. Facing a dog, left arm loose at the side, I rotate my right arm, windmilling it slowly while looking at the subject, perhaps speaking softly. As soon as the arm begins to rotate, the animal's eyes focus on the movement; selecting an appropriate moment at random, while continuing to swing the right arm, I suddenly give the dog a not-too-gentle slap on the side of the face. Too late, the subject tries to go for the left hand, misses, then turns to look at the still-rotating right arm. After a bit of play, or perhaps pausing to stroke and pat the animal, I try again. The really intelligent, quick-witted ones are ready for the left hand during the second test, watching both my right and left arms simultaneously. When I try to slap such an animal, it will either duck out of the way or snap playfully at my hand. Such dogs rate one on my scale; after four I consider the animal to be a relatively slow learner; from five up to ten, I believe that I am dealing with canine dunces; above ten the subject must be half-witted. I call this the Learning-by-Experience Test.

Matta and Wa both passed with flying colors, rating superintelligent when they not only waited for my left hand after the first trial but actually bit it as it started to move. My friend Yukon also rated one; Tundra passed with the second highest score, two. Yet I have met dogs who went all the way from three to uncountable numbers, or who got tired of getting slapped and simply quit playing after fifteen or twenty times.

Using exactly the same test, but now days or weeks later, I score the dogs for memory. The best ones will remember the trick after a time lapse of several weeks; the slow ones, as might be expected, don't recall it at all. In between one finds that some of the intelligent ones suffer from relatively poor memories.

None of this proves much more than the fact that some canines learn more quickly than others and have a better memory than their peers, but when applied to wolves, it seems to me that even minor deficiencies in intellect and memory may well spell the difference between life and death. Domestic dogs can afford to be slow on the uptake and of poor recall; not so a wolf.

Experience teaches a wolf the ways of the animals that it hunts and the element of danger associated with each species. Obviously, there isn't much that a mouse can do to hurt a wolf, but even a small creature like a red squirrel can inconvenience a wolf to some extent if it manages to bite the predator's tongue or even a lip. Minor injuries, true, but they can rub off just that tiny bit of efficiency that can make the difference between success and failure later on.

I have seen the lowly muskrat give a good account of itself when attacked by a single wolf, which did, in the end, kill it; but I have also seen two muskrats, at different times, avoid death by jumping on their quite powerful back legs and slashing at their antagonists with extremely sharp, chisellike teeth. In the first instance it was a coyote, which gave up after only a few minutes, in which time it was bitten twice, once on the muzzle and the second time on the lower lip. On the other occasion, I watched for a considerable time as a big dog fox tried to kill a muskrat that it had caught on top of the ice of its pond. The gutsy little rat, again standing on its back legs, small front paws pressed against its chest, actually became the aggressor, jumping at the fox with squeaks of rage and slashing at it. That fox must have been hungry! I watched it collect five bites before it gave up in disgust and trotted away, blood on its muzzle and chin. Thus, considering the number of different animals that they hunt, I believe it is logical to conclude that wolves must learn the ways of their quarry before they can become expert providers. It is true that certain related species behave in much the same general way, but it is also true that many animals are at least partly individualistic and cannot therefore be counted upon to react predictably. Individuality apart, prey animals also learn by experience, and while wolves such as Matta and Wa are busy trying to kill, the prey animals are busy trying to avoid death.

I considered these things in relation to our two adopted wolves as I tried to put myself in their place, hoping to be able to teach them, or at least to help them to teach themselves, as much as possible about the wilderness and its inhabitants. However, I found consolation in the knowledge that Matta and Wa, if not typical of all wolves, were gifted with an excellent quota of intelligence.

Our party prepared to return to the farm shortly after noon, abandoning the leftover wolf kill to the ravens, who reappeared when we were no more than minutes away from the rock. This time their numbers had increased; nine big black birds chortled and gurgled their pleasure as they landed in the snow and proceeded to dig up bones like demented paleoanthropologists gloating over the remains of *Homo habilis*.

Later, almost home, Matta and Wa ran ahead as we emerged from the maples. The wolves disappeared inside the evaporator house. Tundra, confident that he would manage to coax a bit of lunch out of Joan, preceded us to the house, only half trying to eat one of the blue jays at the window feeder.

CHAPTER TEN

The phenomenon known in our part of the country as the January Thaw arrived at the same time as the first day of the new year. December ended on a night of full moon and clear skies that crackled with the pulsing, mystical lights of the aurora borealis; the mercury fell to 35 degrees below zero. As I snowshoed across the clearing, heading for the evaporator house at midnight to see if the wolves were home, the surrounding forests became suddenly endowed with life. To begin with there was the fascinating refulgence of the northern lights, now creeping, suddenly changing from streaks to visibly expanding fans of green blue luminescence, forever on the move. Two great horned owls were calling, one somewhere within the maples, the other more distant, in the direction of East Ridge; the husky, spaced *hoo* notes assailed the night in multiples of five, the faraway voice creating the illusion of an answering echo of the near one. In the far distance, at least several miles away, a solitary timber wolf howled intermittently. The plaintive, ululating wail was suddenly answered from very close to home — from the sap house, first by Wa, who had a deeper tone, then by Matta. Now Tundra vocalized from the end of his porch chain, and the wild one called again.

I stood still, listening to the combined voices, sensing the power of the night with a primitive awareness that by this point in my experience no longer surprised me. The wilderness has the ability to strike such a response from even the most civilized, touching some deeply hidden spot below the conscious mind and transporting man backward in time to the days of the cave. My purpose was forgotten; the cold was not even felt; the mind romped out there with the wolves and the owls and the moon and the lights and the forest. True freedom must surely be like that.

Even when Matta and Wa emerged into the moonlight, I didn't stir, and I was still standing there when the young wolves loped toward me, silent now, coming to nuzzle my extended hands. Tundra was also quiet, as was the wild one out there in the forest. But the owls still called, and the volatile lights still competed with the moon, and the snow around us gleamed and sparkled like diamond dust spilled haphazardly over white broadloom.

As the spell began, it ended—suddenly. I patted both wolf heads, turned around, and retraced my steps to the house. Matta and Wa followed. At the door, the wolves greeted Tundra, then entered the porch and lay down side by side, Wa keeping his head and shoulders erect, Matta stretching her front legs and setting her muzzle upon them. Tundra also entered the porch and thumped himself down in its doorway.

Joan was sound asleep when I at last went to bed. I was glad, for I didn't want to talk tonight, needing time to think, to debate the next stage in the training of the wolves. Today, aided by hindsight, I know exactly why I felt that I needed time to think, but during the early hours of that new year, I was not aware that I was seeking excuses that would allow me to postpone the next, obvious move. I knew that I was begging the real question, but I pretended to myself that it was important to summarize the progress made by the wolves (which had already been well documented, both in the log and in my notes) and to devote some thought to the program of progressive instruction intended to prepare the wolves better for independent survival in the wild. Because I was quibbling, I had made absolutely no progress when I at last gave up the struggle and allowed myself to sleep. It was already 3 A. M.

The next morning Joan allowed me to sleep in, waking me only when breakfast was ready. As I drank my first cup of coffee, she told me that the wolves were back in the evaporator house and that she had fed them each a portion of raw beaver meat. When I put the cup down and made to rise so as to go out and replenish the bird feeders, she informed me that she had already done so.

"Why didn't you wake me?" I was curious.

"Well, I figured you were tired. You were late going to bed, you know. What time did you go to sleep?"

I was sure that she hadn't stirred during the time I lay awake, but she obviously knew. I started to explain that I had been thinking about the further education of the wolves, but she interrupted me.

"I don't think we should discuss it just now. You'll figure it out, I know you will, but don't let's worry today, all right?"

Conceding her point—it *was* New Year's Day, after all—and knowing that she was at least as concerned about the next moves as I was, and for the same reasons, I let the matter drop—at least outwardly. Inwardly I found that I could no longer continue to avoid the truth. I knew what I had to do, if not today, then tomorrow or the next day. I had to lead our wolves into the wilderness, set them onto a deer trail, and encourage them to go out and make another kill. That first whitetail had been a fluke; they still needed to pit themselves against prey that was not incapacitated by man's interference. And once they had shown me that they could take out a deer in winter, there would no longer be any reason to allow them to remain with us. They would be ready for their freedom, even if Joan and I would not be ready to see them go.

Preoccupied by these matters, I did not at first notice the heavy overcast that had oozed in from the south, blotting out the sky. I rose to look at the thermometer; it had climbed to 20 degrees above zero, a jump of 52 degrees since midnight. By noon the mercury passed the freezing point, hovering at 33 degrees. Three hours later it began to rain. Matta and Wa, perhaps sensing the change in the weather, remained close to home. Tundra asked to come in and curled up in his customary corner in the kitchen. I went to our antique telephone, cranked the handle, and put a call through to my distant office, telling my assistant that I would not be coming in for a few days, that the Thaw had arrived.

Sometimes these sudden moderations in temperature come and go without trace of precipitation and leave the roadways

159

no worse than they found them. But when rain follows the warm-up we know from experience that the highways will be turned into skating rinks. I was at that time commuting eighty miles each way to work, and although I didn't really have to go in on a daily basis, because my staff were perfectly capable of running the show without me, I usually tried to be there three days a week, though with the arrival of Matta and Wa this routine had been abruptly interrupted.

Next morning the landscape was transformed. The rain had stopped; in its place ice sculptures glistened under diluted sunshine. The skies were still overcast, but the cloud cover was thin, allowing the sun to show like a large, glowing orange against a field of light gray.

I opened the door to go outside, but Tundra, no doubt anxious to lift his leg a time or six, brushed rudely past me, galloped across the porch floor, and charged out through the always-open entrance. The next thing I saw was one malamute skittering forward swiftly like some hairy, misshapen curling rock, chest and chin pressed against the glistening white crust, his fore and aft trotters flailing ineffectually as he tried to check his slide. Eventually he came to a stop, running out of momentum. But when he tried to stand, his behavior was reminiscent of the performance of a clown in an Ice Follies spectacle, going through the antics of a rank and very clumsy beginner on skates.

Tundra eventually regained his footing, but only after he had slithered and stumbled into a young evergreen that grew on what passed for our front lawn. Using the tree to lean against, the dog stood, then moved gingerly, trying to raise his leg; and down he went again, and up, and try again with the leg, and down. . . . My loud laughter brought Joan to the door. Seeing poor Tundra trying so desperately to have his first, and much needed, piddle of the day, my wife was not amused by my laughter.

"Don't just stand there and laugh. Go and *help* him!"

Thinking to placate her while aiding the dog in his task, I set out to cross the dividing space. Fate punished me for my levity! Joan claimed afterward that she saw every single movement made by my violently gyrating body, but I didn't believe her. No human eye could possibly follow the blur of movements that my person must have described before I ended on my rump three feet from the porch door. Now Joan was laughing—at me. Emulating her own peevish words, I exclaimed loudly, "Don't just stand there and laugh. Come and *help* me!"

She dove back into the house, to emerge within a few minutes with the hallway carpet, a three-foot-wide rubber-backed strip about eight or nine feet long. With the sangfroid of Raleigh flinging his cloak over the mud puddle, Joan snapped the rug forward so that it furnished me with a skid-proof platform. She didn't wait to see me climb to my feet, but popped back inside to emerge anew, this time clutching three smaller rugs. She gave them to me and ordered me to rescue Tundra, instructing me to place two down, hold the other, walk to the extent of the second rug, put the third down, turn, pick up the second, walk to the end of the third, and so on. In the face of such instant inventiveness and resolve, I had, perforce, to do as I was told.

Tundra, when I reached him, was once again on his feet. That is to say, he was on all fours, but was squatting like a puppy as he tinkled like Niagara on a slow day; but even as I watched, his back paws began to slide. I reached out a foot and placed it as firmly as possible behind one of the dog's sliding pads. His way was checked, but I had not reckoned on the fact that an adult male dog emerging from an all-night session indoors has an unlimited supply of liquid, which he expels with redoubtable vigor. My boot was thoroughly splashed, and so was the lower part of my pant leg. With the stream finally checked, Tundra, like some visiting potentate at the court of Saint James, walked back to the house over the rugs, while I brought up the rear, picking the damned things up as I went. So far, Matta and Wa, sensible beasts, had not emerged from their quarters.

Our farmhouse, built of hand-hewn logs in 1865, was a large affair, almost like two double-story houses side by side and joined together by a single-story kitchen. We used only one side and the big kitchen; the other side was for storage and a workshop. It was there I now went, to make two sets of ice cleats; nothing else would hold me upright outside. Using two small squares of plywood, I drove five roofing nails through each, then attached thongs on the side; these would tie around the boot toe.

I was about to go outside to try my invention when Joan

called from the kitchen, telling me that Matta and Wa had come out of their quarters. At the window, I was in time to see Wa go skating along gaily on his chin, much as Tundra had done. A second or two later Matta essayed a stride, and all four limbs slid out from under her, causing her to do a double split. Wa, meanwhile, got to his feet with near ease, a feat that amazed me, but when Matta also rose with hardly more than a scramble or two, I was really surprised. Nevertheless, both wolves turned around and, walking carefully and retaining their balance, reentered the evaporator house. Either they had a natural grace that allowed them to deal with these slippery conditions or their extra-big paws were better suited for ice-walking. Perhaps both these factors accounted for their ability to walk on the gelid surface once they realized the problem.

I readied a meal for our wards, took it and the cleats onto the porch, and prepared to entrust myself to the roofing nails. When each foot was properly accoutered, I took a careful step out of the porch, let my weight down, and found no difficulty in maintaining balance. Away I went, scrunching abominably with each step, but otherwise able to stride along without the least difficulty. I fed Matta and Wa, waited until they had finished, and lingered awhile to pat their heads and have a chat with them.

At home once more, I had removed one cleat and was about to unfasten the other when Joan opened the house door and told me that since my devices worked so well, I might as well go to the village store and buy some milk and eggs. The village store was a mile and a half away; to reach it I had to climb up two steep hills. My wife, I thought, was showing a great deal of faith in my hardly tested invention. Calling for the packsack, I slipped it on and crunched away. Success crowned my efforts there and back, but I did break one egg and managed to tear my seat and my pants before I got home again. These things, however, were entirely my own fault. Returning from the store and about to descend the second hill, which was long as well as steep, I could not resist the urge to slide down it. Since I didn't want to remove the cleats, there was only one way to try it, and that was on my bottom. I squatted, eased my legs forward and held them up, off the ice surface as I pushed with my hands. And away I went. It was grand, until I was almost at the bottom. A branch had fallen onto the road, and a sharp piece was sticking up through the ice. This sharp end connected with part of my blunt end, and in the antics that resulted I leaned too far back and squashed the packsack against the ice. All in all, I enjoyed the experience. A broken egg, a snippet torn out of my pants, and a gouge on my sit-upon was a small price to pay for the moments of childish glee that I experienced.

After the ice came snow, blankets of the stuff, small fine crystals, large fat flakes, sometimes so quietly one imagined that one could hear them land, at other times lashing and waspish, stinging the cheeks and eyes, seeking entry into all the nooks and crannies of the wilderness. For one entire week it snowed intermittently, covering up the ice at first with a few inches of white, then with more than one foot. At last, overnight, the clouds lifted, and the sun beamed down on a land of white and green and blue. The birds emerged from their storm shelters, and life was once again good.

When I looked out that morning, the temperature stood at the zero mark, and the smothered fields that separated the house from the maple syrup buildings rolled smoothly, undisturbed by tracks, glistening with the brilliance of jewels.

I was sipping my first cup of coffee while Joan was filling the kitchen with the fragrance of buckwheat pancakes and warm, home-produced maple syrup. But while a small part of my mind registered these appetizing aromas, most of my thinking mechanism was busy with the delights that awaited me outside, when, replete with good food and dressed for the weather, I could tramp away on snowshoes and lose myself in the vastness of the wilderness. Those who live in warm climes and who shudder at the mere thought of intense cold do not know what they are missing! I have experienced both habitats, having been raised on the shores of the Mediterranean and having lived in Africa, sometimes right on the equatorial line. Heat is pleasant, but the clean, severe cold of the northland, tempered by the beaming sun and decorated by the pristine snow and the happy greens of the pines, spruces, and balsams, produces a tingling, challenging awareness of life while filling the mind and body with a zest for doing that is rarely experienced in tropical zones. Heat enervates, cold stimulates, provided an organism is healthy and responsive to it. That, at any rate, is my view; but it is one also shared by the wild ones, and some of the tame ones too. Tundra was a cold-lover, and so were the wolves. The difference in their personalities once the temperature dropped was immediately apparent. Feeling good and full of beans, they would play more, charge around, take snow baths, bite at the snow, eat it. And I would join them, as I did that morning after I had carried three modest breakfast dishes to the porch and our canine companions had broken their fast.

At first we were all too carefree for me to think about my earlier worries concerning the wolves and their need to learn to hunt. But when Wa began to play less and started to sniff out scents within the ranks of maple trees, I was returned to the preoccupations of ten days ago. It had to be done. To postpone was only to prolong the agony.

Calling the three to my side, I led them back to the house, ushered them inside, and told Joan what I intended to do. She nodded, but remained silent as she walked into the kitchen to prepare me some sandwiches and a Thermos of hot coffee. While she was doing this, I went upstairs to get the .30-30 Winchester carbine from its scabbard, at first intending to take the gun with me in case the wolves didn't make a clean kill. But as I reached into the closet, I changed my mind. It was unlikely that I would witness a kill if the wolves did manage to make one. I proposed to lead them into the forest and stay with them for a time, or at least until they found a hot scent; then I would probably return home and leave the rest up to the wolves and the prey. Downstairs Joan had put my food in the small packsack I usually carry during day outings. Tundra was put into the basement until the wolves and I left the house.

As we filed out of the porch, I was very conscious of the tears that coursed down my wife's cheeks when she turned away from the wolves and closed the door after us. This enterprise seemed so absolutely final; it was as though we were now saying good-bye to the little blind cubs that came to us one day in early summer. Was it possible that not much more than seven months had passed since then? It seemed as though Matta and Wa had *always* been a part of our household.

Today I allowed the wolves to lead me where they would, and on this occasion it was Wa that forged ahead and Matta who followed in his tracks while I mushed along on snowshoes. Neither wolf was going fast, a circumstance that was due in part to the deep snow, under which the ice still offered treacherous footing, and in part to the absence of fresh scent. From past experience I knew that the snowshoes would allow me to keep up with Matta and Wa until such time as they decided to run; even then, the webs would allow me to catch up with them eventually when they stopped to rest. Using snowshoes, a man traveling in deep snow can actually run down a deer or a moose, or even a wolf pack, if he is fit enough and determined enough to keep going without rest, maintaining an easy pace. This is because animals must continuously lunge and jump when the snow reaches their chests, and such movements are particularly exhausting; an hour or two of this kind of travel will cause an animal to stop and rest, and a determined hunter can eventually slow down the quarry, tiring it, so that he can overtake it. It is not an easy thing to do, and one must be prepared to endure considerable hardship; but it *can* be done.

The beauty of our surroundings receded to the back of my mind as we walked northward. I became only marginally conscious of the trail and its direction as I debated the pros and cons of what I was doing. At first I tried to justify my involvement in this hunt, making excuses for myself and for the wolves, but later I realized that though I was unable fully to accept the thought of being instrumental in the kind of killing that might be done this day, programmed as I was by human sensitivities, I could at least accept the need for what I was doing, because its intent was to prepare the wolves for survival in the wilderness.

Not for the first time, and certainly not for the last, I wrestled with moral conflicts. From a civilized standpoint any animal that kills with tooth and claw is both abhorrent and frightening, while the creatures that are killed by it are viewed with sympathetic affection and are invested with mythical qualities: They are helpless, lovable, cuddly. We think of Disney's Bambi, or our childhood Teddy bears (which we never allow to grow up in our imagination to become ferocious adult bears), and many of us even think of these animals as we do of our children, forgetting that sometimes even the most beautiful and lovable baby can grow up to become a Borgia or a Himmler. So we love the helpless and the cuddly and we hate the "vicious" killers of the wild.

From a natural standpoint, each and every species survives by taking life in some way, shape, or form, Homo sapiens being no exception to this rule. But man has managed to avoid bruising his moral sensibilities by doing most of his food killing by proxy, allowing the butchers in his midst to tackle the bloody and distasteful chore. More and more we are doing this. Granny could probably wring a chicken's neck with the best of them, then slit its jugular, hold the still-kicking fowl over a bowl, and watch its warm blood spurt out.

The farm wife used to help her husband when he batted the pig over the head with the blunt end of the ax, sometimes not killing then and there but only managing a glancing blow, after which the screaming hog would have to be chased around the pen until one more smash would drop it, kicking and grunting. Then the knife would be inserted just above the V of the breastbone, twisted inside, and withdrawn. And the great gouts of steaming gore would be carefully captured in pail or bowl and set aside for making blood sausage and other gustatorial delicacies.

These things still happen, of course, but more and more we are employing specialists to do them for us, and the average Westerner today would not begin to know how to kill a pig or a cow and would be nauseated and horrified if asked to do so.

Yet who shudders as they purchase a roast or a steak or a turkey at the butcher's counter? Or as they poke a finger at a piece of meat lying in the supermarket freezer? What person spares a thought for the truckful of cattle, packed tightly, one against the other, reeking from their own wastes, terrified by the monstrous noise of the truck and of the other vehicles that share the highway while swaying and bumping along in a most unnatural way? I wonder how many of us really take the time to see, in our mind's eye, the terrified beasts inside the truck or to imagine their fate when they are hazed down the ramp into a holding pen within the shadow of the grim building where they will be hung, drawn, and quartered.

Wa picked up a scent. Matta did too. Their behavior told me they had found a hot trail. I returned to my surroundings to realize that we were northeast of the farm and about two miles past East Ridge. The sun was well above the treeline, so I judged it was about 11 A. M. Wa suddenly turned to the right, nose down, his tail rising; but Matta continued on the initial scent for a time. Paying more careful attention to the marks in the snow, I noted that at least two deer had traveled this way recently, then split up. Were the wolves going to separate also? A few minutes later Matta turned and caught up with Wa.

Neither wolf was hurrying yet, and it was only necessary for me to increase my pace fractionally in order to keep up with them. I studied the snow with more care, and I saw that the deer we were following appeared to be having trouble with the ice underfoot, its small hooves punching down and encountering the hard, slippery surface, whereas the broad paws of the wolves, though sinking deeply, compressed enough snow to form a nonskid patch between the ice surface and their pads.

Twice in the last ten minutes snowshoe hares had bounded out of the way of the wolves, but neither Matta nor Wa turned in pursuit, too intent on the deer trail, which was leading us into a region of lowland cedars on the other side of which the country was relatively flat, sparsely treed, and dotted with beaver ponds. We had already passed a number of other deer trails, old ones, made days previously by some of the quite numerous whitetails that inhabited this region. At first I thought that the quarry was seeking the shelter of the heavy forest, and I wondered if it was already aware of the wolves loping behind. After a time, though, the deer angled its course, evidently heading toward the open landscape.

Despite my earlier attempts at justification, I felt more than ever concerned for the deer, until I realized that I was almost on the verge of getting angry with the wolves, which was the same as saying that I was becoming angry with myself. This would not do. I was glad that I could feel sympathy with the whitetail, that I was still human enough to consider the morality of this chase, but my loyalties in this instance had to be with the wolves.

I was suddenly reminded of something written by Bertrand Russell, the British philosopher, in his book *My Philosophical Development*. Explaining some of his concepts of man and morality, he wrote that "it seemed that animals always behave in a manner showing the rightness of the philosophy entertained by the man who observes them. . . . Throughout the reign of Queen Victoria all apes were virtuous monogamists, but during the dissolute twenties their morals underwent a disastrous deterioration."

No one has ever put it better. Recalling the grand old man,

whom I once had the pleasure of interviewing, I concluded that I was being schizoid, seeking to pursue two different sets of values at the same time, while forgetting that the single, most important task facing any organism is the gathering of food. Matta and Wa were seeking to eat; the deer, naturally, would seek to avoid death. The outcome was yet to be determined, but whatever developed, it would do so naturally, within the order of things. This has always been the way, it always will be; at least until the day when our world is destroyed by the madness of our own species.

Predators emerged on earth fitted for a special job within the economy of nature and given the appetite and the "tools" to perform it. It is the predator that keeps the species in good health, just as the species, by seeking to avoid the predator, keeps the latter in good form. One is dependent upon the other. The weak, the congenitally inefficient, of *both* prey and predatory species are weeded out by the unsentimental system that nature decreed long before the first man learned to chip flint in order to make an arrowhead. Since no system is 100 percent perfect, it follows that there are times when a predator will pull down a healthy and splendid prey animal, but the law of averages being what it is in the wilderness, it is usually the unfit that fall to the teeth of the wolves or to the claws of the cats.

Human sport hunters are often heard to say that they are conservationists because the fees that they pay and the efforts that they personally make to replenish game populations help to preserve the species. If such an argument can be accepted— and it is, frequently—the same can be said for the wolf, but with greater credibility. *Canis lupus* belongs to just one of the many natural conservation societies of the wilderness.

Nature as a whole is based upon an intricate system of economy, the main premise of which being that death is the beginning rather than the end of all things. Consider this: From death, in the absence of contemporary man, life invariably springs. An animal is killed and eaten by another, and its meat and bones and sinews give life to the hunter; another may die of disease, accident, or starvation, and its carcass will feed a multitude of creatures, from microscopic organisms to carrion eaters such as the vultures, the rodents, the insects, and even larger animals such as the coyote and the wolf. The remains—

and there are always some remains, no matter who feeds on the carcass—sink into the very earth and make organic matter that will enrich the soil and offer nourishment to plants.

Wherever one looks in the wild, one sees death nurturing life. It may not be obvious perhaps, but it is there for those who would seek it. A patriarchal tree succumbs after 150 or 200 years; it stands sere and decayed at first, offering sanctuary and food to insects and fungi; woodpeckers carve into it to eat the insects, obtaining life from their death just as the insects and fungi obtain life from the tree's death. Squirrels come along and find shelter in the holes made by the woodpeckers, enlarging them and perhaps raising young in them. Then the tree trunk crashes. Now it continues to offer shelter and food to many different organisms; again, insects enter the dead tissue of the forest giant, perhaps an animal like One Ear uses the hollowed trunk as a shelter from its enemies. More fungi feed on the fibrous tissues. Slowly, over decades, more and more of the once-standing tree is used, more and more of the rotten material mixes with the forest soil and enriches it so that it will produce in greater abundance.

Consider the autumn leaves. They turn, weaken on the stem, fall to the ground. In a city or town the homeowner sweeps them up and probably burns them; in the forest the leaves lie where they fall, and tiny creatures come and eat them, turning them into lace; later the lacy fibers break down, become rotten, forming mulch, which mixes with the soil to replenish in measure what the tree has taken in order to sustain itself.

The system of conservation employed by Creation is too marvelous to understand easily. It is there. It works. The wolf is a part of it, as are all those other creatures that share their world with our own species and make it such an interesting place in which to be.

I moved more quickly, gaining on Wa but keeping to one side of him so that I could see the tracks he was following. Only one deer had come this way, but whether the animals had split up for reasons of their own or because they became aware of the presence of the wolves was impossible to tell.

Deer have exceptionally keen hearing and an excellent sense of smell, relying on both to alert them to the presence of a predator. They have good vision also, but this plays a lesser protective role, probably because the animal's forest habitat more often than not obstructs vision; when deer are grazing on cleared land, they use their eyes to good effect, but within the tangle of trees and shrubs in which they normally feed in the absence of man-made fields, vision is restricted to short distances.

A deer's big, jackass ears are continuously on the move, rather like nervous radar scoops, seeking alien sounds whether the animal is feeding, lying down, or merely standing at ease. The ears are its early-warning system, picking up noise disturbance coming from any direction, whereas its nostrils come into effective operation when the wind carries some suspicious scent to them. At the first abnormal sound the deer becomes instantly alert; it may stand like a statue and listen while its nostrils seek to detect a scent, or it may move away, in a direction opposite to that of the sound, walking nervously. If the noise it has heard is close, or otherwise suggests imminent danger, the deer moves swiftly but with remarkable stealth, making little noise even in heavy brush and timber. As the animal runs, it bounds, not only gaining ground in this way, but also allowing its somewhat protruding eyes to observe movement behind and to the sides as well as in front.

While a deer is running, its comparatively long tail, snowy white on the underside, is carried high, revealing the white when viewed from the rear. Commonly, it is said that this white "flag" is displayed in this fashion as a warning, or alarm signal, that will alert other deer to danger. I do not agree with this view. Deer at times congregate in bands and at other times feed alone; in either event, the white tail would serve little purpose as a warning. If the deer is alone, there is no one to warn; if in a band, all the animals are so alert that the first movement made by one of them is immediately detected by the others, so that if one deer begins to run, all the rest will run also.

Pondering this over a number of years, and after having observed a great many deer running away from me, it struck me one late evening that if I were a wolf or some other large predator pursuing such bounding quarry, the flashing, bobbing, snow-white appendage would be particularly distracting to my gaze. It might cause me to miss when I leaped at the target. This, I believe, is the reason for the notorious white flag so blatantly waved whenever a deer runs away from danger.

Indeed, the whole purpose of the white tail, it seems to me, is to attract attention to itself. If one considers the deer's otherwise well-camouflaged coat that blends so well with its surroundings, the waving white flag, held upright during the whole time that the animal is running, is a dead giveaway. I could understand the warning theory better if the deer raised its tail when it was startled and then lowered it discreetly when it was escaping. As it is, I cling to the more logical view that the bobbing, extremely white blur is offered as a distraction to an enemy.

I have observed similar decoy examples in other species. Red and gray squirrels, when startled, or during those times that they must run across a forest opening, wave the end of their bushy tail. I believe that they do this to invite a swooping hawk to strike at the tail rather than at the forward part of the body, giving the squirrel a little better chance of escape. I formed this opinion after watching a red-tailed hawk swoop down on a fleeing squirrel and end its attack clutching one-third of the little animal's tail, while its owner scurried to safety in a tree. In like vein, the prairie antelope, whose white rump is also supposed to act as a warning to its neighbors, offers its startling behind as a distraction. Anyone who has ever seen thirty or forty antelope leaping up and down in a scattered bunch over the prairie will know that all those white patches can become very confusing to the eye. Which one to choose? The hunter *must* be confused by the display.

Deer reach their prime when they are six or seven years of age and are usually old at ten, but the species is prolific. It has been estimated that there are in excess of four million deer in the United States, and although I have not seen totals for Canada, they are certainly numerous in that country as well. A deer needs relatively little land upon which to survive, probably not much more than half a square mile. It is also a polygamous species, that is to say one buck will serve a number of does, which usually start out by producing one fawn, then give birth to twins each year thereafter. Statistically, it has been estimated that one doe could produce one hundred offspring in ten years, if she lived to that age of course. If one halves this figure and considers the fecundity of one thousand does ($1,000 \times 50$), one arrives at fifty thousand offspring in ten years.

Obviously, if it were not for animals like Matta and Wa,

deer would quickly overpopulate their ranges. This would lead not only to the destruction of the deer's food supply, and thus to the extinction of the animal, but it would also seriously damage the land itself and lead to the extermination of many other animals.

In the absence of unnatural disturbances—such as exploitation by modern man—predatory and prey animals have always maintained a healthy economy in accordance with the so-called law of the jungle. This means that the fittest and best live to pass on their traits to their offspring, ensuring that the species remains healthy. Predators like the wolf are not selective hunters; they kill only to eat. In contrast, most human hunters seek trophies first and view the meat as secondary, thus killing the best and leaving the least desirable unharvested. This weakens the species.

Matta and Wa, once they reached their peak of hunting efficiency, would not only keep the herds down, but, by taking out many of the weak and the congenitally unfit animals, would keep the species vigorous, leaving the best to breed with their own kind.

In the absence of man, nature achieves balance. Man, be it through land clearing, industrial or mining development, or because he would seek to protect his livestock, tends to upset the balance. In some cases, misguided men have sought to exterminate the predators in order to keep all the game for themselves. One such example will always endure as a classic case of ecological blundering.

It happened in 1907, on the Kaibab Plateau located on the north side of the Grand Canyon of the Colorado River, in Arizona, where, in that year, there were to be found some 4,000 whitetail deer and an active population of wolves and cougar. State hunters managed to exert enough pressure to institute a maximum effort to "protect" the deer from the predators; the wolves and cougar were hunted down ruthlessly and were soon exterminated from the plateau. By 1925, more than 100,000 deer had developed on the Kaibab, and this horde ate everything within reach of their mouths: tree seedlings, grasses, shrubs, bark, tree boughs. Soon the deer were starving, and there was marked damage done to the vegetation of the plateau. During the winters of 1928 and 1929, vast numbers of deer starved to death until eventually the population fell to 10,000. Thus, *some 90,000 deer died horribly because of man's greed*!

Watching our two wolves while thinking about these things, I finally resolved the conflict within myself. Matta and Wa were natural hunters occupying a necessary niche within the economy of nature. I could feel sympathy for the deer, relate emotionally, as a human, with the "weaker" animal, but I could in no way condemn the wolves for what they sought to do. Having accepted the responsibility for raising them, I had to accept the responsibility for training them for survival. I felt better after coming to these conclusions, but I never managed to quell the emotional stresses entirely. I don't think I ever will.

CHAPTER ELEVEN

It wasn't long after Wa put his nose to the second trail that Matta sought to take over the lead. The scent was evidently strong, and Wa exhibited that tense, alert attitude characteristic of the hunter following a fresh trail. His ears were pricked forward and were held still, his shoulder and hip hackles were partly erect, and his plumelike tail was carried high. He started to increase his pace, only occasionally dropping his nose toward the snow.

It was at this point that Matta tried to take over and received a pointed rebuff. Wa merely glanced at her sideways, but his low, deep growl was ominous. Matta got the message at once, dropping back meekly. A few minutes later the two left me behind, disappearing into a clump of cedars, the small sounds made as they ran soon fading altogether.

I paused for breath, studying the direction of the trail as I inhaled deeply. It was clear that the deer was heading toward the open country, but at this point it was not possible to determine whether Matta and Wa would be successful. I could not now hope to keep the wolves in sight, but I could follow their tracks or take a shortcut that would bring me out at a height of land that dominated the sparsely treed country where the beaver had made their ponds. To do this I would have to go almost due east, then turn sharply north, cross over a narrow but quite long beaver dam, and ascend the rocky slope to the point of vantage above. I opted to follow this course.

Wolves, as has been seen, can bark, and do so when occasion demands, but they usually hunt in silence, conserving their energies for running. This placed me at a disadvantage inasmuch as I could not follow the progress of this chase by sound. But knowing the country as I did, I thought there might be a chance of seeing at least something of the hunt, especially if I climbed a tree that I knew of, a tall white pine with branches that came down within four or five feet of the ground, offering a convenient stepladder up the trunk. Three years earlier I had cleared a number of branches right around the trunk at the seventy-foot level, not denuding the pine but opening "windows" through which I could observe the countryside through 360 degrees. From this perch I had made many interesting sightings. Now it seemed a logical place in which to settle myself, have my lunch, smoke a pipe, and wait to see what I would see, if anything.

It was probably about noon when I negotiated the long dam and ascended the snow-covered rock slope. At the top, I noticed that my vantage tree was already occupied. A big, dark porcupine was sunning itself on a branch about thirty feet up, dozing after having peeled off a goodly amount of bark from the big tree's branches. The ground below was littered with branch tips, little, tender clusters of twigs holding several bundles of needles, five to a bundle.

Because I expected to find it, my eyes soon spotted the snowshoe hare that was feeding on the porcupine's leavings, eating the branch tips with the sideways action of the jaws characteristic of the species. As I approached, the hare loped away, in its mouth a quickly disappearing clump of green. The porcupine dignifed me with a myopic glance from its shoe-button eyes, otherwise it didn't move so much as a quill. From the bottom it looked rather like a slightly misshapen and very untidy football, its quills lying flat and almost concealed by the long winter hair.

I started to climb the tree, keeping to the offside of the trunk so as to disturb the porcupine as little as possible. When I was halfway to the quill pig's level, it began to move, but slowly, as though depicting slow motion on a screen. It had been facing the trunk when I arrived. It turned itself around, clutching at the branch with its long, curved claws and eventually ending up with its tail in the place where its head had previously been. It is not good policy to crowd a porcupine in a tree. The animal will never attack, but if an incautious human seeks to perch on the same branch as the docile rodent, the animal has two choices: to jump off and risk an injury or to rush along the branch and *brush* by the intruder. I had found out the hard way that when a porcupine brushes by, it leaves a number of souvenirs of the event firmly impaled in whatever part of the anatomy happens to encounter the "brush."

Reaching my neighbor's vantage, I paused to peek at the porcupine around the tree and noted that it had advanced farther out along the branch, that its tail was still aimed toward the trunk, and that it was not yet seeking to turn around in order to rush headlong toward the bole. I kept climbing quietly, and by the time I was ten feet above it, the porcupine had curled itself up in a comfortable position again and continued taking the sun. Presently I was more or less at ease seated on my spy branch, the haversack hanging from a broken stub and the field glasses pressed against my eyes. I scanned the countryside through a complete circle and found what I expected, nothing.

I was warm from the walk, and the feel of the air indicated that the temperature had climbed above zero; the sun was comforting on my back as I unpacked the sandwiches, poured a cup of coffee from the Thermos, and commenced my lunch. Below me the porcupine was just visible through the curtain of green branches; it hadn't moved.

Before I finished the first half of the sandwich, I had a visitor. I didn't see or hear it land, but when my ears registered a sweet and rather plaintive whistle, I didn't have to turn my head to know that a gray jay had discovered that I was eating. How these birds are able to spot food so quickly is a mystery to me. This one was evidently an old acquaintance, accustomed to getting handouts from me. When it realized that I was aware of its presence, it hopped forward and landed on the same branch from which the haversack was hanging. I broke off a piece of bread and held it on the flat of my hand. The bird hopped onto my thumb, picked up the tidbit, and sailed away to hide it. Minutes later it was back, this time followed by a companion. I was hungry, and I wanted to eat all my sandwich, so I fished out some peanuts from my pocket and lined them up on a thick, nearby branch, allowing the birds to help them-selves.

North of the pine tree the country was open for about a mile, then gave way to evergreen forest that stretched to the limits of vision. To the east, just a couple of hundred yards away, the ground was littered with great pieces of craggy rock, broken lumps, some of them six feet high and as many broad, others ranging from the size of melons to large pumpkins; these were all loose rocks containing a mixture of feldspar, granite, and milk white quartz. They had broken off from rough out-crops of the same substances formed millions of years earlier during upheavals of the earth; the loosely packed agglomerates were being eroded by the weather. Little grew on such inhos-pitable terrain, and now the snow covered all signs of the rock, but showed the outline of each lump and crag.

To the south, from whence I had come, mixed forests began on the other side of the beaver pond. Here was good cover; it contained plenty of plant growth and was the abode of many animals and birds. About three miles beyond this forest, East Ridge began to take shape. West of my vantage point, about a mile away, was the forest through which the deer had been leading the wolves. If I had guessed right, the hunt might reveal itself to view if the quarry was circling, intent on gaining the shelter of the heavily wooded southlands. Alternately, the deer might head toward the northern evergreens, where there also existed plenty of good cover. In either event, judging from the direction of travel last noted, it would emerge into the open if Matta and Wa didn't catch up to it before the trees thinned out.

When the sandwiches were consumed and the gray jays had removed all the peanuts and left me in order to search the forest for more food, I sipped coffee and made the most of the sun-shine and the commanding view while considering my next moves. At that time of year, in that latitude, the sun starts to set at about three-thirty in the afternoon, and the land becomes dark an hour or so afterward. Returning via East Ridge, it would take me the best part of two hours to emerge from the forest into the farm clearing, so unless I undertook half the journey in darkness, I was going to have to leave by two-thirty at the latest.

Perhaps half an hour was used up musing in this vein. During that time little of interest was noted. Now and then I would catch sight of a bird or two, blue jays, gray jays, chickadees; once a nuthatch flitted past my tree uttering its nasal *yank-yank* call. On another occasion a pileated woodpecker flew from south to north. The porcupine continued to doze on its branch, and I suspected that the snowshoe hare I had disturbed would by now have returned to eat more pine tips. I wasn't cold yet, but I knew I would be before another half hour elapsed, so I determined to stay on my perch only until the first chill made itself felt. I lifted the glasses and trained them on the western trees, saw nothing, and was about to turn toward the north when sudden movement, at first quite indistinct, revealed itself just within the shelter of the trees.

I kept the glasses steady. In another moment the deer emerged, turned toward the beaver pond, and bounded through the snow toward it, its gait appearing to be unsteady; the animal was clearly tired. Before I had managed to swing the glasses back to the place where the deer had emerged, first Wa, then Matta, burst out of the forest. The wolves were about fifty yards behind the deer, going well, as far as I could determine. It looked as though they would catch up to their quarry and make the kill, but I didn't think I would see them do it before the deer crossed the frozen beaver pond and entered the southern fringe of trees. I swung the glasses from the wolves to the deer, back again to the wolves. When I once more looked at the quarry, the animal was just stepping onto the beaver pond.

Wa had lengthened his stride when I next looked at him, pulling steadily ahead of Matta, but now she, too, exerted herself, managing to keep her brother from gaining more yards on her but evidently unable to close the gap. I turned back to look at the deer and was surprised to see it sprawled on the snow, lying on its side, its head and neck upright, neither struggling nor attempting to rise. Leading up to the animal was a long, broad skid mark. Evidently, the small, sharp hooves had punched down through the snow and skidded on the ice of the pond, causing the animal to lose its footing.

I had seen a number of deer and moose do the same thing in other places, and once I had helped a yearling doe back onto her feet and herded her off the ice. But all the animals previously observed during such a predicament had struggled to rise. This deer was not moving. More precisely, its limbs were not moving; its flanks and chest certainly were. Mouth open, the unfortunate whitetail was gasping for breath. As I watched, it lowered its head and rested it on top of the snow, becoming half buried in the white topping. I was still watching when Wa bounded down the slope, landed on the ice, and charged. The picture was all too clear seen through the glasses from less than half a mile away.

Wa, the placid, mischievous wolf cub, was no more. In his place I was now seeing a strong, formidable predator whose entire being was primed for the kill. His hackles were fully erect, his tail so high its tip arched over his back, somehow accentuating the points of his ears. His lips were peeled back to reveal the great fangs shining within the cavernous, gaping mouth, from the left side of which the tongue lolled and flopped loosely as he ran.

I was watching a primeval scene, a playback of prehistory, a spectacle that was at once horrifying and breathtaking. Only seconds elapsed during the time that Wa bounded onto the ice and closed the gap between himself and the quarry, but there was time to spare to note every detail of the wolf, to see the intensity that gripped him, and to observe the smooth, bunching muscles rippling the heavy coat of hair as they drove the wolf forward.

I heard no sound—I wouldn't have expected to do so across the distance—so I don't know if he was growling or not when he closed his jaws on the deer's throat, set his front paws, sloped his body backward, and wrenched suddenly, shaking his massive head from side to side as he exerted the pull. The whole scene was somehow unreal. The teeth disappeared, then great gouts of crimson flooded out, spraying Wa's face and shoulders and chest as his fangs cut through hide and muscle and tendons and larynx and pulled suddenly free. Wa stumbled, tried to recover, and fell on his side. As he scrambled up, Matta dashed in, fastening her teeth on the deer's uppermost haunch. The moribund animal's kicking back legs dislodged Matta, but she recovered quickly and rushed in again even as Wa seized the throat anew. But the deer was dead already. The last jerky kicks came and went, the muscles along the flanks quivered spasmodically beneath the grayish hair, and that was all.

I lowered the glasses, discovering that I was bathed in sweat and that my heart was racing. It was as though I had participated in the kill. A strange excitement filled me, and I felt ashamed of it, because I knew that for some heartbeats I had actually *enjoyed* the kill. It was as though some totally primitive and feral part of me that I never knew existed had taken over for those split seconds and had participated in the hunt. Afterward I began to tremble, and there was a sick feeling in my stomach. I didn't dare begin to descend the tree, but sat there, looking down so as to avoid watching the wolves. When my hands stopped shaking, I reached for pipe and tobacco, filled the bowl, lit the tobacco, and puffed for several minutes. I began to climb down the tree.

As I reached the level of its perch, I was surprised to note that the porcupine had gone, evidently decamping while my attention was elsewhere, for I had certainly neither heard nor seen it leave. At the foot of the pine, the rodent's tracks, ~~ompanied by the marks made by its dragging tail, were ~~d toward the rocky ground, where the animal's winter ~~probably located~~. Retrieving the snowshoes from where ~~y~~ hung on a dead limb, I strapped them on, only to find that I could not yet force myself to go near the wolves and their kill. In fact, I would have preferred avoiding the confrontation entirely, but I needed to learn more about the deer. Knowing that the longer I delayed, the less of the animal would remain undisturbed for my inspection, I still lingered under the tree until I had finished the pipeful of tobacco. Some ten minutes later I moved away from the pine's shelter and directed myself toward the wolves.

Before I was halfway there, both Matta and Wa became aware of my approach, stared at me intently for a moment, then returned to their meal. Even without the glasses I could see that both were well stained with blood and that Wa, in particular, presented an extremely gory appearance. This was not, of course, unusual after the work he had done, but it lent him a rather frightening countenance.

As I got closer, I saw that Matta was working on a back leg, pulling great mouthfuls of meat from it, chewing rapidly and swallowing such big amounts that her throat distended as the food went down. Wa had eaten most of the deer's neck, nearly severing the head from the body; he was now eating into the chest cavity, evidently consuming the heart, lungs, liver, and other offal. These things added to the crimson that already plastered his entire head and neck and chest. Now I could hear both wolves growling almost continuously, but

180

whether they were directing this at me or at each other I could not determine.

In truth, I was apprehensive. Having seen Wa in action, I discovered that I was suddenly afraid of him. But this wouldn't do. I had to control my emotions if I was to approach the kill as an alpha animal might do. But fear is a difficult thing to conquer. I walked more slowly, lecturing myself silently, trying to be clinical. In the end I must have managed to *mask* my fear at least, for when I came at last to stand within three feet of Wa and he growled at me, lifting his bloody muzzle as he hastily gulped whatever he had taken out of the deer's chest cavity, I managed to growl back with what I hoped was equal ferocity and to stare into his eyes as fixedly as he stared into mine. At any rate, he dropped his gaze, reduced the level of his growl, and went into the carcass again. As he did so, I took the last step, paused beside the deer's head, and squatted down. Wa looked at me. I ignored him, but I couldn't stop my right hand from moving to place itself on the handle of the hunting knife that hung low from my waist. I suppose I moved purposefully when I reached out with my left hand and grasped one of the deer's large ears, then bent my head down as though to feed from the animal, but it seemed to me that my movements were leaden, a dead giveaway that Wa would note with his keen senses. If he did, he would attack, I felt; but I shall never be sure about that. He continued eating, as did Matta, and soon I was making my pretend eating sounds while easing the knife out of its sheath, holding it at the correct angle, and slicing through the last of the flesh on the deer's neck. At the bone of the vertebrae I chopped with the heavy knife, once, twice. With the third stroke the deer's head was fully severed from its body. I picked it up by one ear, straightened, and walked away with it, seeking to examine it at leisure from the safety of distance. Before I turned away, I noticed from a couple of the animal's dugs that were still intact that the wolves had pulled down a doe, evidently an old one, or at least one that had not mated last autumn, for she was not big with young and she was particularly thin.

I took the head to the rocky area, cleared snow from one flat-topped boulder, and used this as a dissecting table. Before I cut into the head, I already knew what I was going to find. Near the back of the throat, where Wa's teeth had created a

181

jagged tear, I could see two, inch-long, black-banded maggoty things, flat on one side, rounded on the other, and fat, the larvae of a botfly, a species belonging to the family Oestridae, which infest deer.

The fly itself is about half an inch long, a tough looking customer, yellow gray in color, and hairy. Females of the species are actually able to lay their tiny larvae in the nostrils of deer, even when these are running at top speed. The botfly is thought to be able to travel at fifty miles an hour while chasing after a fleeing deer.

The tiny, whitish larvae have a pair of quite large mouth hooks. They work their way into the nasal passages, sinuses, and other cavities in the bones of the deer's head, anchor themselves with their mouth hooks, and begin to feed off their unwilling host, developing within ten months into the fat, black-banded creatures I was now viewing. Usually, the adult larvae are ready to leave the deer by spring or, at the latest, summer, at which times they unfasten the mouth hooks and leave the host or are coughed or sneezed out when they irritate the nasal and throat passages. On the ground, these revolting, inch-long insects pupate and become flies, which mate and repeat the parasitic cycle.

Various species of these flies attack sheep, cattle, and horses as well as members of the deer family. In Central and South America, one species, the human botfly, or *Dermatobia hominis*, has an ingenious, if malevolent, way of ensuring that her larvae reach a human victim: She somehow manages to attach her sticky eggs to blood-sucking mosquitoes, which transfer them to man or beast when they go to take food from the host! Fortunately this species is absent from North America. I have seen the havoc caused by *Dermatobia*. The rather enormous larvae, also equipped with mouth hooks, burrow deep under the skin and feed on the flesh; only surgery will succeed in removing the brute before it is ready to emerge on its own, and in the meantime quite a tunnel is mined in leg or arm or wherever the beast has burrowed. In Brazil few jungle natives escape the pest, though with the stoicism of a people accustomed to hardship on a daily basis, they appear more or less to ignore the dreadful, weeping sores made by the maggots.

The deer bot may do little harm if only a few of the larvae are deposited on the nostrils of the host. In heavy infestations, the larvae cause loss of weight, difficulty in breathing, and general weakness that can result in death, depending on the amount of larvae present and upon the condition of the deer.

Placing the severed head, forehead down, on the rock, I began to open the thing with the knife, first cutting through flesh and sinews, then chopping through the bone. When the head was split into two halves the severity of the infestation was dreadfully apparent. Every cavity was filled with the larvae, which, on closer inspection and by later measurement, were not quite as large as I had at first thought. The biggest among them, measured with a pocket tape, was five-eighths of an inch long and a fraction under three-sixteenths of an inch wide. All of them were still alive and firmly attached to the raw membranes of sinuses, throat, and the upper portion of the nasal cavity. By the time I had dissected the head, examined the larvae, and dug a few of them out to take back with me, placing them in one of two small containers I carry for just such purposes, the sun was dipping toward the western trees. I left the deer's head on the rock and returned to the scene of the kill.

Wa was lying nearby, dozing. Matta was some distance away, licking herself clean, a task that Wa had already attended to. Both looked at me but didn't rise to approach when I bent over the carcass. The wolves had already taken a large amount of meat. The back leg, the one Matta had been working on, was almost entirely stripped of meat, and the chest cavity, shoulder, and part of one of the front legs had been eaten by Wa, or so I assumed. The paunch and intestines remained more or less untouched.

I stooped to the rather disagreeable task of slitting the stomach so as to examine the contents. I particularly wanted to see if the doe was pregnant. When I opened her, it took but a glance to confirm that she had not been impregnated during the autumnal rut. From the worn grinding teeth, examined earlier, I knew she was old; now her condition indicated that she was barren.

I made a few notes, details of the chase, the kill, and the deer's condition, then I added the larvae count: fifty-seven. There may have been more, which fell out when Wa opened the throat or were chopped up by his teeth. Whatever the total,

183

the unfortunate doe must have been half-choking long before the wolves picked up her trail.

I reached home at dusk to be greeted anxiously by Joan, who asked, "Where are Matta and Wa?"

I was still in the porch, taking off my snowshoes. As I straightened, hanging the shoes on a hook on the wall—out of reach of the wolves and Tundra—I explained briefly what had occurred and told her that our wolves had remained beside the deer carcass.

"I'm sure they won't come back tonight, maybe not to-morrow either," I added, but I did not tell her what I really thought, that Matta and Wa would never come back again.

After walking away from the kill and just before entering the mixed forest, I had stopped and looked back. Neither wolf so much as lifted its head to gaze in my direction. Both appeared to be asleep, tightly curled up in the snow, reminding me of my sled dogs and of Tundra, all of whom could coil themselves in that way and endure temperatures of 30 and 40 degrees below zero without discomfort.

I hadn't wanted to leave them and had been tempted to call them, to coax them to return with me, but I resisted the temptation. We had to allow Matta and Wa the freedom of making their own choice. If, now that they had made this second kill, they elected to return of their own accord to us, all well and good; but if they decided to stay in the wilderness, that, too, would be right. During the journey back I rehearsed again and again those things that I was going to say to Joan, but now that I was home, seeing the tears fill her eyes, and knowing how they would flow when I told the rest of the story, I didn't quite know how to begin.

My own emotions were in turmoil. I was haunted by the vision of Wa making the kill, of the spine-chilling change that had come over him. I was also very much aware of my own excitement as I watched the blood flow, of the sense of actual pleasure that filled me momentarily.

On the pretext that I was tired and in need of a drink, both of which facts were true, I postponed talking to Joan until I had had a hot shower, after which I poured out a good measure of Scotch, added water, and settled myself before the fire. Joan, who refused a drink, sat opposite, looking at me with that frown that I knew so well, her eyes shining with unshed tears. Knowing me as she did, she didn't push, but sat quietly, hands folded in her lap, waiting. I could not put if off any longer.

"They picked up a trail near that big elm where the raccoons den. I think there were two deer. They split up, one going straight ahead, the other turning toward the rock flats. Wa followed that one. Matta followed the other for a while, then turned and followed Wa."

Having started, I found the words difficult to stop. Step by step I took Joan along the route, right up to the pine, along country that she knew well, so that the telling of it was not complicated by territorial explanations. Eventually I described the kill, but I kept a lot back, not wishing to distress her any more than was necessary. Wa had always been her favorite, though she loved both wolves greatly. To be told that he had again done the killing was more than her self-control could handle. She broke down, weeping quietly but copiously. I sipped my drink, letting her get it out of her system. When the flow began to lessen, I got up, put an arm around her shoulder, and held my glass to her lips. She sipped a little, feeling in her apron pocket for a Kleenex. Afterward she dabbed the tears from her cheeks, blew her nose, kept the tissue balled up in her hand, and looked at the fire.

"Don't tell me more," she murmured.

I was glad to stop. Presently she looked at me.

"Do you think they'll come back again?"

I had to be honest. She would know if I wasn't. I said no, I didn't think they would return. Now Joan cried quietly, dabbing away the tears as they came, until the Kleenex was a soggy ball. I got up and went to get the box and put it on the arm of her chair. Then I poured myself another drink and made one for her and put it in her hand. She took it, sipped occasionally, stared into the fire, and continued to cry.

My own eyes were stinging now. I didn't trust myself to speak for fear of breaking down, so I got up to go outside to bring in a fresh supply of logs for the fireplace. Tundra greeted me as always, but sensing that I was preoccupied, he soon desisted and returned downstairs. He came up as I reached the door and went outside with me, waiting beside his chain for me to fasten it to his collar. When I returned with an armful of wood, he was lying down in the snow, looking toward the north expectantly.

Somehow the evening turned into night. We both ate a meager supper, neither of us feeling hungry, listened to the ten o'clock news, and then went to bed. Sleep was a long time coming.

I don't know how long I had slept when I was awakened by Tundra's peremptory scratching on the door. Feeling groggy, vaguely aware that dawn was only just starting to break, I slipped on a robe, stuffed my feet into slippers, and went downstairs. Three glad and expectant faces beamed at me as I opened the door. In another moment there was a concerted rush into the house, and Tundra, followed closely by the wolves, clattered upstairs. When I reached the bedroom, it was to find Joan smothered in her friends, laughing and crying at the same time, and not a bit put out by the rather filthy condition of her darlings.

I pretended to be unmoved. I even pretended that the return of the wolves was a nuisance, because now we would have to go through all the emotions of another, final parting. But, in the end, I had to admit that I was damned glad to have them back.

CHAPTER TWELVE

Looking at the two wolves as they lay stretched out in their old place in the kitchen, it was almost impossible to visualize them as they had been on the first evening at home, when Tundra licked the little blind pups and I watched Wa dragging himself forward with his scrabbling front legs. Matta was twelve inches long then; Wa measured fourteen inches. Now he was taller and longer than Tundra, his head was wider, and his jaws were cavernous. He wasn't as heavy as the dog yet, for he still had to fill out some more, but in all other respects he was bigger. Matta was about the same height and length as Tundra. From handling them and going on my experience after examining dead wolves, I judged that the bitch probably weighed between sixty and sixty-five pounds and that Wa was eighty pounds or more.

It was the third day of March. Winter was old, but still exerting pressure, bringing the mercury down to the 20-below-zero mark almost every night and not allowing it to rise much above the zero point during the day. It had not snowed for the past two weeks, but there was a good four feet of white on the flat and considerably more in those places where drifting had occurred.

I sat at the kitchen table, waiting for supper; Joan was doing something with pots and pans at the stove, filling the room with appetizing aromas. As I watched the wolves—they could no longer be called cubs—Wa raised his head from the floor, stared into space, and yawned prodigiously, revealing four great fangs that gleamed like polished ivory. He closed his mouth with an audible snap, sighed, and dumped his head down again carelessly, the way somebody might drop a ten-pound bag of potatoes. In this, the male wolf was like Tundra; neither seemed sensitive to the pain that I thought must result when they flung themselves down the way they did. Matta, perhaps because she was a female, was more graceful, which caused Joan to point out the niceties of male and female movements, extending the parallel to include the human species, and singling out one of these in particular.

At nine months, the wolves showed the sleek, healthy characteristics of their breed, their lines well sculpted, their fur shiny and long, controlled strength evident in their every movement. I was proud of them—justifiably so, I think—and pleased that they were so ready to take their places in the wild. Not that we were thinking of rejecting them yet, but by now it seemed likely that they would elect to leave of their own accord. Indeed, they came and went as they pleased, sometimes staying away several days at a time, then returning to sleep for a while in the evaporator house, or, more usually, underneath it, where there was a crawl space about four feet high extending all the way under the building. They still came to call at the house, socializing with Tundra on the porch, but we allowed them inside only on rare occasions for fear that they might become too tame. In this, it appeared that they shared our opinion; they seldom tried to come in and were somewhat reluctant to do so when I called them, as I had done that evening.

Observing them, I realized that they looked out of place in the house. It was as though a piece of the wilderness itself had suddenly and magically appeared in one corner of our kitchen, each wolf seeming to be surrounded by an aura of primordial force so compelling that it gave off sensual vibrations. They were utterly *alive*, two organisms tuned to fine pitch, strong, lithe, and absolutely formidable.

I reached behind me to the telephone desk and picked up a note pad, jotting down some of these impressions. Joan looked up, waited until the pencil stopped moving, and asked what I was doing. I shrugged, muttered something about making notes.

"You're doing more than that! Whenever you get that vacant

look, I know you're taking a trip inside your head. You can't fool *me*, kid!"

She didn't notice that the pencil moved as she spoke, and I was saved from taking down more of her words when something made disturbing hissing noises on the stove. She turned back to her cooking and allowed me to continue looking "vacant."

Unnoticed by either of us, Wa's eyes opened while we were talking. I was in time to see him close them again and settle his head a little more comfortably; in front of his nostrils twin pools of moisture made irregular patterns on the shiny boards. Matta had not budged; she lay with her finer head resting on one foreleg, both her back feet pressed against the wall and her tail curving toward her back.

As usual, the wolves and Tundra had already eaten their suppers and the dog was now sleeping off his meal in the basement, a place where Matta and Wa would not follow him, perhaps because they didn't like steps, or perhaps because they recognized that the dark hole below grade was Tundra's sole domain. All three had fared well, but the wolves had eaten a considerable quantity, for I was now feeding them large amounts at irregular intervals to encourage them to hunt for themselves and to accustom them to the feast-famine pattern that they would have to endure when they returned to the wild.

Quite often neither wolf showed much interest when I offered food, evidently having satisfied their hunger during their nightly rambles through the forest, though now I didn't go with them, and thus I could not tell what they hunted, particularly in view of the fact that they usually moved bowels and bladder while in the wilderness, depriving me of the opportunity to examine their scats for fur and bone chips.

Tonight they were ravenously hungry. I could tell when they had fasted for a few days by the way they reacted to the scent of food, but even so, I doled out their rations portion by portion, weighing each amount. Supper for Tundra consisted of a mixture of dog chow and raw beaver meat spiced with some leftover stew; the wolves were given straight beaver, a good supply of which remained in the freezer. By actual weight, Wa polished off twenty-two pounds of meat; Matta ingested sixteen pounds. The rotund contours of their bellies showed they were full.

At this point Joan served our dinner, and I was about to remark that the gorged wolves would not be drawn to the odor of roast beef when four lids popped open to reveal four inquisitive amber eyes. I grinned, shook my head, and wagged a finger at our two pack mates. Wa raised head and shoulders the better to allow his nose to suck in the aroma, but Matta contented herself with sniffing from where she lay. I decided to ignore them, for I had one inflexible rule (which was often broken): Never feed a dog (or wolf!) from the table. But it appeared that Wa's interest was only passing; he soon dropped his head. Matta actually closed her eyes and went back to sleep, but her brother continued to watch us, occasionally flicking one ear while he siphoned the smell of our food.

We enjoyed our meal in relative silence, each busy with individual thoughts. Afterward, because Joan was on a diet and I am indifferent to desserts, we ended with coffee, the dinner plates with their bits of leftovers remaining on the table. It was at this point that Wa rose to his feet, stretched luxuriously, arching his back like a cat, and came padding over toward me. Joan was rising to get the coffeepot from the stove.

I was thinking of putting the plates on the floor and allowing Wa to lick them if that was what he wanted, when he moved close to me and eased his head on top of the table, reaching with his tongue for my plate. This was never tolerated. Indeed, Joan disliked it intensely when I allowed Tundra or the wolves to lick the plates on the floor, but she would become downright angry if any of them tried to help themselves. In my own case, though I couldn't see what there was to fuss about when a canine licked a plate that would in any event be thoroughly washed, I considered it a sheer impertinence for one of our pack members to try to eat what was not offered to them. Now I reached out with my right hand, beginning to phrase a stern rebuke, and grabbed Wa by the shaggy scruff, starting to shake him.

He was unbelievably fast! Emitting a sudden, deep growl, Wa shook his head violently, pulling it out of my grasp, then swung back again swiftly to clamp his teeth on my right forearm. Reflexively, I struck him on the side of the head with my left fist, a hard blow that traveled all the way up my arm. Wa let go and backed away, but his lips were peeled back in a full snarl, revealing those formidable fangs that were now stained by my own blood. There he stood, tail high, hackles raised to their utmost, ears pricked forward, a suddenly savage and dangerous creature, every inch of whom was signaling a challenge. My favorite wolf cub had grown up and was now seeking to challenge the alpha male of his pack, his inherent leadership qualities exerting themselves, perhaps against his will.

Time stood suspended for an endless heartbeat. I cannot recall my thoughts, if, indeed, I had any. But other details are still clear: Joan, her face white, her eyes round and staring, pressing herself backward against the counter top, the coffeepot clutched in one hand; Matta, sitting up, looking at Wa intently; the throb in my arm and the feel of blood running wet and warm toward my wrist. And Wa, no longer himself, was transformed into a fighting wolf, standing ready to leap, and staring intently into my eyes with those uncomfortable yellow lenses of his, while his rumbling growl continued nonstop. His teeth were so fully exposed that his upper lip was wrinkled back to reveal the top of his red gums. He was a superstition come alive, Fenris, the giant wolf of Norse mythology, son of Loki, who had slipped the chain.

Instinct urged me to pick up a chair and to strike Wa with it, to kill him, because I now feared him. Yet some calmer corner of my mind retained the reality of this showdown. This fierce animal was still Wa, the puppy that had sucked milk out of my mouth, the cub that had always been exceptionally close to me and that, during our wilderness walks, had always been the more responsive of the two wolves. Even now I knew that he had no wish to kill me, that his threat was partly bluff and partly motivated by the inherent desire to elevate his pack status. He was rather young to be gripped by such an urge, though he was certainly big enough and confident enough to be capable of trying to win a social contest. It was clear that he had wanted to get his own way with the leavings on the plate and that he rebelled at the scruff punishment, just as some big teen-age boy might challenge the authority of his father or schoolmaster.

I did not, of course, consciously debate these things while facing Wa's noisy and fierce threats; still, the mind being what it is, I seemed to review them with the speed of a computer, and this allowed me, later on, to set down the events in more or less chronological order.

I was still standing beside the table, bleeding, and Wa was still planted firmly on the kitchen floor when Tundra came charging up the stairs. Hearing him, I felt relief at first, believing that the dog would interpose himself between me and the wolf. Then I felt deep concern for both Tundra and Wa, not wanting either one to injure the other. As it turned out, both my relief and my concern were uncalled for. Tundra, entering the kitchen, stopped immediately, evidently reading correctly the cause of the commotion. He stood with tail curled, hackles slightly raised, and ears pricked forward, looking first at Wa, then at me.

A split second later I made my decision. So, evidently, did Wa. We both moved at the same time, each toward the other. The wolf came in low, aiming for my legs, I thought.

Reflex once again guided my actions. As we were about to come together, I swung my right leg outward and forward, bringing it sharply against Wa's front legs with enough force to knock away his underpinnings. He fell on his side, heavily, and was hindered by the slippery foor in his efforts to rise quickly. Taking advantage of this, I threw myself on him, trying to keep my head and face away from his jaws, but aiming to place my weight on his shoulders. I felt the breath go out of him as my chest collided with his; while my body swiveled so as to place my legs in position to allow me to clamp both knees against his sides, both my hands reached for his neck.

I have only vague recollections of what happened next. Joan, who watched in frozen horror, told me later that Wa struggled so violently that he rolled right over, on top of me, and that I crossed my legs over his hips, securing a "scissors" hold. She saw him bite me twice, once on my right hand, another time on my right eyebrow, which bled profusely. I wasn't conscious of these during the heat of the action.

Somehow, using my legs, I rolled Wa over and was able to straddle him, both hands clutching his throat. I must have squeezed hard, because Joan said that he started to gag and that his breath rasped as he tried to inhale. But my next conscious awareness came when I found myself holding his scruff with my right hand, clutching the fur and loose skin as hard as I have ever gripped anything. I suddenly realized that I was silent, and now I made myself growl as I shook Wa's scruff violently, thumping his head against the floor.

Wa maintained his deep growls for a time, then they gradually lost the fierce timbre. He continued to struggle, but by this point I was kneeling and had both knees clamped tightly against his flanks. I knew I had him, and that, if necessary, I could use my other hand to choke him into submission if he didn't give up. How long we maintained this position, I don't know; even Joan could offer no estimate of time. At this stage of our fight I was most conscious of the danger that I faced. I was at a clear disadvantage because I didn't want to injure Wa, while the wolf, gripped by the inherent urge to win, was not so inhibited. If he could, he would rip and tear until I capitulated. That, at least, would have been the pattern during a status contest among two members of a wild pack, but whether or not he would have stopped attacking if I had surrendered will, thank the Lord, always remain a question.

The first real intimation that he gave to show that he felt himself bested came when he avoided my eyes. I kept my own fixed on him, but I eased up on the scruff punishment, maintaining a tight hold on his neck but no longer shaking him. And I began to scold, keeping my voice low, but making it as stern as I could under the circumstances. Afterward I was to bless the training and battle experience obtained during the war, which, once the first mad rush of adrenaline becomes expended, allows one to think coherently despite the continued fear. Such repeated indoctrination puts the emotions in mothballs, takes advantage of the adrenaline surge, and allows reason to dictate the proper moves. One retains memory of these reasoned actions, whereas recollection of the actions undertaken during the initial, instinctive phase is only fragmentary.

I knew myself to be in control of the situation the moment that Wa turned his eyes away. When his growls ended and he began to whine, and when he moved his head back, exposing his throat, the fight was won.

I let go of his scruff but continued to straddle him. Wa remained docile. He stopped whining, but kept his throat exposed. This was the appropriate time to take my eyes off him, lift my head, and examine my surroundings.

Matta was staring at us, but as soon as my eyes encountered hers, she turned her head away and dropped her tail, signaling her subordinate role. Tundra also avoided my gaze, though he kept his tail tightly curled. Joan stood as I had last seen her, pressed against the counter, coffeepot in hand, complexion chalky, and eyes wide-staring. Without looking at Wa, I got up slowly, deliberately turned my back on him, and told Joan that everything was all right now. Trying to make light of the incident, I suggested that she could bring the coffeepot to the table.

"Aren't you tired, holding that thing like that?" I said with a grin, or I *think* I did, but the movement of my lips may have been a grimace instead.

Joan almost broke the glass pot as she set it on the stove and then ran toward me to reach for my head with both hands. She peered at me with tears in her eyes, turned around, and dove into the bathroom. After she was sick, she washed her hands and returned with some Kleenex, intending to dab at the blood on my face. But I stopped her, explaining briefly that this was not the time to fuss. Wa must be made aware that he was, indeed, the loser. Over my wife's protests, I walked back to the wolf, who was now on his feet and looking at Tundra, holding the dog's gaze. The confounded animal appeared to be challenging the dog now!

"Haven't you had enough yet!"

I spoke in a loud tone, fiercely, advancing on Wa threateningly, only half conscious of Joan's soft "*Oh no!*" She didn't understand. She thought that Wa would attack me again. I was quite sure that he wouldn't and that, although *I* was bluffing, *he* didn't know that. I was right. Before I had completed the first step toward him, Wa dropped his tail, averted his eyes, seeming to stare into space, and backed toward a corner of the kitchen, there to lie down. *Now* I could attend to the bites.

As is always the case with me, as soon as the crisis is past, reaction sets in. I felt shaky, he hands began to tremble, and my entire body seemed to be spastic. Walking toward the living room to sit down, I asked Joan to get the first-aid box from the bathroom. As I passed a wall mirror, I caught sight of my face. It was certainly gory looking. No wonder Joan had disgorged her supper!

Lumps of absorbent cotton soaked in alcohol soon removed the surplus gore and returned some semblance of humanity to face and arm. The eyebrow injury was a cut rather than a bite; one of Wa's tusks had evidently connected sideways, opening the skin. The wound was bloody, but not serious. The hand injury wasn't serious either. Wa had opened a cut about half an inch long on the knuckle of my right index. The forearm was another matter. One of his bottom fangs had punched a deep hole, but, somehow, the upper fangs had only scraped the skin. The puncture was on the underside, halfway between wrist and elbow. The scar is faded now, but I have a dimple to remind me of the scrap.

The bite of a carnivore is always a source of potential infection because of the bits of raw meat that may be adhering between the animal's teeth and because of bacteria in the saliva. Between us, Joan and I doused the injuries with alcohol, strong iodine, and, lastly, after I stopped cursing as the fiery disinfectant sank itself into the hole in my arm, sulfa powder was applied liberally and some Band-Aids covered the evidence. During all this, Wa, Matta, and Tundra attended, each seeking to get a taste of the nice red stuff, wagging their tails, behaving as though they were filled with concern. They weren't, of course; they were simply interested in the odor of my blood and gripped by a mild desire to sample some of it. I allowed them to remain nearby, but I decided that my system had enough germs to contend with without those that might be present on three canine tongues.

At one point during these proceedings Joan paused to address herself to my erstwhile opponent, telling him that she was "really ticked off" with him. He replied by wagging his tail and raking her thigh with a loving, but ungentle, paw the size of a saucer.

The first-aid manuals tell you that stimulants should not be administered to patients suffering from shock. Bosh! That must have been written by a medico who belonged to the Temperance Union. After a good, stiff Scotch, a pipeful of rank tobacco, and a relaxed sit in a comfortable chair surrounded by two wolves and a dog, I felt great. I even admitted that I had enjoyed the scrap.

Patting my "enemy's" big head—and perforce having to administer similar treatment to Matta and Tundra—I dressed for the outdoors, ignored Joan's protests, and took the canine trio for a brisk plunge in the snow, keeping to no trail and making sure that they had to expend a good deal of energy bounding through the shoulder-high drifts while I ambled along

195

on top with snowshoes. The moon was full, the night calm. It hadn't been a bad day, after all.

It has always been my practice to look for positive results after negative experiences, and although there are times when I am hard put to find the good that lies concealed in the bad, I know that it is possible to ferret it out if one but tries hard enough. It was even so after my altercation with Wa.

By the time that I returned home leading Tundra, after having left Matta and Wa in the evaporator house, I considered that the knowledge derived from experiencing hand-to-hand (hand-to-mouth?) combat with a wolf was worth the price I had paid. Beyond doubt, this proved that a fit man can get the better of a single wolf if driven to it, although he will certainly receive a number of injuries while doing so. It also proved, at least to my own satisfaction, that an unarmed man stands no chance at all against two wolves or more.

I was able to get the better of Wa while exercising some restraint, not wanting to kill him, but if Matta had also joined the fray, I could only have saved myself by using some sort of weapon; of this I felt sure. Pursuing this trend of thought, I remembered the wolf pack that had bluffed me after I had disturbed its members at their kill. There was no doubt that those big northern wolves could have killed me if they had decided to attack. Why didn't they? I don't really know. But I can offer a guess that may also account for the fact that wolves, despite their reputation to the contrary, do not readily attack humans.

It seems to me that such forbearance is bound up with the inherent caution of the predator. Just as they refrain from attacking a moose that stands at bay and will immediately seek to attack the same animal if it runs, so wolves back away from a human that does not run in panic from them. Added to this, perhaps, is the fact that man is not the natural prey of the wolf; he smells quite unlike any other animal upon which the wild dogs prey, and that fact alone may be regarded with suspicion. He is also built differently, and he carries on his person other alien odors besides his own: the smell of the material of his clothing; the scents of his tools, automobile, and many other subtle aromas that go unnoticed by humans but are quickly detected by the keen noses of the wild ones.

Would a pack of wolves attack a human who ran from it in panic? I don't know, and I do not propse to try to answer this question by experimentation! But, despite the many imaginative horror stories that seek to prove that *Canis lupus* is a man-killer, there are extremely few authenticated cases of such attacks available in North America, and the many such stories that have come out of Europe are so old and so impossible to investigate that most people who study wolves tend to view these tales with extreme skepticism.

Rabid wolves have been known to attack humans on our continent, but so have a variety of other rabid animals. It may well be that because rabies was prevalent in Europe in the days before Pasteur discovered a means of inoculating against the disease, wolves on that continent were frequent victims of hydrophobia and thus more likely to attack humans. However this may be, it is my opinion that the average human walking through a northern forest has less to fear from the wolves than he or she may have to fear from the neighbor's dog. And there is no lack of statistics to prove that people are frequently bitten by "friendly" dogs.

Joan was silent for some time after I returned with Tundra, but when I had finished entering details of the evening's scuffle in the wolf log, she spoke her mind. The gist of it was that though she was greatly attached to Matta and Wa, she was also afraid of what might happen if the wolves were allowed into the house again. What she said made sense and was based upon our commitment to raise the wolves as near to a wild state as possible. In this, she said, we had evidently succeeded to a point where the house was now almost alien territory to Matta and Wa. I didn't quite agree with her there, but she was still upset over the affair, and I saw no point in adding to her concerns. I agreed that the wolves should be kept out of our quarters from now on, although not because of her alien-territory theory.

I felt that there were too many temptations for the wolves within the confinement of the house, things that might cause them to explore, such as food, clothing, furniture, and rugs that they might decide to chew on; they were still young enough to chew in play, and if they "trespassed," I would have to control them, and another altercation could result. It is difficult enough to control a dog in these regards, but it is well-nigh impossible to prevent wolves from physically sampling those things that capture their interest, especially if the animals have been allowed full freedom elsewhere. It was wrong, I felt, to discipline Matta and Wa for doing what they had been designed to do: explore, taste, and investigate their environment. Far from alien, the house was a place that they knew well, but now that they were older and more daring, they would not limit themselves to tentative investigations. For these reasons, it would be better to keep them outside.

Once this question was disposed of, Joan went upstairs to bed, leaving me sitting before the fire. I had not mentioned it to her, but I was now convinced that the time had come to encourage Matta and Wa to return to their own world. They needed to be free and to be divorced from human influence. We would miss them, Wa in particular; like Joan, I had always favored him, probably because he had responded to me so soon, during the very first mouth-to-mouth feed, and because of his calm temperament. He was big and bluff and jolly, a *likable* animal, despite tonight's trouble. Matta, though I was fond of her also, was less trusting, more withdrawn, and, of course, excitable.

Before going to bed, I made up my mind to do all I could to encourage the wolves to leave us. Naturally, such a resolution was not calculated to produce a good night's sleep!

CHAPTER THIRTEEN

Following our fight, the relationship between Wa and myself continued as of old with one exception: I was now more cautious in my dealings with the wolves. As the alpha male of the pack, it was important that my behavior should reflect leadership and dominance, else Wa could well decide to have another go at overthrowing my rule; but my still-tender injuries reminded me that I had to be careful to avoid placing Wa in a position from which he could not retreat gracefully, otherwise I would risk a second confrontation.

It was not fear that prompted caution, but rather it was a deeper understanding of the wolves and of the finely balanced system that maintains lupine hierarchy. We were still good friends, we respected each other; and wolves and dog were quick to acknowledge the status that they themselves had thrust upon me from the beginning of our relationship. But I was now a better, more understanding leader, one who was aware that power should never be abused and who, in the absence of challenge, always respected the needs of his subordinates on a day-to-day basis. In this regard I was helped by the example set by Tundra in his dealings with Wa. The dog, as beta male, was clearly the boss, but, just as clearly, he was always careful to avoid overplaying his role now that the wolves were almost full grown.

Matta and Wa were now ten months old, and it was evident that the increase of daylight was causing them to be restless. Since my altercation with Wa, they had taken to spending more and more time away from the farm, running through the wilderness for a number of days, then returning to the sap house and resting up until they were ready for another trip. They continued to socialize with us, but to a more limited extent, though their relationship with Tundra had not altered. In this regard we had a great deal of difficulty keeping the dog at home, for he naturally wanted to run with Matta and Wa. The poor animal spent rather a lot of time either chained outside or in his outdoor pen, often howling plaintively. But it was necessary. He could not be allowed to go with the wolves. Should he do so, it was almost certain that he would not return; the three would go wild together and form their own pack.

Matta and Wa had become expert hunters. Rarely did they show interest in food when they returned from a foray, and a week before the maple sap began to run, I had decided not to feed them anymore, feeling sure that if they were not offered food, they would one day go away and not come back. Which was what we wanted, wasn't it?

Because of the restrictions that we placed upon Tundra, and because I now rarely accompanied Matta and Wa when they ran the wilderness, a slight change began to develop in the relationship between the dog and the wolves. Around the farm, Tundra quite definitely dominated Wa, but on the few occasions that I led the three of them for an outing around the property, I noticed that Wa usurped Tundra's place, becoming the beta male of the pack. It was a sort of division of power accomplished without rancor, as though each male recognized the position of the other within his own ambient; but it was impossible to know whether this would have continued in such an amicable way if the two males had gone on running together. After my own experience with Wa, I was inclined to think that he and Tundra would sooner or later have become involved in a status fight, but I would not have wanted to forecast its outcome. Both were powerful animals, and although Wa was longer and taller than Tundra, the dog outweighed the wolf, being more blocky in the body and having attained full adult growth. A battle between these two could go either way, and while the clinical part of me was curious about the outcome and would have welcomed the opportunity to witness such a contest, the rest of me recoiled from the idea of a fight between dog and wolf.

Soon after my bites healed, the weather moderated, and the signs outside reminded us that the time had come to make ready for the maple syrup season. The first task was to pound a way through the snow that clogged the pathways through the maple woods.

Early one morning during the second week of March I started the tractor and headed toward the evaporator house more involved with the task ahead than with thoughts of the wolves. I was not yet halfway to the building when Matta and Wa emerged from under it, gave the rowdy machine and me one quick glance, and then ran into the forest at full gallop. Knowing their aversion to mechanical noise, I paid little attention to their behavior, thinking that they would come back that evening or early next morning. But they stayed away. Three days later, when I was about halfway through the job, we were pretty well convinced that the wolves had gone for good, their departure triggered by the sudden and noisy invasion of their domain. But the job had to be done, and I carried on.

With an aluminum snowshovel clipped to one wing of the machine and a galloping malamute running alongside, I continued to attack the trails, chains affixed to the rear wheels. The tractor got stuck often, and then it was necessary for me to climb down, take the shovel, and manually clear the impeding, cloying snow from under the machine's differential housing; then climb back on the seat again and more path making, until we got stuck anew. It was active and sweat-making work, but not unpleasant, just slow. As a reward, I was able to pause now and then and to watch as spring gentled the woodlands, which now seemed full of bird songs.

When all the trails were made, Joan and I worked inside the sap house, where fifteen hundred pails had to be washed with water containing chlorine bleach to kill lingering bacteria, a like number of spiles had to be boiled and drained dry, and the enormous sap and syrup pans on top of the evaporator stoves had also to be washed and disinfected.

Much of the indoor work was accomplished by Joan while I was breaking trail, but the big pans—the largest being six feet square and eight inches deep—were too heavy for her to handle alone. When the trails were cut and all the equipment ready, the drilling of the trees followed. Ideally, if I had been able to hire labor, which I wasn't, the routine of this work would have proceeded in sequence; that is to say, while one or more workers were drilling the trees, the tractor would pull the wagon on which were piled the pails, spiles, and lids; the driver would stop at strategic locations and a gang of spile drivers would tap the spiggots into the trees while other workers would hang the pails on hooks fastened to the spiles, each of which was secured to its own lid.

With just the two of us, this work took a long time. While I drilled each tree—the big ones would take four spiles, the smallest, of a minimum twelve-inch diameter, would take one spile—Joan drove the tractor and kept hopping off to tap in the spiles. This work is delicate; each spile must be driven into the correctly angled hole only so far; put it in too deep, and it stops the flow of sap, too lightly, and the sap leaks around it. I finished hand-drilling fifteen hundred holes long before Joan managed to affix fifteen hundred spiles, so I now took over while she drove the tractor. When this job was done, it was back to the sap house to load pails on the wagon and to hang these on their hooks under each spile.

We worked like Trojans, leaving the house as the eastern sky showed the first traces of pink and returning when the west was similarly hued. Joan ached each night, her back, legs, and hands stiff from guiding the machine over bumpy, narrow trails. I arrived home every evening soaked to the waist from wading through deep, melting snow, my hands raw and peeling after prolonged contact with moisture and cold. But the days were glorious! Blue skies, big sun, crisp-cool in the forest shade, benignly warm outside of it. The raccoons were out and about at night; in daytime it was usual to see one or two sunning themselves high in a tree, like holidaymakers working on a suntan in Florida.

The sap flow was accelerating. The vital juices of the trees leaked out of those holes that were not yet fitted with spiles, dripping out steadily from those spiggots that were already affixed, tap-tapping into the hung pails; this rhythm changed as the little buckets began to fill.

In the end, as the sap rose to flow in full spate and the pails started to fill rapidly, we were exhausted, but very, very satisfied. It took us an entire week to get ready. Now we had to start gathering sap; later we would begin to boil it, to evaporate the water until only the thick, golden syrup remained, reducing the volume of forty-five gallons of sap in order to distill one gallon of syrup.

On a platform covered by a lean-to roof adjoining the evaporator house stood three one-thousand-gallon holding tanks, each connected to the other by two-inch pipes equipped with shut off valves; the last tank fed the evaporator boiling pans by means of a metal tank in which were fitted a float and a valve rather like those used in a toilet tank. By this means the evaporator pans were kept full against the constant loss of sap water, which rose in billowing clouds of steam.

For three days Joan drove the tractor and the long flatbed wagon, on top of which was secured a two-hundred-gallon tank. My job was to struggle through the snow with two five-gallon gathering buckets into which I tipped the contents of each tree's pails, then trudged back to empty the gathered sap into the tank. When this was full, we returned to the sap house and piped the contents into the holding tanks. In due course came the tricky part.

When the first holding tank brimmed with one thousand gallons, I lit the evaporator fire, feeling like Satan stoking the furnaces of Hell. The firebox was eighteen feet long and six feet wide; I fed it logs, previously gathered, farm wood debris, old split-rail fences—anything that would burn! I forget how long it took from the first stoking to the first pouring off of the hot, marvelous-tasting maple syrup, but it was some hours. While the boiling was going on, the tall chimney stack belched smoke continuously and steam escaped from special hatches high up along the eaves of the building, filling the air with its shimmering whiteness and permeating our world with that wonderful smell of cooking maple sap.

As soon as the fire was burning well, we returned to the woods, for by now the pails had to be emptied twice a day. Then, when the first sap was poured from the syrup pan—the last one in a row of five—and the first hot, golden harvest was sampled for quality (a needless task, but done every time we "poured off" because there is nothing more wonderful than maple syrup tasted just at the ready), the furnace was restoked and I would leave Joan in charge of the mammoth cookstove while I went to gather more sap.

So we worked, nonstop for three weeks, having little time to dwell on the departed wolves during the hours of work and being too tired to think when we at last went to bed at night. For now that the boiling had started, the process was continued halfway through the night in order to use up as much of the sap from the holding tanks as possible while the night frost arrested the flow from the trees. I think we averaged about three hours' sleep each night. But the job was done at last.

The syrup was put into pint, half-gallon, and gallon tins, labeled with our own colorful imprints, and stacked, waiting for customers. And . . . all the pails, spiles, and lids had to be collected, washed, and stacked ready for next year! By the time all this was done, it was mid-April and spring had arrived.

Spring . . . how little a word to describe so marvelous a season! Consider the maple woods at North Star Farm toward the end of the third week of April . . .

The trees were bursting with sap that stained the branches a pale saffron color and imparted to the new and tender buds a deep magenta hue. Row upon row of trees, suddenly transformed, actually gained strength and growth as we watched them. And the forest floor . . . grassy or shrubby between the big trunks, but here and there decorated by patches of moss, some of it growing on rotting logs, some adhering to large, gray-granite boulders. Shooting up out of the grass were thousands of broad, apple green leaves with tips shaped like lance points; these were the wild leeks, offering themselves for the picking, not just to us but to many animals of the forest, especially the bears, who loved their piquant taste. The forest smelled like a vast, green salad dressed with the recipe of a cordon bleu chef.

In sunny places grew carpets of delicate hepaticas, little flowers standing guardsman-straight on thin, furry stems, so anxious to sample the sun and the air of spring that they all popped up ahead of their leaves. Beneath each floret last year's dead foliage clung to the grasses, each veined and toned like flakes of bloodless liver; from this unlovely concept the dainty flower takes its official name. But if the name is inelegant, the little blooms more than make up for it; they come in pink, white, blue, and lavender shades, each as delicate and beautiful as the other.

In more shaded places were to be found bursts of columbine, the flowers resembling tiny scarlet jesters' caps with yellow centers; they glowed against the more somber, but no less beautiful, greens and browns of the woods. In many locations, particularly along the pathways, uncountable maple seedlings tinted the understory with their plum-red shoots and stems, delicate little treelets, some but thread-thin stems supporting a tiny pair of opening buds, others two or three years old and already making proper branches and showing enough buds to forecast a cloak of leaves later on. Among these seedlings showed patches of stubborn snow, melting reluctantly and making small tinkling sounds as the massed ice crystals compacted and shifted, spasmodic music that complemented the husky song of small, golden bees that flitted through the air in quest of honeydew.

The big Canada geese had already passed over on their way north, shrilling their return. And the ducks were back, the iridescent mallard drake and his modest mate, the rainbow-colored wood ducks with their reedy voices, and the whistle-winged teal. These came in bunches, perhaps four or six or eight, perhaps only a pair of each, our spring waterfowl who nested in the slews and ponds of the farm and who were not afraid of us.

Standing on the outer edge of the maples, beside the clearing from where the distant tamarack swamp could be seen, I happened to look up as a pair of black ducks gossiped overhead, and I was in time to see the sleek lines of a gyrfalcon heading for the distant north: a white gyr, beautiful, its pointed wings scudding rhythmically and effortlessly. I focused the glasses on the bird and watched it spiral, climbing higher and higher until at last it disappeared in the magnitude of blue sky.

On such a lovely spring day one ought to feel elation, contentment, but though Joan and I took pleasure from this now benign and beautiful environment, we could not help feeling somewhat downcast, for Matta and Wa had left us some four weeks earlier, and we both felt sure that we would never see them again.

One may feel nostalgia on a spring day like this one in such a place as our maple woods; one may feel happy, content, stimulated. But I cannot imagine anyone feeling sad. But Joan was sad, for she missed the wolves; and well ... perhaps so was I, a little.

Behind me, just inside the maples, my wife was gathering young leeks to add to the basket in which she already carried a small bunch of hepaticas. There were literally thousands of these bright little flowers in our woods, but Joan only allowed herself to pick one small bunch each spring, preferring to leave the majority of them to grace the landscape and to multiply more profusely next year. Lying beside my wife, in the shade, was Tundra, his long fur already starting to molt and now hanging in untidy hanks, soft wool that we would pick off and save with the intention, someday, of spinning it and knitting something from it.

Watching Joan harvesting her wild onions and realizing that we had both been rather silent since breakfast, each distressed by the success of our plan to encourage the wolves to leave home, my feelings were mixed. I felt relief at the prospect of returning to a more normal way of life—the coming of Matta and Wa had most certainly upset the tenor of my ways for almost an entire year—and I felt depressed because the wolves were gone. Joan was probably gripped by similar sentiments. But I wasn't so sure about Tundra; it now seemed as though he might be content to be the only canine at North Star Farm, happy that he no longer had to compete for our attention and affection. During the four weeks that the wolves had gone, he showed little desire to run off on his own, and he stayed particularly close to Joan.

At any other time of the year the departure of our wolves would have weighed more heavily on us (as it was to do later), but in the face of the beauties of spring, our depression was tempered by the wonderful rhythms of new life. Walking quietly through the budding woods, we reacquainted ourselves with many of our old friends. Scruffy came for his seeds and peanuts. One Ear arrived at the feeder. Herself, the old female raccoon who I suspected had a permanent springtime tryst with One Ear, arrived, showing by her swollen, milk-tipped dugs that she had again delivered herself of a litter of little masked ones. The yearling deer emerged from wherever it had wintered, sleek and red-coated and quite safe, removing one of our major worries, for we had feared that Matta and Wa might have killed it long since.

Later, sated with the peace and the many miracles of spring, we began consciously to fret over our wolves. We didn't discuss our worries much, but each knew the cause of the other's preoccupation. We didn't have to talk to know that we both shared the same hope, contradictory though it might be: We hoped that Matta and Wa would come back, even if only for a brief visit. It may seem foolish, but we hadn't said good-bye to them before they left!

It is one thing to know that one's emotional wants are impracticable, even undesirable in the long run; it is quite another to think "sensibly" and to be satisfied with the results of such thought. We had raised our wolves, equipped them in such a way that they could now survive in the wild without us; they had attained independence. That was what we had set out to do and what we had told ourselves we really wanted. *Ha!* What we really wanted was to have big, placid Wa and nervous, excitable Matta back with us, to see them as they raced lithely through the woods, to hear them howl their forlorn and haunting songs, to look again into those yellow, intelligent, sparkling eyes, and to see the big wolf grins on their faces.

For my part, aware of the dangers that Matta and Wa faced, I worried a great deal. I was engaged in such fretting a few days after we had strolled through the woods in admiration of the new season, when Joan suggested that we might go for another walk. I agreed at once, knowing that she was hoping to meet Matta and Wa on their way home, though she said she wanted to walk to one of our sloughs to see how many pairs of ducks were nesting there this year.

We strolled along silently, while Tundra, now on his lead, paced beside me, sniffing at the awakening forest and occasionally biting his trailing leather lead, inviting me to play with him. But I was in no mood to play as I reviewed the diseases, parasites, and possible injuries that might already have killed our wolves. And there were the traps of man. Three of our neighbors ran traplines in the wilderness around our farm, the price of wolf fur was up, and the bounty was still being paid; the trappers always set wolf traps, cruel jaws waiting in strategic places for wolf, coyote, or fox to step into. The thought of either Matta or Wa getting caught in this way was abhorrent,

207

and now I found myself hoping more than ever that they would return. If they did, I promised myself, I would lead them far into the wilderness, right away from the haunts of my own kind, where the dangers that they would have to face would all be natural.

It was ironic that now that they had gone I should find myself worrying about the dangers that they must face away from the farm. Despite the fact that I still believed the perils of the wild were preferable to the comforts of unnatural captivity, I had not reckoned with the presence of trappers within their domain. Given a choice of freeing them to die in a leghold trap, or keeping them as pets, I knew that I would accept the second alternative. But I had little choice in the matter just then.

Six days later, during the evening of May 18, the wolves came home, pausing within the maple woods on their return to howl a greeting. We should have known before we heard the howls, for Tundra had shown unusual restlessness for some fifteen minutes, but we had ignored him. Now, when the mournful calls floated through our open windows, all three of us became galvanized. Tundra would have leaped through the kitchen window had I not restrained him, and Joan almost fell as she rushed toward the door. By the time we emerged outside the house, Matta and Wa were galloping toward us across the clearing that separated house from maples. Our reunion was exuberant and lengthy, beginning as a press of five bodies and ending when three canines ganged up on Joan, knocking her down and licking her as she had never been licked before. While this was going on, I slipped back into the house, found three very large beef bones in the freezer, and took them outside. Three sets of very keen nostrils picked up the aroma of raw beef almost as soon as I cleared the porch doorway, and Joan was abandoned as the trio came charging toward me. Wa was leading, so I tossed him the first bone, which he fielded in midair. Tundra got the second in like manner, and Matta accepted hers from my hand.

Later that evening, while the wolves socialized with Tundra inside the porch and Joan and I sat sipping coffee before an unnecessary but merry fire, my wife opined that the wolves had returned home to us "as though they wanted to celebrate their birthday." In any event, they had been absent for almost two months, and whatever their reason for coming home, they were more than welcome!

Two miles from our farmhouse as the raven flies, but perhaps three and one-half over bush trails, there is a lake that is hidden enough to be private, large enough to allow for some good fishing, and small enough to prevent float-equipped aircraft from landing on it. This place was a favorite of mine, and even Joan liked it after she got there, but she wasn't enthusiastic about penetrating the heavy wilderness in order to share my piscatorial pleasure.

On May 25 Joan dared the bush journey to accompany me to the lake. Now, under blue skies, with a small breeze stirring the trees and a warm sun gladdening the land, she sat by my side as I fished languidly, not caring whether one of the fat perch that inhabited the slightly brown waters came in quest of the small spoon I was using. Surrounding the two of us were the wolves and Tundra.

Wa lay beside Joan, his big head on her lap; his eyes were closed and the very tip of his tongue stuck out between his lips, as though he wanted to lick her but was really too comfortable to make the effort; Matta, more independent, sprawled upside down near my right side; Tundra, jealous, lay between us, eyeing my movements as I cast the lure or retrieved it. A few blackflies had already come to sample our juices—nasty little brutes! Mosquitoes buzzed around, but were still slow and easy to swat. High above, sailing magnificently through the blue sky, five turkey vultures scanned the wilderness, seeking carrion.

Near where I was sitting a young spruce had fallen down during the winter. It was a tree about twenty-five feet tall, healthy looking but evidently unseated from its tenuous hold on an outcrop of rock. Inside the thickest part of the already yellowing foliage a female catbird sat on three green eggs, while her spouse, made nervous by our presence, kept up a continuous mewling, first in one bush, then in another, quickly flitting into the concealment of a treetop. On the far shore, at a respectful distance from our wolves, but unafraid, a buck deer was drinking, stopping to look our way now and then, its big ears constantly on the move. Only Tundra showed interest;

the wolves, well fed, were more concerned with relaxing in comfort and in company. I held the dog's collar as the buck turned around and reentered the forest.

I was quite accustomed to the confidence displayed by prey animals when they detect the presence of sated predators, yet the sight never failed to fill me with wonder. The deer, a young buck in his prime who was already sprouting twin, velvet-covered knobs on his head to replace the antlers shed last autumn, was well aware of our presence, and his keen nose must have picked up the smell of the wolves, but he was not afraid. He came to drink, visually checked our group over, smelled us, then stooped to quench his thirst. In just such a way had I seen zebra and other grazers stroll up to a water hole in Africa while a pride of well-fed lions lounged nearby. The prey animals know when the hunter is hungry and when he is not: They read the signs. Hunger sparks aggression, which in turn puts tension in the body as the adrenaline flows; and there is scent, the exudation from the chemicals that the endocrine glands shoot into the bloodstream to prepare the organism for physical action: Wild senses are too keen to miss these things.

Our wolves had been home one week and had been content to stay with us, showing no desire to wander now that I was feeding them again, a decision I had made the evening of their return because I knew that at this time of the year the area around our farm was full of young inexperienced animals that would be easy prey for Matta and Wa. We didn't want the wolves to kill so close to home. So, having a plentiful supply of beaver meat in the freezer, I allowed them to eat as much as they wanted, making them lazy and much less likely to be tempted to run the wildwood in quest of prey.

When they came back after their long absence, and after the excitement of our meeting had died down, I was gratified to note that except for molting and somewhat matted fur, a normal event at this time, both wolves were in top condition. They carried a number of fleas and ticks, of course, but that was to be expected. I also noted that Wa was marked by a couple of recently healed scars; one was on his shoulder, the other on his head, relatively minor injuries that may have been inflicted while hunting or even during a meeting with one of the wild packs, perhaps Lobo's crew. Both wolves were lean, but then, I have never seen a *fat* wolf, nor, indeed, any obese wild animal with the exception of raccoons and bears, who lard up in summer and autumn as a preparation for their long winter's sleep.

Since their return, both wolves had remained more aloof from us, seeking our company when *they* were ready for it, like now, but otherwise responding to us only with a tail wag or two, and a big grin! If we sought to pat them, they avoided our hands, but they were otherwise companionable enough and would follow us if we passed the evaporator house while going for a walk—as they had done today.

During the hours of daylight, when not with us, they would lie beneath the sap house floor, coming out in late evening and trotting to the house looking for their meal. Tundra always told us when they were on their way, and by the time they arrived outside, I would already have started preparing their meal.

Perhaps the major change in their behavior pattern since their return was the way in which they avoided coming near the house during daylight; and they only rarely entered the porch, even at night, to socialize with Tundra. Now, too, they backed away from the house when I opened the door, coming toward me only when they had made sure of my identity and were aware that I carried their food. If, as happened occasionally, the radio was on inside the house, Matta and Wa would not approach the building. I was pleased by their caution: If they behaved in this manner with us, how much more secretive would they be when they detected strangers?

When they had been home for a couple of days, the wolves took to howling during the night. Their voices always elicited a reply from Tundra, and sometimes even Lobo's pack (as I believe it was) would answer from within the wilderness. The nightly serenade lasted a long time, and it was loud. It worried me because it advertised the presence of Matta and Wa to our neighbors.

After the third such concerto, while I was in the village to collect our mail, I was approached by three of the local farmers, who had heard the wolves, were concerned, and were even then suggesting that a wolf posse be formed to "hunt down the varmints." As my stomach did a fast butterfly flip, I made myself laugh aloud at the would-be wolfers, explaining that it was Tundra, made restless by the annual spring urges experienced by so many dogs, giving vent to his unrequited passions

211

during the night. Appealing to their fondness for off-color jokes, I gilded the lily somewhat, thereby giving Tundra a reputation that he did not deserve. But I managed to quash the posse passions.

Nevertheless, I was anxious that night, fearing a repeat performance by the wolves. To minimize the noise, I brought Tundra into the house and made him sleep in our bedroom, where I could shut him up the moment he opened his mouth. Contrary as usual, the wolves remained silent; only occasionally after that did they sing their duets.

When Joan and I set out for the small lake accompanied by our canines, I suggested that we pack a lunch, remain beside the water until two o'clock, and then, while Joan went home leading Tundra, I would take the wolves for a long walk, thinking that this might keep them quiet at night for a little longer. But after we had eaten sandwiches, the wolves and Tundra had chewed a bone apiece, and we had sipped our coffee, Joan decided she wanted to stay where she was for the whole afternoon, and I readily agreed, loath to end the peaceful, enjoyable interlude. This plan evidently also appealed to our wolves and dog; they all sprawled, dozing, the picture of sloth. But I decided that I would take Matta and Wa for a long walk on the morrow.

Next morning Tundra galloped upstairs to tell me that Matta and Wa were outside. It was dawn, the roseate east held promise of another fine, warm day. Remembering my decision of yesterday, I arose, had a fast shower while the coffee was brewing, then took a cup to my sleepy wife. I told her I'd grab a bite, put Tundra inside after he'd greeted his friends and watered the plants, and take Matta and Wa for their postponed walk in the wilderness. We would be back at suppertime.

Accompanied by Tundra's long-drawn-out laments and by the much closer ululation of the two wolves, I walked briskly toward East Ridge, applying mosquito and blackfly repellent as I went—but out of the bottle, not out of those deadly aerosol cans. By the time the dog's howls faded, we were going along the top of the ridge, heading for the flat country beyond.

At first Matta and Wa were content to walk behind me; presently they drew ahead, but stayed close, sniffing and listening and occasionally sticking their noses into a groundhog

212

or chipmunk hole, there to sniff and to push down hard, but, of course, coming away empty mouthed. Some time later, it may have been half an hour, the two wolves began to trot, but their actions suggested that they were not following a particular scent. Soon they disappeared, and presently I could no longer hear the noise of their going. I sat down near the first beaver dam on a convenient rock that was nicely warm from the sun. A beaver was circling the pond; perhaps it had been disturbed by the wolves. Once again I was reminded that beaver are not as nocturnal as they are made out to be and that, like most other animals, hunger, or even boredom, will cause them to alter their mode of behavior, so that they frequently emerge during broad daylight to swim about on the surface of their pond or to feed on tender water plants in the shallows. From where I sat, I could see fresh wolf tracks crossing the muddy dam, almost certainly made by Matta and Wa.

Noon found me still walking through the wilderness and wondering if Matta and Wa would return to me before I retraced my route home. I had no idea where they were now because the ground was covered in vegetation, in which it was impossible to track a soft-footed animal like the wolf. But I was enjoying my solo outing and was in no particular hurry to return home.

At one place, beside the trunk of a downed spruce tree, I found the remains of a snowshoe hare, little more than bits of skin and fur and some red-brown staining on the foliage to show where blood had spattered. It was a recent kill, an hour or so old, according to the evidence: The skin was still supple and moist to the feel, and my fingers came away stained when I touched one of the blood spots. I didn't think that Matta and Wa had done this; they might have, of course, but I was inclined to think that a fox had satisfied its hunger with the hare.

During late afternoon I turned around to go home. I had neither seen nor heard Matta and Wa since they left me, and I couldn't help wondering if they would return. And that, of course, was the first question put to me by my wife when I entered the house in early evening.

On a Sunday morning in June two weeks after Matta and Wa had left me during our walk, I told Joan that I was going to take Tundra for a walk, and she elected to come with us. It

213

was toward the end of the first week of the month, and the blackfly season was over for another year; this was probably why Joan volunteered to come, for the pesky little bloodsuckers always managed to raise great welts with purple centers on my wife's skin. There were mosquitoes, of course, but by now both of us were pretty well immune to their stings, having been punctured by these pests so many times during the years that the anticoagulating agent they inject into the wound to dilute the blood no longer set up a reaction. Nevertheless, we were both coated with Off as we walked, and we kept our heads covered against the advance of deerflies, which so enjoy crawling into the hair and sinking their stingers into the scalp.

Avoiding East Ridge with its heavy foliage, we kept to our own clearings until we came to the end of our property, then cut through a patch of second-growth maples to emerge at the beaver pond beside which I had rested after the wolves went off on their own. Tundra appeared to be backtracking his friends, but the trail was so old that he soon lost interest, preferring instead to dive headlong into the water when a black duck drake hove into view; the squawking bird raced away, feet paddling for some seconds until it gained height. Tundra, now that he was wet, swam to the other side of the pond while we walked over the dam. The dog just *had* to come and greet us as we stepped onto the shore—after all, a whole minute must have passed since he left us! We tried to avoid it, but even though we were expecting it, we both became soaked when Tundra shook his fur vigorously, ridding himself of about five gallons of water, or so it seemed.

Tundra was about to indulge in a second shake, and Joan and I were seeking to put distance between ourselves and the next shower, when the dog stopped, turned around quickly, head held high, and suddenly dashed away, aiming for a clump of evergreens about two hundred feet distant. Joan and I looked at each other; as it transpired later, we thought the same thing at the same time: The wolves were coming. And so they were!

The noise of their galloping feet reached us a few seconds before they emerged from the evergreens. First came Wa, running stretched out, head high and ears forward, that well-known grin on his lips; Matta was close behind her brother, holding a similar pose but smiling more demurely. Tundra went to meet them. So did my wife.

214

Joan ran ahead of me, and when she was within ten feet of the trio, she squatted and opened her arms wide, as had been her habit of greeting the wolves when they were younger and was still her habit when welcoming Tundra. Moments later she was the center of a melee of excited canines, but Tundra, perhaps feeling left out of things as Joan petted first Matta and then Wa, moved away from the crush and trotted back toward me as I slowly strolled toward the scene of activity.

I was watching with considerable interest, a smile on my lips, pleased that the wolves were back, when I noticed that Wa edged into his sister, moving her to one side; as though impatient with the gentle shoving, he suddenly pushed hard against Matta's shoulder. The bitch wolf seemed to understand the portent of her brother's behavior, for she moved around Joan, pressing against her back while my wife looked at Wa with beaming face, holding both wide-open hands in front of her and about to reach out to pull him closer. Wa retreated half a step, arched his spine, and gave a small cough, more like a muffled hiccup. Too late I opened my mouth to call out a warning!

Before Joan could realize what the wolf was intending, Wa opened wide his mouth and dumped into her hands and lap a great load of partly digested meat; red beaver meat, warm and steaming from his stomach; slimy meat, smelling of gore and stomach acid. What a pity that Wa's unselfish act, intended to show his affection for Joan and to prove to her that he was so pleased to see her that he was willing to share the kill with her, had such a shocking effect on my wife! What a pity that I can never seem to control my mirth at moments when discretion is more recommended than levity!

I felt for my wife, of course; I sympathized with her a lot, for I had often been at the receiving end of just such devotional kindness. But to see her face as she stared down in unbelieving horror at the gory red lumps and the slimy juices that had come to rest in her hands and over her stretched skirt (of course, this *had* to be one of those days when she had worn a skirt rather than the usual jeans because, as she had explained, she wanted to get her legs tanned!) was just too much for my sense of humor. I laughed until my sides ached and the tears came into my eyes. But when the tears appeared in Joan's eyes, the affair ceased to be funny, and I became the contrite and helpful husband, even to the point of removing my shirt, dashing to the beaver pond, soaking it, and running back to mop up.

By the time we returned to the house and Joan had plunged herself into a bath reeking of scented salts, I was more or less forgiven. When she emerged garbed in a shocking-pink terry towel robe and saw the deerfly bites on my back and chest and neck, which caused me to look as though I had contracted a sudden and severe case of smallpox, she actually thawed enough to anoint me with her pet concoction for bites, which never did a damned bit of good, but which I endured because it was politic to do so. Wa wasn't so easily forgiven, but by then he was ensconced under the floor of the evaporator house, no doubt sleeping the sleep of the just. Removing my shirt in order to clean Joan up with it, thus exposing myself to the flies, had earned for me an early pardon!

CHAPTER FOURTEEN

It was the end of July, Matta and Wa were now fourteen months old, and they were still with us. Indeed, it was starting to look as though they were intending to make the wilderness around our property part of their territory and the farm itself their headquarters. Joan and I viewed this possibility with mixed feelings; on the one hand, we were happy to see the wolves regularly and to know they were in good condition, but we worried about them a great deal because the forests within a day's journey of our property were not safe for them, including as they did the trapping areas of three local farmers as well as being filled with hunters each autumn.

The wolves were far from being domestic pets by this point in their lives. To the contrary, they went when and where they pleased, but were always glad to see us on their return, wagging their tails and grinning as usual, though they would not allow themselves to be petted, and they would not enter the house or any other building on the farm, not even the evaporator house, in which they had practically grown up.

They were completely independent of us and well able to earn their own living in the wilderness, but there seemed to be some lingering, emotional pull that caused them to return regularly and to stay for periods that varied from a couple of days to a week and more. When "in residence," they slept during daylight in any one of various selected places within the forests that surrounded our property, coming to visit us during the evening or in the early morning. Sometimes they would turn up in broad daylight and stay for an hour or two, always lying in the open, but upon the highest land, which usually was the area immediately opposite the house or a place near the evaporator building.

The relationship between Tundra and the wolves continued more or less the same; Wa and the dog respected each other and were careful not to intrude in ways that might force a confrontation. Within the neighborhood of the house and buildings, Tundra retained his beta status but didn't force any issues. Beyond the boundaries of the farm proper, such as within the maples, Wa usually took the lead, but he, too, refrained from placing the dog in a position from which he could not retreat gracefully. The two were good friends who maintained their relationship on a basis of neutrality rather than equality. Matta, however, continued to be subservient to both the males, except during those occasions when she was the unwilling recipient of their sexual advances; at such times she would turn on either Wa or Tundra with equal fury. But even in her case, the males did not seek to become tyrannical; they played the part of leaders rather than despots. All in all, it was a carefully balanced pack relationship that the trio maintained, giving me a glimpse of the social hierarchy that exists among members of a wild pack.

As the summer developed, Matta and Wa would often usefully employ themselves hunting groundhogs around the farm, committing themselves wholeheartedly to the task and thereby winning our praises.

Taken individually, groundhogs are interesting and even remarkable rodents that are quick of wit and tough enough to survive in an environment where every hunting animal is forever seeking their scalp. In many ways, the groundhog is to the wilderness what the neighborhood "convenience store" is to the city: open at all hours and forever available when forgetfulness or unexpected guests create a shortage in the larder.

Hawks, owls, eagles, foxes, weasels, wolves, dogs, cats, and man are constantly trying to get the better of the lowly woodchuck; and they have all been doing so for a considerable amount of time. Yet the 'chuck survives wherever there is a blade or two of grass, some tender, kitchen-garden vegetables, or a bush or two with sprouting leaves and buds.

The groundhog population around our farm had been a source of concern to us ever since we moved in. The critters had been given the run of the place by the former owner, an octogenarian who grew no crops and who turned a deaf ear, metaphorically *and* physically, when his septuagenarian wife complained that the woodchucks were devastating her meager vegetable patch and consuming her lovingly tended flowers with relish. Faced by such justifiable laments, Ernie would switch off his hearing aid and deliver himself of a homily, the theme of which sought to establish the right of all creatures to a place in the sun on a more or less permanent basis—that is to say, I *think* that was its theme, though after listening to the first version and having been treated to a number of playbacks during the weeks that preceded the conclusion of our real estate deal, I am not entirely certain. Sometimes I was led to believe that it was Ernie's place in the sun that was under discussion, not the woodchuck's, such a view gaining support when the ancient would catch sight of a red squirrel stuffing seeds into its face in the one and only bird feeder that the old gentleman had affixed to a post some twenty paces from the back door. Ernie, it seemed hated red squirrels. The sight of one of the breed would cause him to reach for an aged .22 rifle and to stump over to the window. If the casement was conveniently open, the rifle would be aligned and would soon go bang; if the window was closed, it would be opened quietly before the trigger was squeezed. The squirrel always escaped unscathed, but the wall of the evaporator house across the way would collect a new hole.

As a result of Ernie's views, the resident population of 'chucks prospered, while vegetables and flowers didn't. We took over the farm in early spring and were at first too busy to notice the army of fat, brown woodchucks that watched us from every conceivable hiding place.

Came planting time, I worked hard during the height of the blackfly season to rototill a patch of good soil for Joan's kitchen garden, and she, full of the urge to grow things, spent many hours putting in tiny seeds. Then we stood back and waited for the stuff to show. And it did! Rows of light green, tender lettuce, purply green beet tops, pea vines, and other succulents began to decorate the dark earth. In the flower beds emerged petunias and sweet peas and all manner of other lovely plants. And then we woke up one morning and found that this host of edibles and decoratives had been wiped out; it was as though a giant vacuum cleaner had been passed over the earth and had sucked up each and every one of them. But, wait . . . down at the bottom of the vegetable garden survived half a row of lettuce; about two inches high, each little salad-to-be basking bravely in the sun. Well, we would have at least *something* for our efforts! With chicken wires and stakes I enclosed the lettuce with great care and set the alarm for 5 A. M. that night so as to rise early and stand guard over the survivors.

When I was roused next morning, it was still dark. I got a flashlight and went to examine our garden. All was well, each little lettuce glistened with gentle dew, standing proudly. Back in the house, I made coffee, watched the sun come up, and had almost made up my mind to return to bed when I went to look out of the window. Marching resolutely up our precious row of lettuce was the biggest groundhog I have ever seen, a roly-poly eating machine that was chomping lettuce at the same rate that its short legs were moving it forward. Behind the raider the wire fence had been casually breached in one place.

That was how the North Star Farm Woodchuck War was declared.

At first it was a shooting war, but it soon became evident that three-score-and-ten years would not be long enough for the job at hand if one depended on sharpshooting. There were too many targets, every one of which was just too elusive. Some successes were logged, but not nearly enough. Traps were tried next, the humane kind that caught the raiders alive; but then the varmints had to be carried far into the wilderness and released—and I am sure they returned home ahead of me! Okay, then, I'd try killing traps. A few scores were made. But new woodchucks seemed to arrive to make up for the casualties. I didn't have a hearing aid, but I found my own way to "pull an Ernie," as Joan used to say. *My* homily had a simple theme: "The damned things are impossible to kill!"

Then we got our secret weapon: Tundra. It took time to develop the missile, of course, but when he was six months old, he brought home the first cadaver. From then on, at least in the immediate area of the house, the woodchuck population began to decrease, slowly, it is true, but decrease it did. Finally, when I was no longer thinking about the groundhog problem, finding it cheaper to buy vegetables and more rewarding to bring home flowers for my wife, Matta and Wa arrived.

By the end of their second July at the farm, the groundhog population was under control. Oh sure, a few guerrillas hung on in strategic areas, but the attacking *army* was no more. Where Tundra was proficient as a woodchuck exterminator, Matta and Wa were *superb*. To watch them as they stalked, ambushed, or ran down this elusive quarry was an education in itself. They hunted solo, each selecting a different target and employing the technique best suited to the scene of the action.

The groundhog's Achilles' heel is its voracious appetite; even those of the tribe that have found for themselves veritable fortresses, such as large stone piles in a field, must emerge in order to eat, and the longer they live in the same place, the farther they must travel to find food, for they soon exhaust available green stuff in the immediate vicinity of their dens. Predators, especially experienced ones, as Matta and Wa now were, soon learn the habits of their quarry, and this knowledge, augmented by their fine senses, enables them to plan the strategy most likely to result in a kill.

The wolves employed a variety of tactics to suit a variety of habitats, but most often they would lie in wait until a groundhog emerged, checked his neighborhood for enemies, concluded that the coast was clear (incorrectly, as it usually turned out), and waddled along regular pathways to a feeding area. As a rule the wolves would wait until their quarry was far from the safety of rock pile or burrow, then they would charge, grab the fleeing rodent by the back of the neck, and give it one mighty shake, snapping the vertebrae. The dead prize would then be carried into the shelter of the woods and consumed. Joan, always a "softy" in such matters, eventually admitted that Matta and Wa killed swiftly and cleanly; she even went so far as to claim that the methods used by the wolves were superior and more humane than those that I had used. And she was right! In open country, overpopulated by rodents, wild hunters are much more efficient than human nimrods; and when they catch up to the quarry, they kill quickly, without wounding.

During that summer, Joan and I were busy remodeling the

old farmhouse as well as clearing up a plethora of debris that had accumulated outside and inside the house during the years that the place had been settled. Today, with the antique craze that has swept over North America, I realize that I hauled away a fortune to the garbage dump, but at the time, I was not enthusiastic about old pine furniture, ancient wagon wheels, and other, assorted artifacts left over from the nineteenth century. It was just junk to be laboriously loaded into the back of the pickup truck and hauled to the dump. Meanwhile, I was devoting a lot more attention to the affairs of the newspaper that I was supposed to be running, while also trying to complete a new book. When there was time left over and opportunity presented itself, I greatly enjoyed walking with Matta and Wa through the wilderness, and the wolves, for their part, seemed to like my company. Thus did the summer wax and wane. It was a busy but satisfying time, during which neither Joan nor I discussed the future of Matta and Wa. Both of us worried about them, but neither one of us wanted to make a decision that would upset our relationship with the wolves.

Tundra was getting to be a little bit of a problem by the time that autumn came. He was beginning to show jealousy whenever the wolves were at home, and fearing an altercation between him and Wa, I kept him either on his chain or in his pen more and more often, though I made sure that he and I went for a walk morning and evening.

The dog would be put on his lead at such times, but he clearly enjoyed getting my undivided attention, especially in view of the fact that on those occasions when one of his walks coincided with the presence of Matta and Wa, the wolves did not try to come with us. I puzzled over this, seeking scientific explanations for the anomaly: Why should Matta and Wa be ready to walk with me alone but now refuse to go with me and Tundra? Joan, not burdened with scientific concepts, had a simple and ready explanation. She claimed that the wolves didn't like the lead, that they could sense Tundra's "imprisonment," and that it made them uncomfortable. Maybe she was right; and perhaps one shouldn't seek to probe too deeply into such things. The fact remained, however, that Tundra could not be allowed to run with the wolves and that on this account I was forced to curtail his freedom, even though this was done with regret.

By the time that the autumnal burst of color had come and gone and winter advertised its imminent arrival with a few snow flurries, the future of Matta and Wa began to intrude on my thoughts with increasing regularity. I knew what had to be done, but I kept finding all kinds of excuses for not doing it, and since Joan didn't raise the subject either, it was obvious that she was also guilty of at least equal procrastination. Then came a letter from my wife's parents containing an invitation to spend Christmas with them in Manitoba; it was more of a plea, really, and, in truth, it made us feel guilty, for we had not visited them for a considerable time. Now they were organizing a family affair (something I frankly *hate*), and it seemed that we must go. And we could neither take Matta and Wa with us nor abandon them at the farm.

It was getting toward the end of November when the letter came; we talked about it, got nowhere, postponed a decision. At last, on December 3, following a long-distance call from Joan's mother, I determined to act. Matta and Wa were in residence at the time, having spent the best part of two weeks on or around the farm; but now, for some unknown reason, they had once again elected to sleep inside the sap house—not because of any desire for shelter, certainly, because an empty building retains and builds up cold and is thus more inclement than the shelter of an evergreen forest. The wolves also hung about outside the house and managed to work on Joan's sympathies to such an extent that she fed them when I wasn't at home, a fact that didn't emerge until after they had finally been returned to the wilderness, but for which Joan received a thorough and well-deserved scolding. No wonder they stayed at home!

Taking advantage of the fact that the wolves were once more reconciled with the sap house, I prepared for them that evening a good meal of beaver meat, and since they were outside the house (no doubt expecting Joan's secret handouts), I led them to the evaporator building, put the food down inside, and left, this time locking the door behind me. I wanted them handy in the morning. That night I explained to Joan what I was going to do.

There is no need now to dwell upon the sadness of the affair. Suffice it to say that Joan cried quite a lot and that my own emotions were stirred up. And, naturally, we spent a rather sleepless night, which was something I didn't need on the eve of a long wilderness tramp.

The alarm woke me at 5:30 A.M. to find that it had snowed during the night and that about two inches of the stuff covered the ground. The thermometer showed five degrees above zero, but the skies, or what I could see of them at that hour of the day, appeared clear. Later, when the true dawn began to arrive, it showed that this was going to be a fine day.

Joan got up also. I had tried to get her to stay in bed and play no part in the final act of our own particular little drama. Her reaction to this suggestion—which was intended to ease the sorrow of parting—was swift and to the point. Fixing me with a cold and direct gaze, she shook her head.

"If you think you're going to take *my* Matta and Wa away without letting me say good-bye to them, you're out of your mind, *Mister!*" The way she would say *mister* when she wished to emphasize some point during a discussion with me made it sound like a very naughty word.

So, on the morning of December 4, while I was getting my gear ready, Joan made breakfast and prepared a snack for *her* wolves. Withal, she didn't forget to put together the food that I had requested for myself, enough to last me for three days.

My plan was simple. I was going to lead Matta and Wa due north into country that was uninhabited by man and virtually inaccessible to the majority of people because there were no highways anywhere near it. There I would leave them, some twenty miles from the farm, a round trip that would probably take me three days to do.

Wolves think nothing of journeying twenty miles through the wilderness, and I was aware that if they had a mind to, Matta and Wa could easily make their way back to our farm. But I was betting that they would find the new country so intriguing that they would want to spend time exploring it, heading deeper into the wilderness as they were doing so and eventually settling on a territory of their own, if they didn't meet up with, and become accepted by, one of the wolf packs that lived in the region. But if they did eventually return to the farm, then I was going to have to crate them up, put them on the back of the truck, and take them a long way north before releasing them. I rather hoped I would not have to do that,

224

though. They would have to be tranquilized before they could be put into cages, but even so, they would suffer considerable discomfort and fear while they were being driven away. I tried not to think of this possibility as I went to get the packsack.

Individual people require somewhat different quantities of food in order to get through each twenty-four-hour period. In my case, I can get along nicely on three pounds a day and manage with reasonable comfort on two pounds while traveling through the wilderness. I have never weighed my intake when living a more sedentary life, but I suspect I ingest a lot less at such times. Joan weighted the rations she was preparing for me, increasing the quota by one pound per day to be on the safe side. Because of this, I would take with me a total of twelve pounds of food composed of the following items: four pounds of raw oatmeal-raisins-nuts mix, packed in one-pound plastic bags; two pounds of slab of bacon; one and a half pounds of precooked frozen beans, packed in half-pound bags; three pounds of whole wheat flour; half a pound of tea; half a pound of ground coffee; a little salt, baking powder, and a plastic container of shortening.

In addition to the food, I carried half a pint of brandy in a plastic bottle, one lightweight frying pan, one tin plate and mug, a one-quart aluminum tea-coffee pail with a lid, one spoon, and one fork (I always carry a belt and pocket knife); and I was taking an ax with a two-and-a-half pound head.

For bedding I had my down sleeping bag, which weighs four pounds, and I also packed two pieces of heavy, polyethylene transparent plastic, each ten feet square, to be used as floor and roof covers. The last items packed were a five-cell flashlight with two spare bulbs and a first-aid kit. I carried a compass, of course, but this was hung around my neck. I also carried a spare set of long underwear, two changes of socks, two clean shirts, and a down vest. The total weight of the backpack was thirty-six pounds; this doesn't sound like much, but when such a load is toted through the winter wilderness for several days, it eventually weighs heavy. Fortunately, as food is consumed, the pack gets lighter—that's one of the nice things about eating!

I was also going to take the snowshoes with me. There wasn't enough snow on the ground to bother with them, but on the premise that nothing should be left to chance when

225

dealing with the wilderness, I thought it better to carry them strapped to the pack.

Joan was still weighing and packaging food when I had finished my end of the job, and because I was anxious to complete one last, but important, task before I went down to let the wolves out of the sap house, I asked my wife to finish packing the food for me and arranged to return with Matta and Wa to collect my gear and allow her to say her good-byes.

In the barn, secure from varmints and prying eyes, I kept a metal box that contained a few items of equipment that Joan refused to have inside the house. One of these was ripe beaver castor sealed in a plastic container; another was a small bottle of aniseed oil. These were used as lures during occasions either when I sought to shoot pictures of animals or when I wanted to attract some of the predatory species to a particular location so that I could observe their behavior. I had never used these "lotions" for the purpose to which they were going to be put today.

Aniseed is a powerful attractant for all canines. It was used to nefarious effect during the days of the Klondike Gold Rush, when there was an outbreak of "dognaping" that resulted when unscrupulous men, intent on getting together a team of dogs without paying for them, would douse their pants cuffs with aniseed and walk along in the vicinity of a coveted animal, which would take one sniff and run along at the heels of the thief. The quite powerful, but not unpleasant, extract is often used as a lure by trappers, who make up their own secret recipes with which to entice the animals they seek to entrap. Beaver castor, fresh or aged, plays a prominent role in most of these liquid lures.

That day, of all days, I wanted to make sure that Matta and Wa would follow me, so I slopped a good quantity of aniseed oil on my left pant cuff and a lesser, but more powerful, amount of mashed beaver castor on the right. Before I even emerged from the barn, Tundra, out in his pen, has scented me and was trying to eat the chain-link wire in order to get out and stick his nose against my legs. His reaction, and my own nose, made me realize that Joan might not want me back in the house just now, so instead of going to release Matta and Wa and then walking back with them, I tapped on the window, and when she opened it, I asked her to pass the packsack to me, reporting what I had done and suggesting that she walk down to the evaporator house to say good-bye to Matta and Wa; she could also bring my snowshoes.

The wolves were delirious when they scented my legs; they couldn't sniff me enough and were still contorting with olfactory joy when Joan turned up. While I secured the shoes to the pack, she sought to pat her wild friends for the last time, a task made difficult because Matta and Wa were rather more interested in my pant legs than they were in my wife. But she had been crafty! In her pocket she carried two foil-wrapped packages containing sirloin steak. Now she had their attention all right!

By the time that the wolves had ingested the meat, I had donned the packsack and Joan was kneeling in the snow, crying quietly while hugging both Matta and Wa at the same time. I was about to suggest that she now return home when she stood up suddenly, said, "Good-bye, babes," in a low, choking voice, and whirled around to go running up the path.

All day we traveled north through country in which small game was plentiful. Matta and Wa killed several hares and a good many mice, but continued to follow the lure of my pants when they were not hunting, though several times during the course of the afternoon the wolves left me for varying periods of time, twice catching up to me from behind, on one occasion waiting for me on the trail ahead.

By early evening I estimated that we had covered almost twenty miles, and I started looking for a rock overhang under which to sleep, no longer worrying about the wolves because I felt that if they went away now, we were already far enough for the purpose I had in mind. If they didn't show up by morning, I would turn around and go home again.

Camping light in the winter wilderness is not a dreadful experience if one obeys a few simple rules. In the absence of a convenient rock "cave," one can construct a comfortable bivouac with poles and evergreen bows, in front of which a long fire is kept going during the night. By a long fire I mean a blaze that is perhaps four or five feet from left to right, usually made by placing two good-sized logs side by side, some eighteen inches apart, and setting the fire between them, piling wood to whatever length is desired. This throws a lot more

227

heat than a conventional, round blaze. For good measure, one may construct a reflector wall behind the fire, sloping slightly toward the bivouac, but set back far enough so that it won't be ignited by the flames; this throws the heat forward.

A rock overhang is my favorite sleeping place if I can find one early enough to allow for suitable preparation. In this case, I light a long fire inside the rock shelter, making a big blaze and letting it burn while I am getting supper ready on another long fire set about three feet in front of the entrance to the overhang. By the time I have eaten and washed up with snow and made tea or coffee, the fire in the rock cave is down to coals, which I rake out carefully. By now the rock is good and hot, but not enough so to burn my bedding, which I spread over the melted ground on top of a sheet of plastic. Building up the frontal fire, I crawl into my warmed-up shelter and go to sleep. A good fire inside such a rocky den will put enough heat into the granite to last until three or four o'clock in the morning, by which time one has already enjoyed a good, long sleep (lights out comes early under those conditions).

I found an ideal rocky nook deep inside the shelter of a thick section of mixed forest that came complete with plenty of dry, blowdown firewood. Here I made camp. Probably because they had already eaten enough on the journey, Matta and Wa settled down near me, but outside the area of the fire, evidently prepared to spend the night. After supper, sipping a last cup of coffee while sitting on the sleeping bag, facing the night fire, I made notes of the journey, using the flashlight. Then I turned in. I hardly had time to notice that the wilderness was extremely quiet before I fell into a deep sleep.

I awakened at three o'clock, cold. The fire was still alight, but down to a bed of coals; after I added fresh fuel and the flames were shooting six feet into the air, I looked for Matta and Wa; they had gone. I got up and went to examine their beds, easily seen as two depressions in the snow, now frozen hard; the heat of their bodies had melted the snow and kept it thawed, but when they got up to go, the frost soon returned, making a hard crusty "bowl" in each place. This told me that they had been away for more than an hour. It also suggested that Matta and Wa had left me for good.

I tried to get back to sleep, but what with thinking about Joan, alone and sad at home, and Matta and Wa, whom I was going to miss greatly, I was not in a happy or relaxed mood. Eventually, tired after the long tramp of yesterday, fatigue conquered my emotions.

It was dawn when something wet and cold and dreadfully smelly poked me in the face. It was Wa, come to greet me. Matta stood behind him, evidently awaiting her turn. But I didn't really wish to be greeted by either of them, for they reeked of fox musk. Those fortunate ones who have never smelled pure, unadulterated fox musk be advised that while this substance is not as acrid or as long lasting as skunk oil, it is equally nauseating. It seemed that the wolves had killed and eaten a fox during the time that they were away from camp.

The second day out was almost a repeat of the first, except that Matta and Wa didn't appear to be as hungry and hunted less while exploring more, and except, also, that the temperature had dropped during the night. It was another sunny day, but since the hairs inside my nostrils became frozen with each breath I took and thawed when I exhaled, I knew it was now below zero, though just how much below I didn't know. I made tea for breakfast, put a plastic bag of oatmeal, raisins, and nuts in my parka pocket, and we set out, once more heading north. As I walked, I munched dry rations.

By late afternoon, as I was starting to look around for a good place to camp, the wolves put up a deer, giving chase. By the way that the whitetail was traveling I didn't think they would catch it, but I knew they would run it for some time and that they might not return on this occasion. I started cutting poles for a bivouac.

By suppertime Matta and Wa were still away. I had made my shelter by first draping the poles with plastic to keep out the wind, then covering the structure with spruce bows; this while the fire was gaining strength. Afterward I fried thick chunks of bacon and a good dollop of frozen beans, made coffee, and mixed up some bannock dough, which was then rolled into a long, round "snake," entwined around a green stick and baked over the coals. When all was ready, I dined, treating my coffee afterward with a good shot of brandy. While I sipped the heady brew, I recorded the day's events. Then, after piling a good quantity of wood on the fire, I crawled into the sleeping bag.

Sleep was a long time coming that night. Again my mind was filled with my wife and with Matta and Wa, all three of whom played havoc with my emotions. After an hour or so I sat up suddenly when wolf howls reached my shelter. They were distant, at least a couple of miles away, but I could tell that only two wolves were singing. Matta and Wa? I reached for the brandy and swigged from the bottle. Then I filled and lit my pipe and propped myself up against the lean-to poles, staring into the fire, listening, my mind out there, running with my wolves, seeing them as they stood or sat somewhere and bayed their primordial song at the stars above. Inside my head ran a movie. It opened beside the Mattawa River as I lifted the bloody sack out of the Cree's canoe. The mind camera zoomed in for a close-up of two tiny, bedraggled, and shivering wildings that were soaking wet and covered in the blood of their mother and sibling.

I saw myself carry the pups to my canoe, there to wipe them as dry as possible and to cover them up, placing them in the sun. The scenes continued to play; the pups grew, became cubs, became young wolves. I could feel Wa's tusk in my arm, sense the power of him as he stood ready to fight me for pack position. It went on and on, and I sipped more brandy and asked myself the questions that I had so often asked before at such times: Why did I do these things? Why go through these agonies of mind each time they return to their wild world? And I knew the answers as surely as I knew that I would do it again next time. At last I went to sleep, clutching an empty plastic bottle.

I was awake before dawn, regaining consciousness with the knowledge that Matta and Wa would not be near me. They weren't. After replenishing the fire, I started breakfast, then packed sleeping bag and clothing before taking down the lean-to and stacking the materials. My head ached, but I supposed that I deserved it for drinking some eight ounces of brandy. I wasn't hungry, but I forced myself to eat. Was I trying to delay my departure?

An hour after rising I was walking toward home. Day had dawned cloudy; by noon it began to snow, but lightly, and I was grateful, for a blizzard was the last thing I wanted to face this day. As I walked, head down in order to follow my outward-bound tracks, I viewed again the mind movie I had seen last night, try as I might to avoid doing so. Occasionally I would stop, sit and rest awhile on fallen tree or rock, and listen for the wolves without hearing them. Then I would go again, on and on, 'hrough a wilderness that at any other time would have enchanted me but that now seemed somehow alien. Evening came; darkness found me still on the trail. I kept going, using the flashlight because clouds hid the moon and stars. I was tired, but I wouldn't stop, too anxious to get this over, to sleep in my own bed tonight and to seek solace from my wife while I offered her my own comfort.

Almost seventeen hours after starting, I arrived home. It was after ten o'clock, but the lights were on. Joan was waiting. Before I reached the door, it opened, and Tundra came bounding out, offering his exuberant love; behind him, no less exuberant, came Joan. We all entered the house together, and I was forced to sit, drink whiskey (I *hated* that, of course!), while Joan grilled a steak. We didn't talk much. We didn't need to, each knew perfectly well how the other felt. So did Tundra. He sat upright beside me, pressing close, only occasionally lowering his head to sniff at the now weakened lures that adhered to my pant legs.

Afterward, replete with steak and a number of other special things that Joan had held in readiness, I sat before the fire drinking strong coffee and sipping warm brandy out of a large snifter, bone-weary in body, but all too awake in mind. Because we had been silent for too long, I was about to remark that it must have been hard on Joan to stay at home and wait, when she spoke first.

"It must have been really awful for you, out there alone after our wolves had gone!"

It was a statement, not a question. Once again I marveled at the way that two beings who are compatible and who have a close relationship can sense what the other is feeling.

"I was just going to say the same to you. . . . I wouldn't have wanted to stay here, waiting as long as you did."

We were silent again. Tundra had been lying at my feet; now he rose and walked over to Joan and put his big head in her lap. She stroked him, and tears came to her eyes. I felt I should speak to her, but I didn't know what to say. Then I realized that it didn't matter what words I chose to utter; she knew how I felt, and I knew how she felt. Both of us were now certain that we would never see Matta and Wa again. As the future showed, we were correct in this assumption.

"You know, love," I said after some moments, "they came to us in secret and they've gone in secret. But they're healthy, strong, and free. We gave them those things, you and I, and Tundra."

She came and sat on the floor beside my chair, and Tundra sat at my feet. The fire was warm, the brandy was good. It was a night to remember. Always.

ABOUT THE AUTHOR

R. D. Lawrence is the author of sixteen previous books about wildlife and ecology, including *The North Runner*, Lawrence's account of his relationship with an extraordinary half-wolf, half-Alaskan-malamute sled dog. Born in Vigo, Spain, and educated partly in that country and partly in England, he moved to Canada twenty-five years ago. He now lives in Ontario.